"This text is admirably amongst the first to take on the massiv[e] and competency for practitioners in applied behavior ana[lysis ...] backgrounds, it constantly calls us to action through self-awareness and case study exercises, reminding behavior analysts that we 'don't know what we don't know' – unless we seek this knowledge. I recommend this text to be an integral component and required reading in every behavior analytic course sequence and supervision framework. We cannot be successful as behavior analysts unless we develop the multicultural humility repertoires outlined here. Capell, Conners, and colleagues promote discussion and debate that may at times feel uncomfortable but are truly necessary in moving forward as a culturally humble field."

Noor Y. Syed, Ph.D., BCBA-D, LBA/LBS-CT, PA, NY, Faculty and Clinical Director, Lehigh University Autism Services; Research Coordinator, Global Autism Project

"In a time when many are screaming for diversity and inclusion, very few do more than just talk about their experience or offer strategies of change. In this book, Brian and Shawn have gone the extra step that is needed within our field of ABA and in society. With a wonderful collection of authors, subject matters of importance, historical references, and methodologies to change the landscape, this book will be used as a potential blueprint for many moving forward. Fantastic efforts by a few to help create change for many. Greatly needed and appreciated."

Dr. Antonio M. Harrison, BCBA-D, University of West Florida

"This book eloquently provides an updated view on the importance of knowledge about group memberships and characteristics, empowering the reader to engage in more cultural humility and effective practice. Context is *everything*, and culture is *everywhere*. Now it's up to *you* to bring that knowledge into practice!"

Ryan O'Donnell, M.S., BCBA, The Daily BA

"This book tackles a number of issues that are at the forefront of discussion in applied behavior analysis; I expect this book will be of great interest to practitioners in our field."

Matthew T. Brodhead, Ph.D., BCBA-D, Assistant Professor, Michigan State University

Multiculturalism and Diversity in Applied Behavior Analysis

This textbook provides a theoretical and clinical framework for addressing multiculturalism and diversity in the field of applied behavior analysis (ABA).

Featuring contributions from national experts, practicing clinicians, researchers, and academics that balance both a scholarly yet practical perspective, this book guides the reader through theoretical foundations to clinical applications to help behavior analysts understand the impact of diversity in the ABA service delivery model. Chapters contain learning objectives, literature reviews, practice considerations, case studies, and discussion questions and are all aligned with the current BACB® Professional and Ethical Compliance Code and BACB® Task List. Accompanying the book are online test materials for students and instructors to assess the knowledge they have learned about various diversity topics.

This book is a must have for graduate students in ABA programs, faculty to incorporate diversity topics into graduate preparation, supervisors looking to enhance a supervisee's understanding of working with diverse clients, and practicing behavior analysts in the field wanting to increase their awareness of working with diverse populations.

Brian M. Conners, Ph.D., BCBA, maintains a private practice, *Brian Conners, BCBA, LLC*, and is a senior faculty associate in the special education and applied behavior analysis programs at Seton Hall University.

Shawn T. Capell, M.S., BCBA, LBA, is owner of *Covenant 15:16 LLC* and maintains an adjunct faculty position in the applied behavior analysis program at Seton Hall University.

Multiculturalism and Diversity in Applied Behavior Analysis

Bridging Theory and Application

Edited by Brian M. Conners
and Shawn T. Capell

Routledge
Taylor & Francis Group

NEW YORK AND LONDON

First published 2021
by Routledge
52 Vanderbilt Avenue, New York, NY 10017

and by Routledge
2 Park Square, Milton Park, Abingdon, Oxon, OX14 4RN

Routledge is an imprint of the Taylor & Francis Group, an informa business

Library of Congress Cataloging-in-Publication Data
Names: Conners, Brian M. editor. | Capell, Shawn T. (Shawn Thomas) editor.
Title: Multiculturalism and diversity issues in applied behavior analysis : bridging theory and
    application / edited by Brian M. Conners, Shawn T. Capell.
Description: New York, NY : Routledge, 2020. | Includes bibliographical references and index.
Identifiers: LCCN 2020001508 (print) | LCCN 2020001509 (ebook) | ISBN 9780367208783
    (paperback) | ISBN 9780367208776 (hardback) | ISBN 9780429263873 (ebook)
Subjects: MESH: Applied Behavior Analysis—methods | Cultural Diversity | Cultural
    Competency | Culturally Competent Care
Classification: LCC RA418 (print) | LCC RA418 (ebook) | NLM WM 425.5.A7 |
    DDC 362.1—dc23
LC record available at https://lccn.loc.gov/2020001508
LC ebook record available at https://lccn.loc.gov/2020001509

ISBN: 978-0-367-20877-6 (hbk)
ISBN: 978-0-367-20878-3 (pbk)
ISBN: 978-0-429-26387-3 (ebk)

Typeset in Bembo
by Apex CoVantage, LLC

Visit the eResources: https://www.routledge.com/9780367208783

Acknowledgment

We would like to thank Kevin Marks, M.A., BCBA, behavior analyst working at *Spectrum 360* and Cayden Halligan, graduate student in the Ph.D. Counseling Psychology program at Seton Hall University for their time and expertise in assisting us with the development of exam questions for the test bank for this book.

Contents

Figures

Tables

Biographies of Editors

Brian M. Conners, Ph.D., BCBA, is a New Jersey Department of Education certified school psychologist and a Board Certified Behavior Analyst. He is Chief Executive Officer of his private practice, *Brian Conners, BCBA, LLC* where he provides consultation and training services to schools, organizations, and families and sells products to assist behavior analysts in their daily practice. He originally developed the graduate program in applied behavior analysis at Seton Hall University. He has worked in various sectors as a behavior analyst and consultant including public and private schools, psychiatric hospitals, and community agencies. He also was the former owner and chief executive officer of a nationally recognized Behavioral Health Center of Excellence for four years in private practice. He specializes in providing behavioral treatment to clients with severe developmental disabilities, emotional and behavioral disorders, and psychiatric conditions. His clinical areas of expertise include crisis intervention, behavioral assessment, and providing treatment and interventions for clients with the severe problem behaviors of physical aggression and self-injury. He has presented at state and national conferences and has published articles and book chapters in school psychology and special education on multiculturalism and diversity issues in the field of behavior analysis, behavior management strategies, crisis intervention, restraint and seclusion practices in schools, and ethics and supervision issues in behavior analysis.

Shawn T. Capell, M.S., BCBA, LBA, holds a Master of Science degree in psychology with a concentration in applied behavior analysis (ABA) and is currently working toward a Ph.D. within the same field. In addition to his current full-time position, he is the owner and clinical director of Covenant 15:16 LLC, an agency with the mission to ensure all families, regardless of socioeconomic status receive the highest quality ABA care possible. His clinical and research interests include parent/staff training, multicultural and diversity issues within the field of ABA, and physical aggression within adult learners. With over 10 years of experience working in the field of ABA, he joined the graduate program in applied behavior analysis at Seton Hall University and continues to work at the university as an adjunct faculty member. With a love and passion for the field of ABA, he has adopted as his personal mission to increase the presence and impact of minority professionals within the field of ABA (specifically African Americans).

Biographies of Contributors

Juliana Aguilar, M.S., BCBA, LBA, Utah State University Juliana Aguilar is a doctoral student in the applied behavior analysis program at Utah State University under the mentorship of Thomas Higbee, Ph.D., BCBA-D. She received her master's degree in applied behavior analysis from the University of Missouri–Columbia and is a BCBA and a licensed behavior analyst in the state of Utah.

Wafa Aljohani, M.S., BCBA, Endicott College Wafa Attallah Aljohani is a Board Certified Behavior Analyst (BCBA) from Jeddah, Saudi Arabia. She received her bachelor's degree in special education with an emphasis on autism spectrum disorders (ASD) from Dar Al-Hekma University. In 2009, Wafa was elected to be the Saudi Youth Ambassador for the Arab Thought Foundation, where she worked alongside 22 young Arab professionals to promote and empower youth to engage in cultural and educational initiatives in their communities. She provided behavior analytic services at different levels and in different countries including Saudi Arabia, Kenya, Indonesia, and the United States. She is currently a doctoral candidate at Endicott College under the supervision of Dr. Justin B. Leaf.

Isaac L. Bermudez, M.S., BCBA, Brett DiNovi & Associates, California Isaac L. Bermudez has worked in the field of ABA since 1998 and became a BCBA in 2005. Isaac has over two decades of experience working with individuals with autism and managing ABA programs. He has co-founded an ABA agency and most recently opened up a branch for Brett DiNovi & Associates.

Kwang-Sun Cho Blair, Ph.D., BCBA-D, University of South Florida Kwang-Sun Cho Blair is Associate Professor in the ABA Program, Department of Child and Family Studies, University of South Florida. Her primary research interests include school-based and family-centered interventions. She currently serves as consulting editors of the *Topics in Early Childhood Special Education* and *Remedial and Special Education* journals.

Fabiana Cacciaguerra-Decorato, M.A., BCBA, Lyndhurst Board of Education Fabiana Cacciaguerra-Decorato has been a Board Certified Behavior Analyst since 2018. She became interested in issues surrounding cultural competency within the field of applied behavior analysis during her graduate coursework. Currently Fabiana serves as the BCBA for a public school and works primarily with elementary students on the autism spectrum. She is a first-generation Italian-American and considers how her own culture influences all the diverse families she has the pleasure of working with.

Casey J. Clay, Ph.D., BCBA-D, LBA, University of Missouri–Columbia Casey J. Clay is an assistant professor in the Department of Special Education at the University of Missouri. He earned his Ph.D. from Utah State University. He is a Board Certified Behavior Analyst – Doctoral (BCBA-D) and a licensed behavior analyst (LBA) in Missouri.

Elizabeth Hughes Fong, Ph.D., M.A., BCBA, LBS, Saint Joseph's University Elizabeth Hughes Fong is a Board Certified Behavior Analyst and licensed Behavior Specialist in Pennsylvania. She works as faculty at Saint Joseph's University and has published in the area of behavior analysis, culture, and diversity. She is the founder of the Culture and Diversity SIG of ABAI.

Ksenia Gatzunis, M.S., BCBA, Endicott College Ksenia Gatzunis is a Board Certified Behavior Analyst (BCBA) and current Ph.D. student at Endicott College. Her primary interest is collaborating with ABA professionals around the world. Through the Global Autism Project, she has worked with centers in Kenya, Nicaragua, the Czech Republic, Ecuador, and the Dominican Republic.

Michelle P. Kelly, Ph.D., BCBA-D, Emirates College for Advanced Education Michelle P. Kelly is a Board Certified Behavior Analyst – Doctoral and holds a Ph.D. in applied behavior analysis (ABA) from the National University of Ireland, Galway. She is an assistant professor and ABA graduate program coordinator at Emirates College for Advanced Education, Abu Dhabi, United Arab Emirates.

Ashley Knochel, M.S., BCaBA, University of South Florida Ashley Knochel is a recent graduate of the Master's in ABA Program, Department of Child and Family Studies, University of South Florida. Her primary research interests are in the areas of culturally adapted interventions and the dissemination of ABA in non-Western settings.

James Donggeun Lee, M.S., BCBA, University of Illinois at Urbana-Champaign James Donggeun Lee is a doctoral student in special education at the University of Illinois at Urbana-Champaign. His research interests focus on providing training and coaching to parents of young children with autism spectrum disorder in low-resource settings.

Worner Leland, M.S., BCBA, LBA, Upswing Advocates and Empowered: A Center for Sexuality Worner Leland (they/them pronouns) is a Board Certified Behavior Analyst with Empowered: A Center for Sexuality in St. Louis, Missouri, and Upswing Advocates in Chicago,

Illinois. They are past president and current research and dissemination liaison of the Sexual Behavior: Research and Practice SIG of ABAI.

Sara Gershfeld Litvak, M.A., BCBA, Behavioral Health Center of Excellence Sara Gershfeld Litvak completed her graduate degree from Claremont Graduate University and is a Board Certified Behavior Analyst. As the CEO and founder of Behavioral Health Center of Excellence, she spearheaded the creation of the first ABA-specific accrediting body and oversees the creation of standards for behavior analytic organizations.

Paulina Luczaj, M.A., Ed.S., Seton Hall University and School District of the Chathams Paulina Luczaj, M.A., Ed.S., began her role as a school psychologist in 2019. She received her Bachelor of Arts in honors psychology from Seton Hall University. She then continued her journey at Seton Hall, where she also received her Master of Arts in psychological studies and Education Specialist degree in school psychology. It was during her graduate career when she discovered her love for applied behavior analysis and received training through Seton Hall's certification program. In addition to her career in school psychology, she serves as an adjunct professor at Seton Hall University training graduate students in cognitive assessment. She is a multilingual, first-generation Polish American who uses her lifelong multicultural experiences to help children and families of various backgrounds with their social, emotional, and behavioral needs.

Kozue Matsuda, Ph.D., BCBA-D, The Chicago School of Professional Psychology Kozue Matsuda, Board Certified Behavior Analyst – Doctoral (BCBA-D), is a New York State licensed behavior analyst. Kozue is CEO of Children Center Inc. in Tokyo, Japan. Kozue has been publishing ABA-related books and journals both in Japanese and English. Kozue is on the faculty of BCBA VCS pathway course in Japan.

Kristine Melroe, Special Education Credential, Morningside Academy Kristine Melroe attended Luther College, Pacific Oaks College, and received her special education credential from the University of Washington. As assistant director of Morningside Teachers' Academy, she worked with Indigenous faculty in Canada, Hawaii, Oklahoma, Montana, and South Dakota. She has remained politically active since the Wounded Knee occupation in 1973.

Pamela M. Olsen, Ph.D., BCBA, Mohammed bin Rashid Center for Special Education Operated by The New England Center for Children Pamela Olsen is a Licensed Special Educator, a BCBA, and an International Psychologist with 20 years of experience working with individuals with autism. She serves as the Chief Program Officer of the Mohammed bin Rashid Center for Special Education Operated by the New England Center for Children.

Jose D. Rios, M.S., BCBA, Private Practice Jose D. Rios, a BCBA since 2000, has over 45 years of experience with children and adults with developmental disabilities, including owning group homes, teaching graduate and undergraduate courses, conducting parent training with hundreds of families, and serving on professional boards (including being president of CalABA). He has made ABA his life.

Joanne Robbins, Ph.D., Morningside Academy Joanne Robbins earned her PhD in educational psychology at the University of Illinois at Chicago. She is the Principal and Associate Director of Morningside Academy. Dedicated to educational excellence and research, she co-founded PEER International to increase the academic achievement of students in historically disenfranchised environments.

Adriana Rodriguez, M.A., BCBA, Rollins College Adriana Rodriguez earned her master's degree in applied behavior analysis and clinical science from Rollins College. Adriana has experience working in an early intervention clinic with children with a variety of problem behaviors. She is currently working as a behavior analyst for a school district.

Hanna Rue, Ph.D., BCBA-D, LEARN Behavioral Dr. Hanna C. Rue holds a Ph.D. in clinical psychology and is a Board Certified Behavior Analyst. She has worked with individuals with developmental disabilities across the lifespan in a variety of settings. Her publications span basic and applied behavior analytic research. As the chair of the National Standards Project II, Dr. Rue spearheaded completion of a systematic review of evidence-based interventions for children and adults with autism spectrum disorder. She currently works at LEARN Behavioral as the vice president of clinical development.

Mawule A. Sevon, M.A., NCSP, BCBA, The Key Consulting Firm, LLC Mawule has earned board certification as a behavior analyst and a specialist's degree in school psychology. She uses her behavioral approach to impact racial disparities in the educational system. Currently, she is the executive director of the Key Consulting Firm, an organization focused on fundamental justice in education.

August Stockwell, Ph.D., BCBA-D, Upswing Advocates and Empowered: A Center for Sexuality August Stockwell (they/them pronouns) received their bachelor's degree in social work from the University of Missouri – Columbia in 2004. They received their Master of Arts in clinical psychology with an applied behavior analysis specialization in 2008 and Ph.D. in applied behavior analysis in 2011, both from the Chicago School of Professional Psychology. They are the founder and executive director of Upswing Advocates, a nonprofit organization that provides education and research opportunities that focus on the LGBTQIA community, and the associate director of research in the Applied Behavior Analysis Department at the Chicago School of Professional Psychology. Over the past decade, their research and applied work have focused on topics including cultural diversity, polyamory, communication in relationships, gender, sexual behavior, mindfulness, and effective skill-building strategies. They have a vision of using precise measurement and an individualized approach to connect people to affirming, accessible interventions that create meaningful change. They are a Board Certified Behavior Analyst – Doctoral (BCBA-D).

Rebecca Tagg, Psy.D., MSCP, NCSP, BCBA-D, Del Mar Center for Behavioral Health Rebecca Tagg has engaged in formal education and training in a variety of complementary fields to best support those with whom she works. She has graduate training and experience in school psychology, behavior analysis, clinical psychology, and clinical psychopharmacology. She works in a variety of clinical and training settings.

Mary Jane Weiss, Ph.D., BCBA-D, Endicott College Mary Jane Weiss is a professor at Endicott College, where she has been for 9 years, and where she directs the Department of ABA, including the master's programs in autism and in ABA, and the Ph.D. program in ABA. She has worked in the field of ABA and autism for over 35 years. She received her Ph.D. in clinical psychology from Rutgers University in 1990 and she became a Board Certified Behavior Analyst in 2000. She previously worked for 16 years at the Douglass Developmental Disabilities Center at Rutgers University. Her clinical and research interests center on defining best practice ABA techniques, exploring ways to enhance the ethical conduct of practitioners, teaching social skills to learners with autism, training staff to be optimally effective at instruction and at collaboration, and maximizing family members' expertise and adaptation. She serves on the Scientific Council of the Organization for Autism Research, is on the board of Association for Science in Autism Treatment, is a regular contributor to the ABA Ethics Hotline, and is an advisor to the Cambridge Center for Behavioral Studies. She is a regular reviewer for several professional journals and is a frequent member of service committees for a variety of organizations.

April Michele Williams, Ph.D., BCBA-D, Rollins College April Michele Williams earned her doctorate in behavior analysis from West Virginia University and has developed early intensive behavior intervention for children with autism spectrum disorders. She is the director of the master's program in applied behavior analysis and clinical Science at Rollins College in Winter Park, Florida.

1

An Introduction to Multiculturalism and Diversity Issues in the Field of Applied Behavior Analysis

Brian M. Conners

This book is the first of its kind to be published on the topic of multiculturalism and diversity issues in the field of applied behavior analysis (ABA). Within the ABA field, not much has been done around the topic of diversity. It has only been within the past few years that diversity issues have even been discussed. Therefore, this book seeks to contribute to the growth of the field by offering a scholarly work that can be used in graduate classrooms around the nation and the globe to help educate others about diversity issues that are relevant to our practice as behavior analysts.

The aspect of diversity is so broad in nature and one book cannot encompass all aspects of diversity. Therefore, this book is the first step in providing an introduction to the general topic in the field of ABA. While we were not able to cover every area of diversity ranging from race and ethnicity, gender and gender identity, sexual orientation, disability, socioeconomic status, age, disability, religious and spiritual backgrounds, and so forth in one book, we attempted to provide readers with a variety of theoretical, conceptual, and clinical chapters that would serve as an initial primer to the topic. Hence, the book provides readers with some understanding of working with specific diverse populations while other chapters offer guidance on clinical applications along with professional issues, such as supervision and ethics.

Terminology

With current discussions about diversity happening in the ABA community, there has been much conversation and debate about terminology and language used when it comes to diversity in terms of cultural awareness, sensitivity, humility, and competence. Table 1.1 outlines some terminology to keep in mind when reading the book.

TABLE 1.1 Definitions of Cultural Terms

Term	Definition
Cultural awareness	Encompasses the ability for one to examine their own cultural beliefs and values and understand how the culture of others can shape behavior and interactions with others (Danso, 2018; Horevitz, Lawson, & Chow, 2013).
Cultural sensitivity	Ability to understand and embrace cultural differences, recognize how one's own culture can influence professional practice, and be able to design interventions with clients that take culture into consideration (Danso, 2018; Nassar-McMillan, 2014; Ben-Ari & Strier, 2010; Burchum, 2002).
Cultural competence	Capability to develop an awareness of one's cultural beliefs, values, and biases while acquiring knowledge of the norms and behaviors of other cultures and displaying professional skills that combine awareness and knowledge of said cultures (Danso, 2018; Sousa & Almeida, 2016; Mlcek, 2014).
Cultural humility	Focuses on individuals and organizations to examine culture and recognize continual learning as practitioners from other cultures and that we do not know everything and need to learn from the client. It is the ability to maintain an interpersonal stance where the practitioner is "other-oriented" and is learning about cultural identity that is most important to the client. Cultural humility often encompasses self-reflection and personal critique and is an ongoing, lifelong process (Wright, 2019; Abell, Manuel, & Schoeneman, 2015; Fisher-Borne, Cain, & Martin, 2015; Hook, 2014; Hook, Davis, Owen, Worthington, & Utsey, 2013).

There has been much debate on whether or not cultural competence can be achieved; therefore, the term of "cultural humility" has been used in the field of ABA and other related disciplines, such as nursing, education, psychology, health care, and so forth, to indicate that it is a lifelong process of learning and that competence may never fully be achieved (Wright, 2019). A newer term of "cultural competemility" has recently been introduced in the research literature and is a merger of cultural competence and cultural humility (Campinha-Bacote, 2019). Cultural competemility can be defined as "the synergistic process between cultural humility and cultural competence in which cultural humility permeates each of the five components of cultural competence: cultural awareness, cultural knowledge, cultural skill, cultural desire, and cultural encounters" (Campinha-Bacote, 2019). This newer terminology of cultural competemility seems to be a more encompassing view instead of having cultural competence and cultural humility being viewed as opposing that instead they are working together to improve a practitioner.

Therefore, we recognize no reader is going to become culturally competent in working with diverse populations just from reading this book, but that readers will gain a level of cultural awareness that they can put into practice as behavior analysts to display cultural sensitivity and work toward competence while engaging cultural humility. In essence, our hope is that the book will inspire you to foster knowledge and skills where you are striving as a behavior analyst to have cultural competemility in order to provide high-quality ABA services to the diverse populations of clients you work with.

References

Abell, M. L., Manuel, J., & Schoeneman, A. (2015). Student attitudes toward religious diversity and implications for multicultural competence. *Journal of Religion & Spirituality in Social Work: Social Thought, 34*(1), 91–104. https://doi.org/10.1080/15426432.2014.943920

Ben-Ari, A., & Strier, R. (2010). Rethinking cultural competence: What can we learn from Levinas? *British Journal of Social Work, 40*(7), 2155–2167. https://doi.org/10.1093/bjsw/bcp153

Burchum, J.L.R. (2002). Cultural competence: An evolutionary perspective. *Nursing Forum, 37*(4), 5–15. https://doi.org/10.1111/j.1744-6198.2002.tb01287.x

Campinha-Bacote, J. (2019). Cultural competemility: A paradigm shift in the cultural competence versus cultural humility debate – Part I. *The Online Journal of Issues in Nursing, 24*(1). https://doi.org/10.3912/OJIN.Vol24No01PPT20

Danso, R. (2018). Cultural competence and cultural humility: A critical reflection on key cultural diversity concepts. *Journal of Social Work, 2*(4), 410–430. https://doi.org/10.1177/1468017316654341

Fisher-Borne, M., Cain, J. M., & Martin, S. L. (2015). From mastery to accountability: Cultural humility as an alternative to cultural competence. *Social Work Education, 34*(2), 165–181. https://doi.org/10.1080/02615479.2014.977244

Hook, J. N. (2014). Engaging clients with cultural humility. *Journal of Psychology and Christianity, 33*(1), 277–280.

Hook, J. N., Davis, D. E., Owen, J., Worthington, E. L., & Utsey, S. O. (2013). Cultural humility: Measuring openness to culturally diverse clients. *Journal of Counseling Psychology, 60*(3), 353–366. doi: 10.1037/a0032595

Horevitz, E., Lawson, J., & Chow, J.C.C. (2013). Examining cultural competence in health care: Implications for social workers. *Health & Social Work, 38*(3), 135–145. https://doi.org/10.1093/hsw/hlt015

Mlcek, S. (2014). Are we doing enough to develop cross-cultural competencies for social work? *British Journal of Social Work, 44*(7), 1984–2003. https://doi.org/10.1093/bjsw/bct044

Nassar-McMillan, S. C. (2014). A framework for cultural competence, advocacy, and social justice: Applications for global multiculturalism and diversity. *International Journal for Educational and Vocational Guidance, 14*(1), 103–118. https://doi.org/10.1007/s10775-014-9265-3

Sousa, P., & Almeida, J. L. (2016). Culturally sensitive social work: Promoting cultural competence. *European Journal of Social Work, 19*(3), 537–555. https://doi.org/10.1080/13691457.2015.1126559

Wright, P. I. (2019). Cultural humility in the practice of applied behavior analysis. *Behavior Analysis in Practice, 12*(4), 805–809. https://doi.org/10.1007/s40617-019-00343-8

2

ADDRESSING Cultural Complexities

Rebecca Tagg

Learning Objectives

- Learn about the components of Dr. Pamela Hays's ADDRESSING model
- Explore one's own culture using the ADDRESSING model
- Gain an understanding of how one's own culture could impact service delivery

Introduction

Behavior analysis is a science that aims to understand behavior through identification of the factors that reliably lead to the occurrence or non-occurrence of the behavior of an individual, group, or organization (Association for Behavior Analysis International, 2019b). Behavior analysts are the professionals who are tasked with implementation of this science to produce meaningful change in the lives of the individuals, groups, and organizations served. Applied behavior analysis was first applied as an intervention for individuals with developmental disabilities and autism spectrum disorder, and so this area of practice has the most evidence base, and likely related to that, it is the area where many behavior analysts practice (Behavior Analyst Certification Board, 2019).

Working in this capacity, to help improve the lives of others means that behavior analysts are likely to interact with a variety of individuals, some of whom may be similar to the behavior analysts and others who may be quite different. Baio et al. (2018), in an update of the Centers for Disease Control and Prevention (CDC) Autism and Developmental Disabilities Monitoring (ADDM) Network's data that the autism prevalence rate, as of 2014, was 1 in 59 children. The male to female prevalence was 4:1. Autism spectrum disorders are reported across all racial and ethnic groups, although children from white or Caucasian families tend to be identified more than those coming from families of other ethnicities. Data obtained from the Baio et al. (2018)

update from the ADDM Network indicated that while these disparities continue to exist, the differences are decreasing since the previous update to the ADDM Network in 2012. These data indicate that behavior analysts, many of whom are serving individuals with autism and related disabilities, are likely to interact with a variety of individuals.

The Professional and Ethical Compliance Code for Behavior Analysts is produced by the Behavior Analyst Certification Board® (BACB®) and serves to guide behavior analysts certified by the BACB® to ensure ethical and professional behavior across the field. The BACB® further guides the practice of behavior analysts with the BACB® Task List, of which the fourth edition is current at the time of this chapter; the fifth edition is scheduled to be released January 2022. The BACB® embedded professional and ethical behaviors under a variety of sections of the Task List (Behavior Analyst Certification Board, 2014). Many of the principles of these guiding documents reference working with others in different contexts such as supervisor, clinician, and researcher. In order to work successfully with others, one must have an understanding of the other person whose perspectives and beliefs are derived from one's own learning history. Culture can be viewed as a component of an individual's learning history and has been described as such by B. F. Skinner (1981) as a "third level of selection by consequences," where he stressed the importance of social and cultural factors when seeking to understand the behavior of an individual or group. De Melo, Camila, and De Rose (2015) reference Interlocking Behavioral Contingencies (IBC), where social behaviors are maintained by specific contingencies and then learned and maintained by others on the basis of the same contingencies. These IBCs could be viewed as one way in which cultural norms develop and persist. Through viewing culture through a behavior analytic lens of learning histories, behavior analysts may be poised to apply the science of behavior analysis to gain greater understanding of these behaviors and thereby become better able to recognize them in oneself and others, and to use that knowledge to more sensitively and successfully serve in the varied roles of a behavior analyst, clinician, supervisor, and researcher.

The purpose of this chapter is to introduce a model that can be used as a framework for systematically and intentionally assessing culture in oneself and in others, particularly as it relates to being a member of the dominant group or minority group. Information gleaned from this framework can then be used to guide culturally sensitive and culturally competent practice, as it applies to each individual involved in each context. The framework was developed by Dr. Pamela A. Hays as a model to assist those in mental health professions consider ten different aspects of culture that could impact their work with individuals (Hays, 2016). The ten aspects spell out the word ADDRESSING, using the first letter of each aspect of culture included in the model; **A**ge/Generation, **D**isability (Congenital), **D**isability (Acquired), **R**eligion and Spiritual Identity, **E**thnicity and Racial Identity, **S**ocioeconomic Status, **S**exual Identity, **I**ndigenous Heritage, **N**ational Origin, and **G**ender Identity and Expression. This chapter will review the ten aspects of culture included in the ADDRESSING framework and provide suggestions for applications of its use to support culturally sensitive and culturally competent behavior analytic practices.

Dr. Hays (2016) described in her text, *Addressing Cultural Complexities in Practice: Assessment, Diagnosis, and Therapy* (3rd ed.), that this model and her work in this area came about from her own experience of not quite fitting into the Anglo-European identity, which was dominant in the United States where she was trained and working as a psychologist. It was her observation that the Anglo-European culture was dominant and that being a member of the dominant group could create blind spots in practice for clinicians. Those blind spots could lead to behavioral missteps, albeit unintentionally, due to not fully understanding the cultural contingencies that may be at play. Relatedly, the ADDRESSING model can be most appropriately applied to the United States and Canada where the Anglo-European culture can be viewed as being dominant. It is not a universal framework, as there are so many cultural complexities and cultural norms dependent upon where one may be located geographically (Hays, 2016).

A place to begin may be to more clearly, more operationally define the concept of culture from the standpoint of the author of the ADDRESSING model. Hays describes culture as the learned behaviors, beliefs, norms, and values that a group holds true and passes from generation to generation in an attempt to preserve those behaviors, beliefs, norms, and values. She elaborates that this definition focuses on the interpersonal and socially constructed aspect of culture rather than on physical similarities between members (as does race). Hays's belief in using this definition is that it is specific enough to include groups that share at least some biological heritage but general enough to apply to groups that do not share a common biological heritage (Hays, 2009). The language of learned behaviors aligns well with the behaviorist view of acquiring and maintaining behavioral repertoires. When one exhibits a behavior and contacts reinforcement after engaging in that behavior, that behavior is likely to occur again in the future, becoming part of an organism's behavioral repertoire. Further, Hays's emphasis on the interpersonal and socially constructed aspect of culture also matches a behavior analytic view, as it suggests the behavior is maintained or changed through interaction with others. The connection with and interplay of an individual's behavior and one's environment is a key tenet of behavior analysis and is apparent in Hays's conceptualization of culture as well, suggesting the ADDRESSING model as one that may fit well within the behavior analytic framework and practice.

Individuals are members of at least one culture and many may belong to multiple cultures. These different cultures may have complementary or oppositional contingencies when compared to those of other cultures. These competing contingencies are likely to impact how successful one is in interacting with another. One set of contingencies may lead to a specific set of behaviors that may be reinforced or viewed as acceptable in one culture, while the same set of behaviors may be punished or viewed unfavorably in another culture. Being aware of these different contingencies and how they may be similar or different from one's own is likely to occasion a response more congruent with the culture in question. This in turn leads to more positive interactions with others. When one is in the position of interacting with others or attempting to guide others in behavior change processes, positive interactions are paramount.

Through greater awareness of and understanding of one's own culture and the learning history from which it was created, one may be better equipped to account for its effect on interaction with others. Interactions with others are a key component in the provision of behavior analytic services and treatments, particularly for the many behavior analysts working with individuals with autism and related disabilities. The components of the ADDRESSING model are not to be viewed as exhaustive of the types of areas that may contribute to the cultural identification of an individual. They are culled from those identified as important by the American Psychological Association (APA) and the American Counseling Association's Division of Multicultural Counseling and Development, as that is the field in which Dr. Hays was seated. The APA's Ethical Principles of Psychologists and Code of Conduct, which were created to guide the behavior of psychologists and to protect those who receive psychological services, specifically reference aspects of culture, age, gender, gender identity, race, ethnicity, culture, national origin, religion, sexual orientation, disability, socioeconomic status, or any basis proscribed by law in Section 3.0, Human Relations. The General Principles are aspirational in nature and meant to guide psychologists toward values of the highest ethical ideals of the profession (American Psychological Association, 2016). Principle E is Respect for People's Rights and Dignities and specifically calls psychologists to action in these statements:

> Psychologists are aware of and respect cultural, individual, and role differences, including those based on age, gender, gender identity, race, ethnicity, culture, national origin, religion, sexual orientation, disability, language, and socioeconomic status, and consider these factors when working with members of such groups. Psychologists try to eliminate the effect on their work of biases based on those factors, and they do not knowingly participate in or condone activities of others based upon such prejudices.
>
> (American Psychological Association, 2016)

Looking to the organizational bodies within the field of behavior analysis, one can see direct reference to cultural competence and diversity in the updated diversity statement from the Association for Behavior Analysis International (ABAI):

> The Association for Behavior Analysis International encourages diversity and inclusiveness in the field of behavior analysis broadly, and within the organization specifically. Diversity refers to differences in race, ethnicity, sexual orientation, gender identity, age, country of origin, religious or spiritual beliefs, ability, and social and economic class.
>
> (ABAI, 2019a)

Fong and Tanaka (2013) suggested Standards for Cultural Competence in Behavior Analysis. Standard 2 identified "Self-Awareness" and defined the concept as follows: "Behavior Analysts shall be aware of their own personal, cultural values and beliefs as one way of appreciating the importance of multicultural identities in the lives of people" (Fong & Tanaka, 2013, p. 19). The ADDRESSING model may provide a framework to guide behavior analysts in moving toward that standard.

Comparing between the different aspects of culture across the different groups outlined above, one can see common characteristics of culture that are well represented in Hays's ADDRESSING model, suggesting they may be relevant features across disciplines and populations and relevant to focus on as areas for addressing, understanding, and self-awareness in developing culturally aware and competent behavior analysts.

ADDRESSING Framework

This section will detail the ten different components of the ADDRESSING framework and how it may be used in the field of applied behavior analysis (ABA). It should be noted that for the purposes of this section, the examples will focus predominantly on the cultural domains within the United States and Canada due to the majority of ABA practitioners working within these countries. Some adaptations to this framework may be needed for areas outside of these cultures.

Age and Generation

This domain is quite straightforward. When looking at the minority group related to this cultural domain, this could be considered children, adolescents, and older adults. What follows are some guiding questions to think about this domain after determining whether one identifies with the dominant or minority group in this area. Some examples of questions to ask yourself are:

1. What is one's own age?
2. What generation does that put one in, and what are some of the cultural contexts of that generation? How might that be stereotypical? How might it be accurate? How might it impact how one is perceived by others?
3. What is the similarity/difference in age between one another?

In review of one's responses to the questions above, how might that information impact one's own view? If a behavior analyst is far younger than a parent of a child with autism, one might want to be aware of the difference in age as it relates to the different perspective of each individual. The cultural context of growing up in the 1960s or 1970s may be different than growing up in the 1990s or early 2000s. These additional contextual factors may be helpful to consider when engaging in treatment planning, particularly the parent guidance or parent training piece of treatment provision.

Disability (Congenital)

This cultural domain relates to any disability that has been present since birth. The minority group for this domain, in the United States and Canada, would be someone who has experienced a congenital or developmental disability. Some guiding questions to evaluate this area after determining whether one identifies with the dominant or minority group could include:

1.   What challenges has one faced since birth?
2.   Is there a known disability that has been present since birth?
3.   What impact has that had on one's life?
4.   How does that impact one's view of self or another's view?

An example of a congenital disability could be a behavior analyst identified as having a learning disability. In application of the ADDRESSING model in this area, one's own experience of going through life with a learning disability may impact interaction with a child or adolescent who may also have a learning disability, or it could impact interaction with a teacher consultee who may serve gifted and talented students. Awareness of these similarities or differences provides context to one's behavior, allowing one to either continue with the behavior or make modifications.

Disability (Acquired)

This cultural domain relates to any disability that has not been present since birth but rather has been acquired. The minority group in this case would be someone who has experienced an acquired disability. Some guiding questions for this domain after determining whether one identifies with the dominant or minority group could include:

1.   What challenges has one faced since acquiring the disability?
2.   How has one's life changed?
3.   How has one's view of self changed or how has the perceived view of another changed?

An example in this area of the ADDRESSING model may be a behavior analyst who has experienced a traumatic event, such as sexual assault, and through that experience one's perception of a particular group of individuals may have changed. This change in perspective is a normal reaction to trauma and it may also impact one's ability to interact sensitively and competently with individuals who share traits of the assailant. Awareness of this residual impact may open the door for dialog with supervisors or organization owners to determine if reassignment is best or what supports the behavior analyst may want or need to serve the individual should one feel it manageable to do so.

Religion or Spirituality

This cultural domain relates to formal religious affiliation and also any spiritual beliefs, including not believing in any spiritual construct. Information from the 2008 US Census Bureau, specifically the American Religious Identification Survey, indicated that 76% of respondents self-identified as Christian, lending support to Hays's classification (2016) of the dominant group as Christians within this domain. Some guiding questions for exploration after determining if one identifies with the dominant or minority group could include:

1. What has been one's experience with religion and spirituality?
2. In what ways does religion and spirituality affect one's daily life and interactions with others?
3. How might others view one's spirituality and religion?

An illustration of the impact this may have could be a behavior analyst, who was raised in a family of origin who subscribed to the Jehovah's Witness religion, and is assigned to provide in-home ABA services for a family believing in the Catholic faith. As the Christmas holiday season approaches, this may become uncomfortable for the behavior analyst, as the recognition of this holiday is markedly different for the different religions. Being aware of one's own beliefs and the different belief of the client's family allows one to engage in a dialog with colleagues and perhaps even the family to determine how to move forward with respect and honor for all parties involved.

Ethnic and Racial Identity

This domain of culture relates to how one identifies with a group that shares national or racial origins. Data obtained from the US Census Bureau (2009) indicated 79% of respondents identified as white or Caucasian, supporting Hays's classification (2016) that the dominant group for this domain is European Americans. It is pertinent to note, in reviewing the data from the US Census Bureau, that this is fluid. With each completed census, differences in the ethnic makeup of the United States is clear. For example, from 2000 to 2009 there was an increase of 36.6% of individuals self-identifying with two or more racial groups. Some guiding questions for exploration after determining if one identifies with the dominant or minority group could include:

1. What experiences has one had related to his or her ethnic and racial identity?
2. How have those experiences shaped the view of self or given insight into how others have viewed oneself?

An example of this characteristic of culture and the possible implications on practice could be a behavior analyst raised in a racially homogenous area, with little exposure to individuals of other racial or ethnic groups. The behavior analyst is then assigned to provide school consultation services to a school district with a different racial group as the majority than what the behavior analyst is familiar with. Through acknowledgement of this difference, the behavior analyst may engage in some cultural exploration to gain more information about how this may or may not impact the behavior analyst's service provision and gather information that may help to avoid this blind spot becoming an impediment to service provision.

Socioeconomic Status

This domain of culture relates to a person's standing in a society and can be viewed as a combination of income, education, and occupation (APA, 2019). The dominant group in the United States and Canada is upper and middle class for this domain (U.S. Bureau of Labor Statistics, 2016). Some guiding questions for exploration after determining if one identifies with the dominant or minority group could include:

1. How has one's belonging in this area affected the opportunities and/or interactions one has had?
2. How does one view his or her standing in this area?
3. Has one remained in the same standing in this area, or has there been change over time?

A behavior analyst who came from a family of origin in the upper socioeconomic class assigned to provide in-home ABA services for a family whose socioeconomic status different greatly and fell into the lower socioeconomic class may encounter different experiences from which one may be used to. These different experiences may be reflective of different cultural norms while atypical to the behavior analyst, may be completely "typical" for the status of the client. Awareness of potential differences at the onset permit the behavior analyst to seek consultation to ensure cultural sensitivity and competence for the client served.

Sexual Identity

This domain of culture relates to a person's sexual orientation, sexual identity and expression. Hays (2016) suggests that cisgendered, heterosexual individuals make up the dominant group in this domain. Because the US Census does not yet ask about gender identity, confirmation data to this end was unable to be attained. Meerwijk and Sevelius (2017) attempted to extrapolate an estimate of the population of individuals identifying as transgendered, and their estimate came to 390 adults out of every 100,000. National Health Statistic Reports (2014) indicated that 96% of adult respondents self-identified as heterosexual. This data is in process of being updated and this may be another area where fluidity can be observed in the data sets over time. Some guiding questions for exploration after determining if one identifies with the dominant or minority group could include:

1. What are one's own views related to sexual identity, orientation, and expression? How has this affected one's own experiences?
2. Have these views remained stable over the lifespan or has there been fluidity?

A behavior analyst coming from a family of origin with two female parents, assigned to serve a family who is vocal about their beliefs that heterosexuality is the only acceptable form of sexuality, may experience significant discomfort. Awareness of this difference and the knowledge that competing beliefs may impact treatment can lead the behavior analyst to an open dialog with supervisors about whether this case may or may not be a good fit for this analyst for ongoing treatment and if it is, the needed supports to help ensure cultural sensitivity, competence, and respect for all involved parties.

Indigenous Heritage

This domain of culture relates to people who can be viewed as being the original inhabitants of a specific area. In the United States and Canada, this would refer to American Indian or Alaska Native individuals. The U.S. Bureau of Labor Statistics (2016) data reports that 2.09% percent of respondents self-identified as a member of this group, which supports Hays's (2016) classification as this group is the minority, not dominant group, in this area. Some guiding questions for exploration after determining if one identifies with the dominant or minority group could include:

1.   What are one's own experiences related to individuals of indigenous heritage?
2.   What stereotypes does one have related to individuals of indigenous heritage?

A behavior analyst who grew up in the lower 48 states moves to Alaska and begins providing ABA services. Living in Alaska, the behavior analyst encounters more individuals who identify as Alaska Natives. Awareness of this difference can lead the behavior analyst to delve into the literature of the culture and history of the area to be better equipped to be sensitive to the needs of a population that may be new to the behavior analyst. Seeking out mentorship from a behavior analyst who identifies as a member of this cultural group may also prove beneficial.

National Origin

This domain of culture relates to whether one was born in the country where they live. In 2009, the US Census Bureau indicated that 1.3% of the respondents were born outside of the United States, which supports Hays (2016) classification of US-born Americans as the dominant group in this area. Some guiding questions for exploration after determining if one identifies with the dominant or minority group could include:

1.   What are one's own experiences related to immigrants, refugees, and other individuals who were not born in the United States?
2.   What stereotypes does one have related to individuals born outside of the United States and who are currently living in the country?
3.   Are these beliefs consistent over time, or have they changed?

A behavior analyst who was born in the United States is assigned to work in an area with a high concentration of individuals who were born in Colombia and immigrated to the United States. The behavior analyst may have blind spots related to the experiences that led families' decisions to immigrate or the experience itself of immigration or living in one place while perhaps considering another culture and country "home." Upon recognition of this, the behavior analyst may choose to learn more about the immigration process in the United States and perhaps specifically as it relates to those coming from Colombia and Colombian history and culture.

Gender

This domain of culture relates to which sex an individual identifies with, and as more is learned about gender and its expression and identity, it would be remiss to not include those who identify as genderfluid or non-binary. Males would be considered the dominant group in this area. Some guiding questions for exploration after determining if one identifies with the dominant or minority group could include:

1.   What experiences has one had related to gender, gender identity, and gender expression?
2.   What beliefs does one hold about male or female roles and responsibilities?
3.   How might that impact one's work?

An illustration of this in practice could be as follows. A behavior analyst who identifies as male is assigned to work with an adolescent who identifies as gender non-binary. The behavior analyst is not familiar with the language around individuals identifying as non-binary. Awareness of this knowledge deficit can lead to the behavior analyst seeking out more information to be better equipped to speak and behave in a manner that prioritizes the culture of the client in this situation and models culturally sensitive and competent behavior, validating the client's identity.

CASE STUDY

Miss Carolina Martinez is a 23-year-old behavior analyst working in a school setting serving children identified as having a disability and requiring specially designed instruction. She provides services directly to students and also serves in a consultative capacity to classroom teachers, helping them to strengthen their classroom behavior management strategies.

Mr. Cory Sydes is a fifth-grade general education classroom teacher who has submitted a referral for support from Carolina related to a few students in his classroom who have been engaging in challenging behavior, such as calling out and making noises during instructional time. Mr. Sydes is a 48-year-old Caucasian male who has been teaching in the same school for the last 12 years.

(continued)

(continued)

Miss Martinez arrives for the first meeting and is prepared to gather information about the antecedents, behaviors, and consequences of the students in Mr. Sydes's class related to the behavior of calling out and noise making. She previously sent Mr. Sydes an electronic version of a behavior questionnaire to complete prior to their first meeting. She had not received it prior to the first meeting. Miss Martinez was angry that the questionnaire had not been completed as she is currently serving multiple schools and there never seems to be enough time. She was running late to the meeting coming from another school in the district across town where a meeting ran later than expected.

When she arrived at the classroom, Mr. Sydes was feeling irritated that she was late. He had agreed to meet during his planning period and was feeling his time was not being valued. He had received the electronic forms and is not very technologically savvy, so he did not complete them and was embarrassed to ask for help. When Miss Martinez began speaking, she spoke with an accent that was unfamiliar and difficult to understand for Mr. Sydes. After about 10 minutes, Miss Martinez and Mr. Sydes both felt the consultation was not going very smoothly. After 30 minutes, the appointment time was over and both professionals left feeling unheard, unappreciated, and disinterested in moving forward with a collaborative relationship.

Case Study Questions

1. Using the ADDRESSING model, identify some areas where Miss Martinez's and Mr. Sydes's own cultural identity may have impeded his or her ability to understand the other person.

2. How might he and she move forward and repair the situation to be able to help support the students Mr. Sydes were concerned about?

3. How does a better understanding of each of their cultural membership, as well as that of the other person, improve the interaction and thus the collaborative efforts to support the student?

4. What components of the Professional and Ethical Compliance Code could be jeopardized without adequate cultural awareness and competence?

Self-Reflection Activity

Creating a Cultural Sketch. Now that you have been able to apply the ADDRESSING framework to a practical case in behavior analysis, take some time to reflect on yourself as a behavior analyst. Review the different cultural groups outlined in the ADDRESSING framework. Fill in your membership in the different groups, identify if this is the dominant or minority group, and think about how this may impact your work as a behavior analyst.

Reflect on the information entered into Table 2.1. Membership in each area, whether dominant group or minority group, is likely to create biases in each individual. The goal, in

TABLE 2.1 Creating Our Own Cultural Sketch

ADDRESSING cultural group	How I identify in this group Am I in the dominant or minority group in this area?	Implications for my work Where does my privilege lie? What groups may be easy/difficult for me to work with based on my membership in this area?
Age/Generation		
Disability (Congenital)		
Disability (Acquired)		
Religion and Spiritual Identity		
Ethnicity and Racial Identity		
Socioeconomic Status		
Sexual Identity		
Indigenous Heritage		
National Origin		
Gender (identity and expression)		

Source: Hays, P. A. (2013). *Connecting Across Cultures: The Helper's Toolkit.* Thousand Oaks, CA: SAGE, pp. 15–16.

an exercise of this nature and in the ADDRESSING framework as a whole, is to become aware of where one stands in each of these groups and how that may impact one's worldview. Even more integral, as behavior analysts, is to gain insight where one's view may be different than that of an individual with whom one is working. Behavior analysis is the interaction between an organism and its environment. Culture can be conceptualized as environmental interactions that persist, over time, for specific groups, creating cultural norms. When one is missing information about that culture of which a client or family or supervisee belongs, one may be missing important contextual factors that could impact behavior analytic intervention for that individual, family, or group.

Gaining awareness is the first step. The next is to seek out more information. This is the parallel process to what behavior analysts are encouraged to do before working in new areas, in the BACB's® Professional and Ethical Compliance Code, specifically Section 1.02, which encourages behavior analysts to obtain more education and supported experience before taking on different clinical roles. In identifying gaps in cultural knowledge, one could go to cultural literature to gain more information about the norms and histories to better understand the contingencies that may differ from one's own. Another way to increase cultural competence would be to seek out supervision or consultation by another behavior analyst who has more experience with the specific cultural domain where one is noticing a blind spot or a deficit of knowledge.

For those serving in supervisory capacities, embedding activities such as the activity in this chapter can serve as additional learning opportunities for students and supervisees. Supervisors can model cultural competence and cultural sensitivity in interactions with others and share their experiences from practice related to cultural differences and similarities. Emphasizing the importance of talking about cultural variables and being open to those discussions, when brought up by students and supervisees, also helps to ensure cultural competence. Cultural sensitivity is seen as a value for behavior analysts and behaviors aligned with those values are highly valued by the supervisor and the organization and perhaps even the field as a whole. These additional activities endeavor to increase one's own knowledge, resulting in greater success in interactions between the behavior analyst and identified clients, ultimately leading to greater outcomes of the application of the science of behavior analysis.

CHAPTER DISCUSSION QUESTIONS

Now that you have learned about the ADDRESSING framework, please answer the following questions:

1. In what areas of culture, as defined by the ADDRESSING framework, do you find yourself in the minority? In the majority? How does reviewing this information align with or is dissonant from your previous ideas of your own cultural membership?

2. Think of a time when you were engaged in practice with someone whose cultural membership differed from your own in one or more areas. Discuss your experience in that situation.

3. Give three examples and three non-examples of culturally sensitive interactions with someone whose cultural membership differs than yours in at least one area from the ADDRESSING model.

4. How could failing to be aware of one's own cultural belonging lead to increased likelihood of violations to the BACB® Professional and Ethical Compliance Code?

5. Create a plan for how to continue to enhance your learning and awareness around cultural members.

References

American Psychological Association. (2016). *Ethical principles of psychologists and code of conduct.* Retrieved from https://www.apa.org/ethics/code/index

American Psychological Association. (2019). *Socioeconomic status advocacy.* Retrieved May 1, 2019, from www.apa.org/advocacy/socioeconomic-status/index

Association for Behavior Analysis International. (2019a). *Diversity policy.* Retrieved from https://www.abainternational.org/about-us/policies-and-positions.aspx

Association for Behavior Analysis International. (2019b). *What is behavior analysis.* Retrieved from https://www.abainternational.org/about-us/behavior-analysis.aspx

Baio, J., Wiggins, L., Christensen, D. L., Maenner, M. J., Daniels, J., Warren, Z. . . . Dowling, N. F. (2018). Prevalence of autism spectrum disorder among children aged 8 years – Autism and developmental disabilities monitoring network, 11 sites, United States, 2014. *MMWR Surveill, 67*(6), 1–23. http://doi.org/10.15585/mmwr.ss6706a1External

Behavior Analyst Certification Board. (2014). *Professional and ethical compliance code for behavior analysts.* Littleton, CO: Author.

Behavior Analyst Certification Board. (2019). *About behavior analysis.* Retrieved from www.bacb.com/about-behavior-analysis/

de Melo, C. M., de Castro, M.S.L.B., & de Rose, J.C.C. (2015). Some relations between culture, ethics and technology in B. F. Skinner. *Behavior and Social Issues, 24,* 39–55. https://doi.org/10.5210/bsi.v24i0.4796

Fong, E. H., & Tanaka, S. (2013). Multicultural alliance of behavior analysis standards for cultural competence in behavior analysis. *International Journal of Behavioral Consultation and Therapy, 8*(2), 17–19. https://doi.org/10.1037/h0100970

Hays, P. A. (2009). Integrating evidence-based practice, CBT, and multicultural therapy: Ten steps to culturally competent practice. *Professional Psychology: Research and Practice, 40*(4), 354–360. http://doi.org/10.1037/a0016250

Hays, P. A. (2013). *Connecting across cultures: The Helper's toolkit.* Thousand Oaks, CA: SAGE.

Hays, P. A. (2016). *Addressing cultural complexities in practice: Assessment, diagnosis, and therapy* (3rd ed.). Washington, DC: American Psychological Association.

Meerwijk, E. L., & Sevelius, J. M. (2017). Transgender population size in the United States: A meta-regression of population-based probability samples. *American Journal of Health, 107*(2), e1–e8. https://doi.org/10.2105/AJPH.2016.303578

National Health Statistics Report. (2014). *Sexual orientation and health among U.S. Adults: National Health Interview Survey,* 2013. Retrieved from https://www.cdc.gov/nchs/data/nhsr/nhsr077.pdf

Skinner, B. F. (1981). Selection by consequences. *Science, 213,* 501–504.

U.S. Bureau of Labor Statistics. (2016). *Race, economics, and social status.* Retrieved from www.bls.gov/spotlight/2018/race-economics-and-social-status/pdf/race-economics-and-social-status.pdf

3

Standards for Culturally Sensitive Practice of Applied Behavior Analysis

Elizabeth Hughes Fong

Learning Objectives

■ Provide a background on the diversification of the United States and how it might impact service delivery.

■ Describe the development of multicultural services in behavior analysis.

■ Describe at least one way to apply multicultural practice to behavior analysis.

Applied behavior analysis (ABA) came to light as a field, discipline, and practice beginning in the late 19th century (Morris, Altus, & Smith, 2013). While it may be argued that behaviorism existed prior to this, many important publications around behaviorism came out during this period. Some of the notable authors include B. F. Skinner, John B. Watson, J. R. Kantor, and Fred Keller (Morris et al., 2013; Gilmore, 2019). While these were not the only significant contributors to ABA, they are some of the early prominent ones whose contributions to the field are widely acknowledged. Another common thread among these early pioneers in ABA is that they are all Anglo-American men. In fact, if we look at the demographics of the United States around this time period (1910), 88.4% of the population were white, 10.9% were Negro, 0.3% were Indian, 0.1% were Chinese, 0.2% were Japanese, and 0.1% other (United States Census Bureau, n.d.a). Fast forward to the establishment of the Behavior Analyst Certification Board® (BACB®), which was established in 1998, and the demographics of the United States continued to diversify. Around this time period (1997), 82.6% were white, 12.6% were black, 0.8% were American Indian or Eskimo Aleut, and 3.75% were Asian or Pacific Islander (1998 United States Census Bureau, n.d.b). In those 78 years, the change in the demographics of the US population is prominent.

Examining the US Census in 2018, 76.5% of the population were white, 13.4% of the population were African American, 1.3% were American Indian and Alaska Native alone, 5.9% were Asian, and 0.2% were Hawaiian and other Pacific Islander (2018 United States Census Bureau, n.d.c). By examining this data, it is clear that the United States is continuing to diversify. This means that both the population a behavior analyst might serve and the behavior analyst themselves are not part of the same demographic as when Watson and Skinner first began to discuss behaviorism. With this change in demographics, it is important for behavior analysts to educate themselves and know how to be effective practitioners in serving an increasingly diverse population of clients.

While the topic of culturally competent services has circulated for decades, mental health professionals have more recently taken a strong interest in the development of resources, training models, laws, and guidelines required to achieve appropriate standards (Sue, Zane, Hall, & Berger, 2009). In addition, as a result of health disparities within the United States, there have been changes at the federal and state levels (e.g., US Department of Health and Human Services) and within organizational structures, where more employers are seeking out professionals who have greater experience and training working with diverse populations (Bhui, Warfa, Edonya, McKenzie, & Bhugra, 2007). The guidelines that currently exist within the framework and bylaws of the Behavior Analyst Certification Board® (BACB®) are similar to those upheld by the American Psychological Association. What remains to be determined is whether or not those simple guidelines can be sufficient to ensure behavior analysts are capable of confidently providing culturally competent services on a national and global level. The development of multicultural guidelines would more clearly ensure that clinicians are providing multicultural sensitive services since they would be given a with a framework to guide their practice.

In a 2015 survey of behavior analysts by Hughes Fong, Jarmuz Smith, Dogan, Woolery, and Serna, 987 BACB® certificants completed a 33-question online survey. Subjects included practitioner demographics, client demographics, cultural training and experience, as well as qualitative data about practitioner opinions on training and experience needed for competency. The majority of respondents reported spending less than 10% of their time working outside of their culture. The second highest among of time spent working outside of the respondent's culture was 41%–60%. Similarly, the largest number of respondents indicated that they spend 41%–60% of the time working with a different race/ethnicity. Most respondents viewed themselves as mostly competent or somewhat competent. This is interesting, as the majority of respondents also reported to have received fewer than five hours of further training via webinars, seminars, workshops, and so forth in cultural training/education since receiving their degree. The second and third largest number of respondents reported receiving at least one years' experience working with culturally diverse populations and no cultural training/education since receiving their degree. These results are interesting, as how are respondents classifying themselves as culturally competent when there are no adopted standards for culturally sensitive practice of behavior analysis, or no definition in behavior analysis as to what culturally sensitive practice of behavior analysis should look like?

What Is Culturally Sensitive Practice?

Culturally sensitive practice has historically gone by many names for similar concepts, such as cultural competence, cultural adaptation practice, culturally informed practice, cultural awareness, cultural humility, or culturally appropriate practice, just to name a few. Cultural sensitivity may be conceptualized as awareness and ability to utilize and apply information (e.g., race, culture, gender, sexual orientation, religion) when working with clients (Unver, Uslu, Kocatepe, & Kuguoglu, 2019). Culturally sensitive practice might involve ensuring appropriate communication across cultures; this might include eye contact, body contact, vocal language, written forms, body language, and so forth. A lack of culturally sensitive practice can impact the client-clinician relationship and cause difficulties with implementing programs (Unver et al., 2019).

History of Multicultural Guidelines in Psychology

Before examining multicultural guidelines in behavior analysis, it might be useful to see how they have developed in other closely related fields, such as psychology. In 1964, the Civil Rights Act improved equality in education, employment, and housing for minorities (Arredondo & Perez, 2006). Around this time, the Association of Black Psychologists (ABPsi) was formed, and later the Asian American Psychological Association, the National Hispanic Psychological Association, and the Society of Indian Psychologists. These groups were formed in order to promote their heritage and fight against the marginalization that the groups felt from the American Psychological Association. Over the next 40 years, a multicultural movement developed in psychology. As a part of this movement, psychologists, with guidance from the American Counseling Association, developed their multicultural guidelines for the field of psychology. The first multicultural guidelines called *Guidelines on Multicultural Education, Training, Research, Practice, and Organizational Change for Psychologists* were published in 2002 and approved at the 2002 annual conference by the American Psychological Association (APA) Council of Representatives (American Psychological Association, 2017). The purpose of the guidelines was to highlight the role of diversity and multiculturalism in impacting individuals and groups. There were six guidelines developed, each one with a specific intent to address an area of concern in practice, teaching, research, organizational development, and change (Arredondo & Perez, 2006). A few years after the development of the multicultural guidelines in 2005, Dr. Ron Levant established a task force to address diversity within the APA (Arredondo & Perez, 2006).

In 2017, the APA revised the multicultural guidelines in response to changing times from the first version in published in 2003. Among the changes, additional guidelines were added bringing the total number of guidelines up to ten and broadening the conceptualization of what it means to be multicultural (American Psychological Association, 2017). The focus of the guidelines continues to be on "contextual factors and intersectionality among and between reference group identities, including culture, language, gender, race, ethnicity, ability status, sexual orientation, age, gender identity, socioeconomic status, religion, spirituality, immigration status, education, and employment, among other variables" (American Psychological Association, 2017, p. 8).

History of Multicultural Guidelines in Behavior Analysis

The history of multicultural guidelines in behavior analysis is short. In 2011, the Multicultural Alliance of Behavior Analysts (MultiABA) was approved as a special interest group (SIG) as part of the Association for Behavior Analysts International. The mission of this SIG was

> to connect behavior analysts who have interest and/or experience in serving multicultural/minority populations – whether they be ethnic, religious, geographic, socioeconomic, or linguistic. The hope is to create a network of behavior analysts who speak a language or have a skill set relevant to a given population with people who need those services, as well as to connect behavior analysts with others who share common interests.
>
> (Association for Behavior Analysis International, n.d.)

As part of their mission, two of the founding board members wanted to develop guidelines or standards to help guide clinicians on how to be ethical and culturally sensitive clinicians. In 2013, Hughes Fong and Tanaka developed and published the "Multicultural Alliance of Behavior Analysts Standards for Cultural Competency in Behavior Analysis." As part of that article, the authors proposed seven standards for cultural competence in behavior analysis, which centered around ethics and values, self-awareness, cross cultural application, diverse workforce, language diversity, and professional education and referrals. These guidelines were then shared with the BACB®, ABAI, and the Association of Professional Behavior Analysts (APBA); however, they were not official adopted by any of these groups. However, MultiABA as an organization did adopt them. In 2019, MultiABA rebranded as the "Culture and Diversity SIG" in order to have a more inclusive and broader platform, and they may look to revise these guidelines and push for greater acceptance in the field.

Going one step further, standards from culturally sensitive practice could elaborate on what makes the practice of behavior analysis sensitive to diverse populations. While further work needs to be done in this area, one would assume that these would include education and training, advocacy, cross cultural communication, cultural competency, and self-reflection at a minimum. By including education and training, behavior analysts could ensure that a culturally sensitive practitioner is able to obtain the necessary training to know what culturally sensitive practice is. Advocacy would allow for behavior analysts to advocate for the needs of their client where appropriate. Cross-cultural communication would help ensure that a culturally sensitive behavior analyst is able to understand and communicate in meaningful ways with their clients. Cultural competency would build on the standards described by Hughes Fong and Tanaka (2013) by ensuring that behavior analysts have the skills necessary to be culturally competent behavior analysts. Finally, self-reflection as a proposed standard for culturally sensitive practice would ensure that behavior analysts are able to reflect on their values, beliefs, and biases and how these might impact service delivery.

Another notable development in behavior analysis relating to diversity, was the ABAI Task Force on Diversity, Respect, and Inclusion, which organized a diversity panel discussion held at the ABAI's 2018 annual conference. Various members from the behavior analytic community came together to discuss steps that have been taken in increasing respect and inclusion, as well as to answer questions and concerns from the participants. From this panel discussion, a task force for inclusion and development was developed in order to make recommendations to the ABAI Executive Council on the topic. The development of this task force led to the recommendation to develop a more permanent committee on diversity and inclusion as part of ABAI.

Ethics and Multicultural Guidelines

As previously stated, there are currently no widely adopted standards for multicultural competency. There are a number of ethical guidelines from the BACB® that are applicable, specifically from the BACB's® Professional and Ethical Compliance Code for Behavior Analysts (2019) codes 2.02 (Boundaries of Competence) and 1.05 (Professional and Scientific Relationship). These codes describe how behavior analysts should only work in areas that they are familiar with, via education, training, or experience, or, if they are unfamiliar, to first obtain the necessary education, training, or experience from an expert. Similarly, discrimination should not be occurring, and if a behavior analyst feels that they may be biased and this impacts their work, to make referrals where necessary.

While codes of ethics are a good starting point, they do not fully address the needs that multicultural guidelines would. In addition, some argue that professional codes of ethics minimize multicultural issues, are missing a moral philosophical framework, and may promote unintentional racism (Pettifor, 2001). There are additional ethical concerns relating to multicultural guidelines and competencies and ethical practice. The APA's original multicultural guidelines were developed to specifically address some of the ethical issues related to diversity. These include issues around categorization, stereotyping, color blindness, ignorance of within-group differences, policy development, acculturation, ethnic and racial identity, oppression, use of inappropriate research designs, failure to conduct research in the participants' primary language, importance of context and socialization in treatment, and ethnicity and race as variables in research to be explored (Arredondo & Perez, 2006). By not having a set of multicultural guidelines, our field is not fully addressing some of these issues and leaving behavior analysts to problem-solve them independently.

Challenges and Strengths

There are a number of challenges in establishing multicultural guidelines. The first challenge is that there is as yet no task force or committee formally established to address multiculturalism in behavior analysis. ABAI has taken steps to create such a task force, but it is still in its infancy and there is much work to be done.

Another challenge is that the lack of a committee may indicate that there may not be a universal consensus that multicultural guidelines need to be established. For some, the statements in the codes of ethics might be enough to address this topic. Behavior analysts should recognize on a more universal level that culture impacts practice and research. It is only by taking that step and advocating on how to be culturally sensitive behavior analysts that such a committee might be created under the major behavior analytic organizations.

A third challenge is defining what multiculturalism and cultural sensitive practice means in behavior analysis and how this might be related to culturally sensitive in both practice *and* research. Often times multiculturalism includes race, gender, ability, socioeconomic status, and religion, but this would need to be decided. In addition, the field should look to not only focus on culturally sensitive practice but also explore what this looks like in research. For example, including more information about client demographics for social validity or social validity reporting at all to know how interventions were accepted (or not) by clients, caregivers, staff, and so forth. In research conducted by Lee, Hughes Fong, and Catagnus (2016) examining social validity, they found that overall, the reporting of social validity is inconsistent and the data was inconsistent. However, there was a notable increase in social validity reporting in 2015. Similarly, in 2006, there was a significant increase in the reporting of social validity, specifically in the reporting of the social importance of the effects.

Not reporting social validity or demographics makes it difficult to know the generalizability of interventions and one could even argue if they were ethical, as the BACB® Professional and Ethical Compliance Code for Behavior Analysts (2019) states that should include obtaining client consent and input.

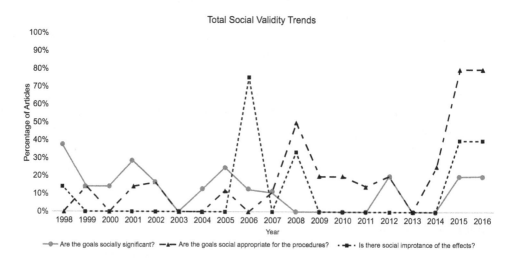

FIGURE 3.1 Social Validity Trends, 1998–2016

One of the strengths is that some of the current codes that behavior analysis has may be good starting points for the development of such standards on multiculturalism and diversity issues. For example, the APA's guidelines also include language around the need for psychologists to obtain training, experience, consultation, or supervision to help ensure that they are competent in providing services to diverse clients. Similar, discrimination is also prohibited (American Psychological Association, 2017). This is a strength for two reasons: (1) the thought is that these are needs for ethical services provision and (2) as mentioned, these can be reused when creating multicultural guidelines.

Another strength is that steps are already being taken in behavior analysis to start to address some of these issues. Conference presentations, journals, and webinars are already discussing some of the deficits and needs in addressing diverse populations. In addition, as previously stated, ABAI created a task force on inclusion and diversity and held formal meetings at their annual conferences in 2018 and 2019 to address these topics.

Conclusion

Behavior analysis is a relatively new field and it is not surprising that multicultural guidelines have yet to be developed. However, now is the time for behavior analysts to think about the direction they want the field to go. As the population continues to diversify, this is going to impact the clients that are seen as well as the behavior analysts in the field. It would be to the advantage of the field to begin to think about how they want to position themselves to provide the most ethical and comprehensive services as possible. The main initial step would be through the development and acceptance of a standard set of multicultural guidelines and defining what culturally sensitive practice means in behavior analysis.

CASE STUDY

Tanya is a new behavior analyst located in the United States and she has been asked to provide remote services to a 6-year-old boy recently diagnosed with autism spectrum disorder. The family is located in Jamaica. While Tanya is familiar with providing home base services and using telehealth to deliver ABA services, she has never worked with a family from Jamaica. While doing her intake, Tanya noticed that she sometimes has difficulty understanding the family due to differences in communication. The family speaks Jamaican Patois as well as Jamaican Standard English. In addition, the mother described significant barriers such as fear of her son being stigmatized as unruly in the community and his behaviors stemming from a lack of discipline in the home. In addition, the family also experiencing hardships. For example, community members believe the child is "plain rude" and needs to go to church more regularly and that the child gets away with "murder". The boy is unable to attend a specialized school for children with autism due to overcrowding, so he is not currently in school because of a lack of staff training. The family is looking for a "shadow" to accompany the boy to school, which Tanya would also supervise remotely.

DISCUSSION QUESTIONS

1.   Do you feel Tanya should accept this case? Why or why not?
2.   What BACB® Guidelines for Professional Conduct should Tanya be aware of?
3.   What additional steps do you feel Tanya should take in order to provide sound ABA services as well as to ensure she is engaging in culturally sensitive practice?

References

American Psychological Association. (2017). *Multicultural guidelines: An ecological approach to context, identity, and intersectionality.* Retrieved from www.apa.org/about/policy/multicultural-guidelines.pdf

Arredondo, P., & Perez, P. (2006). Historical perspectives on the multicultural guidelines and contemporary applications. *Professional Psychology: Research and Practice, 37*(1), 1–5. http://doi.org/10.1037/0735-7028.37.1.1

Association for Behavior Analysis International. (n.d.). *Special interest groups: Multicultural SIG: Multicultural alliance of behavior analysts.* Retrieved from www.abainternational.org/constituents/special-interests/sig-details.aspx

Bhui, K., Warfa, N., Edonya, P., McKenzie, K., & Bhugra, D. (2007). Cultural competence in mental health care: A review of model evaluations. *BMC Health Services Research, 7*(1), 15.

Fong, E. H., Jarmuz-Smith, S., Dogan, R., Serna, R., & Woolery, K. (2015). *The behavior analyst and cultural competency.* REDCap (Research Electronic Data Capture).

Fong, E. H., & Tanaka, S. (2013). Multicultural alliance of behavior analysis standards for cultural competence in behavior analysis. *International Journal of Behavioral Consultation and Therapy, 8*(2), 17.

Gilmore, H. (2019). *Brief history of applied behavior analysis.* Psych Central. Retrieved November 4, 2019, from https://pro.psychcentral.com/child-therapist/2019/02/brief-history-of-applied-behavior-analysis/

Lee, H., Hughes Fong, E., & Catagnus, R. (2016). *Social validity reporting in behavior analytic journals from 1998–2016.* Unpublished manuscript.

Morris, E. K., Altus, D. E., & Smith, N. G. (2013). A study in the founding of applied behavior analysis through its publications. *The Behavior Analyst, 36*(1), 73–107. https://doi.org/10.1007/bf03392293

Pettifor, J. L. (2001). Are professional codes of ethics relevant for multicultural counselling? *Canadian Journal of Counselling and Psychotherapy, 35*(1), 26–35.

Sue, S., Zane, N., Nagayama Hall, G. C., & Berger, L. K. (2009). The case for cultural competency in psychotherapeutic interventions. *Annual Review of Psychology, 60,* 525–548. https://doi.org/10.1146/annurev.psych.60.110707.163651

United States Census Bureau. (n.d.a). *1910 Census: Volume 1. Population, general report and analysis, Chapter 2. Color or race, nativity and parentage.* Retrieved from www2.census.gov/library/publications/decennial/1910/volume-1/volume-1-p4.pdf

United States Census Bureau. (n.d.b). *Statistical abstract of the United States: 1998. Section 1. Population.* Retrieved from www2.census.gov/library/publications/1998/compendia/statab/118ed/tables/sasec1.pdf?

United States Census Bureau. (n.d.c). *Quick facts: People.* Retrieved from www.census.gov/quickfacts/fact/table/US/PST045218

Unver, V., Uslu, Y., Kocatepe, V., & Kuguoglu, S. (2019). Evaluation of cultural sensitivity in healthcare service among nursing students. *European Journal of Educational Research, 8*(1), 257–265. https://doi.org/10.12973/eu-jer.8.1.257

CHAPTER

4

Applied Behavior Analysis Within the African American Community

Shawn T. Capell and Mawule A. Sevon

Learning Objectives

- Effectively identify and define culture specific to African American communities.
- Describe the historical impact of trauma as it relates to African American communities and how this trauma can impact applied behavior analysis service delivery.
- Identify existing behavior analytic literature describing the impacts of ABA within the African American community.
- Pinpoint ethical and professional standards related to service delivery specific to African American communities.
- Address community-specific concerns related to African American communities

---

Introduction

Developing culturally responsive and just practices for serving African American communities requires an understanding of culture and race. Typically, both race and culture are used interchangeably to label a collective group's identity. Evidence shows a difference in these two constructs and how knowledge of these differences impact clinical work. Culture is the established shared values, beliefs, and customs developed through experiences (Wilson, 2014; Kashima, 2014). It grows into a system of rules that are the core of communities (Sue, Sue, Neville, & Smith, 2019; Fong, Catagnus, Brodhead, Quigley, & Field, 2016). Wilson (2014) outlines two aspects of culture, which include deep versus surface culture. Surface culture includes the practices of a group, which are seen and observed from the outside. Underlying these practices are the unspoken and shared rules of the group. These unconscious processes are considered deep culture (Myer, 1987).

Early studies in behavior analysis included the impact of the environment on the organism. Skinner (1981) stated that human behavior is a product of the contingencies of survival and are responsible for the natural selection of the species. The contingencies of reinforcement are responsible for the repertoires acquired, and the particular contingencies are maintained by the social environment (Skinner, 1981). These contingencies are influenced by the culture of the person's environment and also how cultural practices grow over time (Wilson, 2014; Kashima, 2014).

Historically, developing cultural competency included practices developing a list of cultural practices within each group resulting in operating in a model of stereotypes. Helping fields have moved from competence in the work of multiculturalism to a responsive approach (Clauss-Ehlers, Chiriboga, Hunter, Roysircar, & Tummala-Narra, 2019). Sue and colleagues (2019) state that culturally responsive service delivery includes openness and acknowledgment of beliefs associated with the identities and sociodemographic differences of clients. Fong and colleagues (2016) defined cultural awareness, particularly in the science of behavior analysis, as understanding the importance of the behavior to the person and society.

African American Identity

The shared identity of a group is impacted by the culture of the individual group and factors rooted in their environment. The racial and cultural labels of a community are largely influenced by the time, cross-cultural influence, and the shared beliefs of the inner group (Sue et al., 2019; Wilson, 2014; Kashima, 2014). The racial labeling of the African American cultural group is an example of shifts in group labeling. During history, multiple names were used to describe those of African descent. Some of these names were determined without acknowledgment or input by people of African descent. Other names were established by the group in response to historical oppression. Currently, black and African American are used interchangeably in scientific literature, popular culture, and throughout political conversations (Agyemang, Bhopal, & Bruijnzeels, 2005; Zilber & Niven, 2000). As with any group, every person in the group will not identify in the same manner. As a culturally responsive professional it is important to refer to individual preferences in reference to all labels of identity for all racial, cultural, ethnic, and other social groups. For the purpose of this chapter, we will use the label of African American to identify people of African descent living in the United States.

Knowledge of African Americans has been researched in the United States to create or combat harmful narratives. As noted in this chapter, culture includes shared beliefs and values (Kashima, 2014; Boykin, 1986), which differs from racial identity, the significance and meaning of connection to the membership of the group. The identity of African American differs from other group to the history of oppression, resulting in race playing a large role in their everyday lives. Assimilation of a more Eurocentric culture and maintaining their original cultural systems and values was not completely optional and was carried out somewhat as a method of survival in turn resulting in an expression of individualized identity (Sellers, Smith, Shelton, Rowley, & Chavous, 1998). Seller and colleagues (1998) define this unique racial experience as the Multidimensional Model of Racial Identity (MMRI) racial development framework. The MMRI is particular to those who identify as African American and aims to integrate a comprehensive exploration of the impact of racial oppression and consists of four dimensions.

The first dimension within the MMRI is racial *salience* of race for an individual in relation to their self-concept at a moment in time. The second dimension, racial *centrality*, describes how a person defines themselves based on their race. Salience is fluid and changes across situation, while centrality is constant. The third dimension, racial *regard*, is the feelings and judgments attached to membership within a racial group, whether negative or positive. Lastly, Seller and colleagues (1998) define the final dimension of racial *ideology* as the thoughts on the expected behaviors of others within the same group in relation to the mainstream society. Racial regard and ideology are both highly impacted by the environment. The MMRI states race has a significant influence on the behavior of individuals across various settings and situations (Sellers et al., 1998).

Development of Race in the United States

Individuals with African descent within the United States have histories that extend across multiple countries and continents around the globe, producing complexities within the shared group. For the purpose of the text, the culture and historical experience of African Americans will be discussed. It is important to remember that not all people that identify racially as African American will share the same cultural experiences. African American culture in the United States is unique due to weaponization of race in this nation (Sellers et al., 1998; Boykin, 1986). Race is a social construct that is used to define the physical characteristics of a shared group (Degruy-Leary, 2017). As described earlier in the chapter culture is the shared rules, values, and beliefs develop by a group (Sue et al., 2019). Race relations in the British colonies and throughout what is now known as the United States creates a deep intertwining of race and culture for African American people (Milner, 2007; Boykin, 1986; Tatum, 2017b).

History indicates slavery was not initially built on the construct of race; those of African and European descent could arrive to the British colonies and work their way out of servitude. A shortage in labor during the 17th century left plantation owners looking for methods to maintain labor and capital. Additionally, around this time in US history in the state of Virginia, a racially mixed group of enslaved people rebelled. In efforts to deter different race-enslaved people from joining together in opposition to slavery, the system of racism interconnected with slavery was created (Tatum, 2017b). Social division based on race became integral to the success of the newly developing nation, which remains until present times (DeGruy-Leary, 2017; Tatum, 2017a). Since this act, policies and laws have been developed to undermine the humanity of African American people in the United States. It is important to start a discussion of a people's history with an acknowledgment of their origins leading back to the continent of Africa (Boykins, 1986; Sellers et al., 1998).

The transatlantic slave trade removed people from various regions of Africa and spread them across modern-day North, Central and Latin America (Marques, 2016). Historians noted enslaved Africans arrived with different languages, religions, and customs yet shared large foundational cultural beliefs such as communalism (Marques, 2016; Sellers et al., 1998; Boykin, 1986). Throughout their time enslaved, cultural traditions and practices were stripped of Africans, often by harsh punitive actions, resulting in a merging of maintained African core beliefs and European expectations and norms (Sellers et al., 1998). Oppression has also created shared practices among diverse communities due to historical treatment in the United States. Medical historians reported significant maltreatment of enslaved Africans and African American people stretching back as far as the birth of the nation (Thomas & Casper, 2019).

African American culture is considered dynamic due to the integration of African indigenous culture and conforming to the systems required with living in the United States and developing within the mainstream culture (Sellers et al., 1998; Boykin, 1986). Systems of oppression previously did not allow for the maintaining of indigenous culture, which resulted in the merging of African and European/American culture creating an original cultural experience (Sellers et al., 1998). The African American cultural expression includes three experiences: (1) being of the African American racial group, (2) acculturating to the mainstream culture, and (3) being considered a minority (Boykin, 1986). These foundational theories outline the development of deep structures of African American culture and the practices that follow.

African Americans and the Impact of Bias and Racial Trauma

African American identity and values shape the practices typically distinguished as distinct to the group. Bias has an unusual impact on African Americans leading to disparities in medical access (Faye, 2005), educational attainment (Baker, 2005), interactions with law enforcement (Wilson, Wilson, & Thou, 2015), and other societal conditions. While bias is a natural part of human interaction, the behaviors shaped by bias that follow have damaging outcomes. Bias in the medical field contributes to delays in the treatment and diagnosis of autism among African American children, which represents a substantial health care disparity in the United States (Burkett, Morris, Manning-Courtney, Anthony, & Shambley-Ebron, 2015).

A lack of awareness and access to treatment continues to negatively impact the effectiveness of behavioral interventions within the African American communities it can most benefit. The impact of early diagnosis and intervention has been shown to be the most effective intervention to educate children affected by autism (Rosenwasser & Axelrod, 2001); however, how can this be accomplished if the individuals requiring these services are not made aware of their existence? When a racial group is not provided with accurate and appropriate medical treatment (diagnosis, medication, interventions, etc.), it is impossible for the group as a whole to address generational health concerns and overcome them. African Americans have received substandard care for generations, and it is partially due to these factors that the majority of children within this community do not receive appropriate interventions until the later years (Burkett et al., 2015).

The misdiagnosis of African American children can be considered a contributing factor to the lack of understanding of applied behavior analysis (ABA) within the culture. African American children are more likely to be diagnosed later and misdiagnosed with severe autism in comparison to their Caucasian counterparts (Burkett et al., 2015). As a medical professional is considered to be an expert in their respective field of study, African Americans rarely seek second opinions and/or question a diagnosis once given (Burkett et al., 2015). This reliance on professionals at times can rob a child of years of effective intervention or subject them to inappropriate interventions.

Within the African American culture, the subject of mental health continues to be taboo. The African American culture possesses a zeitgeist that views the discussion of items considered "family topics" outside of the family to be disrespectful and inappropriate. The statement "What goes on in this house stays in this house" is something a large percentage of African American children encounter during development. This understanding within some African American families can restrict willingness to seek assistance regarding children engaging in stereotypic behaviors (Burkett et al., 2015). At times symptoms of autism and family interpretations of these symptoms are different from the cultural group, which compromises their willingness to seek assistance (Burkett et al., 2015). The act of obtaining the appropriate services for some African Americans is seen as going against the established culture, which in itself is very challenging. In addition to perceptions of diagnosis, ABA treatments are at times considered to be very intrusive to the norms within the family, and this can elicit historical traumatic responses from families, which was discussed earlier in this chapter (Roche, Bush, & D'Angelo, 2018).

When implementing ABA services within the African American community it is important to consider the role of the family within the learner's daily life. Some families within the African American community do not reflect the traditional mother, father, and siblings composition. Like other racial groups the family can comprise extended family members, non-related family friends, and community members. Each family unit is composed of a unique set of individuals; however, the total inclusion of all family members is critical in the dissemination of ABA and the improved outcomes for the individuals within this community. According to Robertson (2016), the parent is within a unique role as they are both recipients of interventions and are at times the individuals implementing interventions for their child. This role can serve a dual purpose within the African American community. Parents who have been newly introduced to the science can often have misconceptions of the outcomes and procedures involved. The effective and appropriate inclusion of parents into the intervention procedures assists the behavior analyst in educating the family and community while simultaneously ensuring the most appropriate outcomes for the learner. For the purposes of this chapter, parents are not defined as the traditional biological individuals but rather the individuals charged with the care of a specific learner. Behavior analysts should incorporate a learner's larger community as often as possible to ensure skills developed during intervention are generalized and maintained within the learner's community.

According to Wilson et al. (2015) African Americans have been stereotyped as criminals for years, been viewed as criminal predators, seen as physically threatening, and hold a "biological flaw" in their makeup, causing a predisposition to violence. These preconceived ideas can cause law enforcement to enter into a situation with an established bias against an African American when one is not warranted. The behavior of law enforcement officials can at times additionally serve as a historical trigger for African Americans, causing individuals to engage in specific behavioral responses that from the outside can be viewed as non-compliant, maladaptive behaviors; however, when viewed through the lens of historical trauma can elicit an alternative understanding. Studies conducted by the US Department of Justice indicate approximately 11.9% of current law enforcement officers are of African American heritage (Wilson et al., 2015). Behavior analysts should make all possible efforts to include law enforcement in behavioral interventions and provide positive interactions when possible. Teaching African American learners how to effectively interact with law enforcement, identifying possible culturally sensitive teaching targets related to law enforcement, and incorporating community law enforcement into generalized programming can effect change within the African American communities specific to law enforcement views.

Additionally, bias can have an impact on the perception of behavior challenges in schools. The overuse of suspension and expulsion to address student behavior is most pronounced for children of color, particularly African American students. Moreover, early childhood expulsions and suspensions are matters of health and education equity. This early pattern is linked to further problems in kindergarten and beyond including underachievement, retention, exacerbated behavioral problems, and negative internalized messages during such a critical time in brain development (Gilliam, Maupin, Reyes, Accavitti, & Shic, 2016). This crisis is titled "the discipline gap" and is contributing to the well-known achievement gap. The discipline gap refers to African American students, across gender, who are suspended more often, for more subjective infractions, and with harsher consequences (Gregory, Skiba, & Noguera, 2010). Behavior analysts are in a position to reduce racial discipline disparities by helping educators objectively observe behaviors.

The discipline gap is also connected to the adverse experiences during childhood. Experiences during childhood have lasting effects on life up into adulthood and beyond. In 1991, health professionals found a connection between adversity experienced before the age of 18 and health outcomes. These detrimental events were named adverse childhood experiences (ACEs) and include abuse (i.e., physical, sexual and emotional), neglect (i.e., physical and emotional), and family challenges (Felitti et al., 1998). More recently, the Philadelphia Urban ACE Survey expanded the list of ACEs to include neighborhood violence, racial discrimination, bullying, and living in foster care (Wade, Shea, Rubin, & Wood, 2014). The topic of childhood adversity is shared across all racial and cultural groups, yet due to a system of racial oppression it is worth discussing in this chapter. Philadelphia's inclusion of racism as an ACE increased the possibility of exposure within the African American community. Additionally, with the noted structural barriers, the likelihood of obtaining these forms of adversity are increased.

This information presented is not to create bias but rather to seek the empathy of clinical professionals. Evidence has shown an empathy gap, the inability to see another's beliefs and feelings based on bias, when providing ABA services to African Americans. When educators were given information indicating adversity exposure of African American children, their behaviors were still deemed in need of harsh punishment (Gilliam et al., 2016). Implicit bias and the empathy gap are documented as contributors to the racial disproportional use of exclusion in educational settings. Improving outcomes for students requires a clear understanding of trauma and its impact on behaviors and development. Behavior analysts should continue to see additional training and knowledge on trauma-informed care and integrate their knowledge within behavior analytic practices.

Clinical Applications

Within the previous sections of this chapter we have explored the African American culture within its historical context and intersection with the science of ABA. The information presented within this chapter provides critical competencies of behavior analytic service delivery specific to African American communities. Although this information is critical, the field of ABA has struggled in its full inclusion of these concepts. One such struggle has been the lack of inclusion within the educational and supervision requirements of the field.

Each year hundreds of students receive education in the science of ABA; however, few make tangible contact related to the areas of cultural awareness and diversity. Social validity is considered a cornerstone of science; however, how can one achieve the required levels of socially valid cultural awareness and effectively navigate these areas if they are never exposed to this subject matter? Culturally aware behavior analysts should understand their own cultural values, preferences, characteristics, and circumstances and seek to learn about those of their clients (Fong et al., 2016). Simply put, a good behavior analyst is someone who is culturally aware and can synthesize cultural components into individualized service delivery. A full understanding regarding the impact of culture related to individualized service delivery will produce a well-versed behavior analyst who can be effective in the African American communities they serve.

Within the African American culture, the subject of mental health continues to be taboo. The African American cultures poses a zeitgeist, which views the discussion of items considered "family topics" outside of the family to be disrespectful and inappropriate. The statement "What goes on in this house stays in this house" is something a large percentage of African American children encounter during development. This understanding within some African American families can restrict willingness to seek assistance regarding children engaging in stereotypic behaviors (Burkett et al., 2015). At times symptoms of autism and family interpretations of these symptoms are different from the cultural group, which compromises their willingness to seek assistance (Burkett et al., 2015). The act of obtaining the appropriate services for some African Americans is seen as going against the established culture, which in itself is very challenging. In addition to perceptions of diagnosis, ABA treatments are at times considered to be very intrusive to the norms within the family and this can elicit historical traumatic responses from families, which was discussed earlier in this chapter (Roche, Bush, & D'Angelo, 2018).

When implementing ABA services within the African American community it is important to consider the role of the family within the learner's daily life. Some families within the African American community do not comprise the traditional mother, father, and siblings composition. Like other racial groups, the family can include extended family members, non-related family friends, and community members. Each family unit is composed of a unique set of individuals; however, the total inclusion of all family members is critical in the dissemination of ABA and the improved outcomes for the individuals within this community. According to Robertson (2016), the parent has a unique role as they are both the recipient of interventions and at times the individual implementing interventions for their child. This role can serve a dual purpose within the African American community. Parents who have been newly introduced to the science can often have misconceptions of the outcomes and procedures involved. The effective and appropriate inclusion of parents into the intervention procedures assists the behavior analyst in educating the family and community while simultaneously ensuring the most appropriate outcomes for the learner. For the purposes of this chapter, parents are not defined as the traditional biological individuals but rather the individuals charged with the care of a specific learner. Behavior analysts should incorporate a learner's larger community as often as possible to ensure skills developed during intervention are generalized and maintained within the learner's community.

Roche and colleagues (2018) provided a clear analysis of the current treatment of autism as it relates to an examination of culture. Within this article the authors provide clinicians with an understanding of the required actions needed for effectively working within cultural communities. Examples of these actions include: (1) clinicians should explore personal biases, (2) clinicians should be aware that parents' concerns may differ from theirs, and (3) clinicians should remain flexible. It is through these actions that we will examine how behavior analysts can effectively address treatment among the African American community.

According to the study published by Roche and colleagues (2018), the delivery of ABA services can take on many forms ranging from 40 hours per week of direct specialized intervention to short, targeted sessions related to specialized behavioral issues. These interventions can include multiple members of a community that can directly improve behavioral outcomes. Let us look at the clinical recommendations presented within this study and apply them to the African American community.

Clinicians Should Explore Personal Biases Regarding the Nature of Their Role

Within our personal lives, we all hold specific biases regarding the stimuli we encounter each day. These biases at face value can seem simple; however, they can seriously impact service delivery within the African American population.

Within today's social media culture, it is very easy to establish implicit biases against a culture or group that you do not have regular access to or interaction with. Media attention and coverage at times can contribute to the general belief that African Americans are criminals, with a disproportionate amount of coverage specific to African Americans demonizing them as violent criminals (Wilson et al., 2015). In the event a behavior analyst holds the bias of African Americans being criminals, this will negatively impact their ability to accept cases within this community, provide the appropriate amount of services to this population, and incorporate the community into behavioral interventions.

Within our professional responsibilities, there is no place for bias. Due to a family's lack of understanding, it is easy for a behavior analyst to cut corners, provide substandard care, or provide additional services when not needed. It is the responsibility of the behavior analyst to be an ambassador for the field and educate families regarding appropriate behavioral intervention services.

Clinicians Should Be Aware That Parents' Concerns About Their Children May Differ From Theirs

During the assessment process, the behavior analyst traditionally utilizes a wide range of behavioral tools to identify targets for behavioral intervention. These tools include formalized assessment protocols, direct observations, baseline data collection, and indirect assessment procedures. Following the assessment process, goals are presented to the family for approval regarding targeted behaviors for increase, targeted behaviors for decrease, and skill acquisition. When a behavior analyst does not take into account the wishes of the family, this process can become contentious and negatively affect the professional relationship between clinician and family. Some families will request specific skills be addressed prior to skills identified within the assessment period, and these skills may not be identified as a priority by the behavior analyst. This inability to incorporate a family's wishes can manifest itself as a rigidity within behavioral program implementation. Rigidity within implementation is appropriate for some skills but not across the entire service delivery process.

In the event a parent does not agree with the goals being implemented, their family can at times be classified as "difficult". African American parents who seek out ABA services for their child are looking to increase socially appropriate skills and decrease maladaptive behaviors, and they often vary in their understanding of the science. According to Fong and colleagues (2016), the culturally aware behavior analyst may assist in the increased probability that behavioral analysts will engage in behaviors that are socially acceptable to people from diverse cultures and backgrounds. Yes, there are varying levels of parent involvement and understanding; however, the more African American families and communities are involved with the behavioral interventions in place, the better the generalized outcomes for the learner over time.

Clinicians Should Remain Flexible in the Service Delivery of Interventions

The African American culture is one of rich heritage and substance. Providing services within this community can be challenging due to the lack of understanding of ABA principles, historical trauma, and the general cultural influence within this racial group. Within the area of service delivery, flexibility is key. For example, if a family requests you work with an African American child regarding a specific culturally relevant goal, it is okay to say yes. Within the study conducted by Fong and colleagues (2016), the authors utilized the example of attending a religious service to demonstrate a clinician's flexibility in the area of service delivery. Within their example, a behavior analyst providing in-home and community services for a child with severe autism was asked by the family to assist the child within the area of attending a religious service. The typical service lasted approximately three hours, and because of this the behavior analyst did not feel the child attending church was an appropriate goal at that point of intervention. After intensive conversations in addition to several direct requests from the family, the behavior analyst still did not comply with the family's request. The role of spirituality and religion within the African American community has served as a survival and coping mechanism for ongoing racism, adversity, and loss (Boyd-Franklin, 2010). In the event the behavior analyst does not hold the same views regarding religion, it would be bias not to incorporate goals regarding religious practices into treatment when specifically requested by the family.

Applied Behavior Analysis Training

Currently the field of ABA adheres to Behavior Analyst Certification Board's® (BACB®) *Professional and Ethical Compliance Code for Behavior Analysts* (BACB®, 2016). This code provides practitioners with detailed ethical standards regarding the practice of the science. These ethical practices are interconnected with the BACB's® 4th and 5th edition Task Lists (BACB®, 2017). These provided documents are the basis for coursework completed within the field of ABA. Students receive education across both ethical and technical applications of science; however, there remains no requirement for instruction related to cultural diversity and multicultural concerns within the field. According to Fong, Ficklin, and Lee (2017), the field of ABA needs to recognize the cultural diversity of consumers (specifically those historically marginalized) while examining the role of culture in effective service delivery, practice, and design. According to Beaulieu, Addington, and Almeida (2018), behavior analysts holding a master's degree reported their behavior analytic courses included little (47%) or no (35%) materials related to diversity. This lack of training related to cultural competency and diversity demonstrates a clear area of improvement regarding our science.

New coursework standards should be implemented to address culturally responsive teaching. This term refers to the extent of educators utilizing a student's cultural contributions in transforming their lives, the life of the family, and community at large (Kauffman, Conroy, Gardner, & Oswald, 2008). Courses should encourage students to utilize their past experiences with their identified cultural group and evaluate the effectiveness of their clinical application to other groups. Making a student aware of self-held biases can assist them to address these beliefs prior to interacting with a family outside of the academic setting. These negative inter-actions only serve to paint the field of ABA with a negative connotation within communities where it can be most effective.

Within the already established coursework requirements, an infusion of culturally relevant topics should occur. This increase of culturally relevant topics will assist students in addressing personal deficits regarding culture. The current social climate has made discussions surround-ing topics of race difficult; however, within the field of ABA these conversations are critical to ensure we provide the highest levels of clinical support possible to each client we interact with. Some strategies for increasing self-awareness that can be incorporated into coursework include discussing diverse client interactions with other professionals, reading literature regarding cul-tural issues, self-reflection, mentorship meetings with professionals of diverse backgrounds, and verbal feedback sessions (Fong et al., 2016).

Behavior Analytic Service Delivery

According to the landmark paper, "Some Current Dimensions of Applied Behavior Analysis" (Baer, Wolf, & Risley, 1968), the field of ABA and its interventions should be generalizable across a wide variety of environments. Although this is true, it is not always possible within the real-world application specific to African American families. Each cultural subset possesses their own set of social norms that must be factored into effective behavioral intervention. As behavior analysts it is our ethical and professional responsibility to identify the social norms practiced by our client, their families, and their community and effectively incorporate them into our interventions. According to Fong et al. (2017), the field of behavior analysis continues to serve consumers from increasingly diverse ethnic, racial, and socioeconomic backgrounds, and this increase is anticipated to continue as the field expands.

African Americans oftentimes do not receive the appropriate levels of education regard-ing the benefits of ABA or are not made aware of the science in its entirety. Generally, little to no effort is placed into the education of the African American community related to the benefits of the science and how these benefits can affect the community at large. At times a family's first direct contact with the field of ABA results from a request for services for a family member. The goal of these intake meetings is to obtain specific information related to the client (i.e., insurance information, preferences, possible schedule identification); however, oftentimes a family is never provided with a basic understanding of the scientific journey they are embarking upon. Practitioners of the science must ensure the basic concepts of the science are explained in a language appropriate for the family from the onset of service delivery.

Additionally, within the area of service delivery behavior analysts must understand the cul-tural identity and/or expression of each family they interact with. African American families often express their cultural identity through their belief structure, attire, foods eaten, or hairstyle (Fong et al., 2016). At times these cultural identity expressions can be in direct conflict with the cultural identity expressions of the behavior analyst and/or their current understanding of a family's culture. One of the best tools a behavior analyst can utilize when addressing these concerns is to ask respectful questions to gain further clarification.

Within some African American communities, it is considered a sign of respect to address others by their last names (i.e., Mr. Smith, Ms. Johnson). This cultural norm is not considered an isolated value within the African American community; however, it is widely practiced. When teaching a learner a skill related to greeting and/or identification of others (i.e., expressive and receptive), it might be requested by a family to have the learner address the individual presented in this same manner (which might include the behavior analyst and therapist). Although the behavior analyst might be comfortable with the learner addressing them by their first name, it is important to identify the family's preferences related to this matter. Within the African American community it is considered a sign of respect, and the act of addressing someone who is not a peer by their first name can be considered a sign of disrespect. This might be considered a small programming change; however, it could allow a learner greater access to their community and ensure they engage in socially significant behaviors specific to the African American culture.

Ethical and Professional Considerations

Behavior analysts are provided with strict guidelines related to ethical practices within the field. The BACB's® *Professional and Ethical Compliance Code for Behavior Analysts* (Behavior Analyst Certification Board, 2016) serves as the standard for all ethical conduct within the field. However, this code (revised in 2019) does not address areas of cultural competency. As the field of ABA continues to grow and reach new populations, the ethical code must be adapted to fit the real-world concerns surrounding cultural awareness and diversity. In 2002 the American Psychological Association published *Guidelines on Multicultural Education, Training, Research, Practice and Organizational Change for Psychologists*. Topics discussed within these guidelines include assessment, service delivery, education, and research specific to minority groups. Practitioners are provided with five specific guidelines related to the topic of multicultural service delivery. This document (in conjunction with the APA's professional standards) provides practitioners with a clear framework under which all practice should be conducted. To date, the field of ABA has not undertaken such an endeavor; however, this would provide useful to both students and practitioners of the science. In the absence of such a document within the field of ABA, let us evaluate some aspects of the current ethical code as it relates specifically to the African American population.

The BACB's® *Professional and Ethical Compliance Code for Behavior Analysts* (Behavior Analyst Certification Board, 2016) states that behavior analysts rely on professionally derived knowledge that is based on science and behavior analysis. When viewing the service delivery of ABA through this lens of African American culture, it is very possible for the behavior analysts to hold specific biases against the African American community. These biases are in direct contradiction to the ethical code. When presented with an African American family a behavior analyst should exclude all biases and preconceived notions regarding the family as they are not science based or grounded in the principles of ABA. These internal beliefs can cause negative impacts in service delivery that can ultimately affect the learner. Behavior analysts must examine their own belief system prior to working with clients to ensure personal beliefs are not impacting professional responsibilities.

A universally held belief within the field of ABA is a learner's entitlement to effective treatment. Treatment should be research-based and individualized to fit the needs of the client (Behavior Analyst Certification Board, 2016). As we have discussed previously within this chapter, the African American community extends across the United States, representing various socioeconomic statuses, educational levels, religious beliefs, and other social groups. The needs of one family do not reflect the needs of another, and it is unethical to make this assumption. Behavior analyst must rely on science, observation, and assessment to identify behavioral targets that are appropriate for each individual learner. The inclusion of parent goals is also critical, as this will ensure parents buy into the services being provided.

Lastly, we will look at a behavior analyst's responsibility to the field of ABA. According to the BACB's® *Professional and Ethical Compliance Code for Behavior Analysts* (Behavior Analyst Certification Board, 2016), behavior analysts have an ongoing responsibility to make information regarding the science publicly available to those who need it most. For some behavior analysts, the ultimate goal of their professional career is to present original research within a conference setting; however, this is not the highest level of dissemination. With the increase of African American professionals engaging the field of ABA, dissemination has become more and more important. This dissemination within the African American community by those who are African American can potentially open the door for the next generation of behavior analysts of African American heritage to contribute to furthering the field of behavior analysis.

Best Practice Recommendations

We understand we do not live in a perfect society, and it is impossible for the authors to anticipate your full understanding of working with African American learners after reading this chapter. It must be noted that the African American community is not a monolithic group with one set of needs. Each family unit presents an individual set of strengths and challenges. This chapter is not designed to be a handbook on working with all African Americans; however, it is designed to provide you with some tools to assist you in your process of moving forward in working with clients specific to the African American community.

Within the paper published by Beaulieu et al. (2018), the authors stated:

> The behaviors that embody a culture include the way we socialize with others, the language we use and the specific words within a language, our religion or lack of religion, the way we solve problems and make decisions, the gestures we use, the things we eat, the clothes we wear, gender roles, the way we parent, our values, our beliefs, and our priorities.
>
> (p. 337)

Within the area of best practice, it is critical for behavior analysts to keep this statement in mind across all interactions, specifically within the African American community. Our preconceived biases regarding the African American community are often incorrect and can negatively impact our effectiveness. One African American family does not directly reflect the next family you interact with. It is impossible to generalize your experiences with one African American family across the entire racial group. It is important for clinicians to understand the biases held and address them. Within the Beaulieu et al. (2018) study, the authors provided a detailed questionnaire utilized to evaluate current behavior analysts' training and practices regarding cultural diversity. The questionnaire included questions specifically assessing the respondent's training within the area of cultural diversity, current practice with diverse populations, and their overall feelings toward working with diverse populations. Practitioners should apply this and other self-assessments within daily practice to identify their potential effectiveness in working with individuals from diverse backgrounds, specifically African Americans.

Within the field of ABA, the Association for Behavior Analysis International (ABAI) oversees the science worldwide. Within this organization there are opportunities for professionals to join special interest groups (SIGs). Additionally, outside of the SIGs there are several social media groups specifically geared to African Americans within the field of ABA and service delivery within this community. It must be noted that not all social media groups are created equal; however, they can be utilized as a resource to identify possible solutions to presenting concerns related specifically to the African American population. It would be useful for professionals in the field to maintain active membership and participate in SIGs and social media groups to stay aware of issues related to diversity in the field.

One of the current requirements to maintain a certification within the field of ABA is the completion of continuing education (CE) credits. In addition to practitioners identifying personal biases and joining professional organizations, practitioners should continue to receive training regarding African American populations by contacting CE events specifically geared toward this population. The behavior analyst has the ability to access CEs across a multitude of settings within today's society. From conference attendance to online video reviews and publications, CEs are offered consistently. In the event a behavior analyst is unsure and/or uncomfortable with working with African Americans, they should consider attending CE events to address the concerns presented.

The final best practice recommendation for practitioners specific to the African American community is to get involved within community programs and conduct outreach within this population. As a practitioner of the science, we should consider ourselves to be ambassadors, especially within the African American population. African American children are often diagnosed 1.6 years later than their Caucasian counterparts, and in addition to this delay in diagnosis they are more often misdiagnosed with an adjustment disorder or conduct disorder (Burkett et al., 2015). As behavior analysts we understand the importance of an early diagnosis and early intervention regarding the overall trajectory of an individual's learning. With increased education of health care professionals and the African American community, we can provide socially significant change specific to the service delivery of ABA.

Conclusion

The African American culture is one derived from a rich tapestry of diverse backgrounds and experiences. Although the term African American is utilized to describe this group, in actuality this group is composed of people who come from many ethnic backgrounds and lands who were transported to the United States and through resilience formed a social culture. Through hardships, struggles, oppression, and adversity, the African American race has moved from a substandard class to the place of prominence they hold today. Although great strides have been achieved, more work is still required, especially within the area of ABA.

After reading this chapter, we hope you have identified several solutions to addressing concerns directly related to the African American community. It is important to remember that when working to become culturally responsive, you must remember to gain authentic knowledge. This is not just knowledge generated from a textbook but also from the application of the principles presented within a textbook in clinical application and under the supervision of a competent behavior analyst. Not all African Americans submit to the concerns presented within this chapter, and it is not the authors' intention to communicate this. The authors understand these solutions are not a one-size-fits-all model, and this chapter should not serve as a step-by-step manual to address all concerns related to African Americans and ABA. This chapter and the entire volume should serve as a starting point for practitioners to have an open and honest dialogue surrounding the issues and concerns within the field surrounding cultural diversity specific to diverse populations. It is our sincere hope that the next time you interact with an African American family, you are able to utilize the information presented to provide the highest level of culturally competent service possible.

CASE STUDY

You have been asked to provide behavior analytic services for a 3-year-old African American boy named Devon. He was recently diagnosed with autism and currently lives with his father and mother (who is currently pregnant with a girl). Devon is able to make many vocalizations and is able to say approximately 10 recognizable words. During the assessment period you observed Devon engaging in non-compliance behavior, however the intensity and duration of this non-compliance was approximately 10 seconds of the total duration of the assessment period (10 days). Dad is a police officer and mom is a stay-at-home mother. During the parent interview both mom and dad expressed the following concerns:

■ Devon is very spoiled and does not like to share. With the introduction of an additional child within the home, they feel very nervous regarding Devon's reactions toward the new child.

■ According to Devon's academic setting, he is very behind within his milestones; however, both parents feel it is the school and the lack of structure that is holding Devon back.

(continued)

(continued)

- Dad expressed his desire for Devon to interact with others within the community; however, the family does not live in a safe area, so this can be difficult.

- Devon is extremely intelligent; however, both parents communicate they feel he was misdiagnosed.

- The family attends church services each week; however, Devon is not able to attend due to non-compliance during service.

CHAPTER DISCUSSION QUESTIONS

Now that you have reviewed this chapter and reviewed the information presented within the case study, please use that information to address the following questions.

1. This is your first experience addressing behavioral concerns with a learner of this racial background. What steps/activities can you engage in to ensure you are providing appropriate and effective behavioral interventions?

2. Within the chapter we spoke about the incorporation of the community into behavioral intervention specific to the African American community. How would you go about identifying and incorporating the community into programming while maintaining the privacy and dignity of the learner?

3. How can you address historical trauma related to the African American populations within behavioral intervention?

4. How could you navigate this situation regarding the parent's requests to produce the best possible compromise for the parents while maintaining the integrity of behavioral intervention?

5. What information/resources would you provide the family specific to the last point of concerns raised during the assessment process?

References

Agyemang, C., Bhopal, R., & Bruijnzeels, M. (2005). Negro, Black, Black African, African Caribbean, African American or what? Labelling African origin populations in the health arena in the 21st century. *Journal of Epidemiology & Community Health, 59*(12), 1014–1018. http://doi.org/10.1136/jech.2005.035964

American Psychological Association. (2002). *Guidelines on multicultural education, training, research, practice, and organizational change for psychologists.* Retrieved from www.apa.org/about/policy/multicultural-guidelines-archived.pdf

Baer, D. M., Wolf, M. M., & Risley, T. R. (1968). Some current dimensions of applied behavior analysis. *Journal of Applied Behavior Analysis, 1*(1), 91–97. https://doi.org/10.1901/jaba.1968.1-91

Baker, P. B. (2005). The impact of cultural biases on African American students' education: A review of research literature regarding race based schooling. *Education and Urban Society*, *37*(3), 243–256. https://doi.org/10.1177/0013124504274187

Beaulieu, L., Addington, J., & Almeida, D. (2018). Behavior analysts training and practices regarding cultural diversity: The case for culturally competent care. *Behavior Analysis in Practice*, *12*(3), 337–575. https://doi.org/10.1007/s40617-018-00313-6

Behavior Analyst Certification Board. (2016). *Professional and ethical compliance code for behavior analysts.* Retrieved from www.bacb.com/ethics/ethics-code/

Behavior Anlayst Certification Board. (2017). *BCBA/BCaBA task list* (5th ed.). Littleton, CO: Author.

Boyd-Franklin, N. (2010). Incorporating spirituality and religion into the treatment of African American clients. *The Counseling Psychologist*, *38*(7), 976–1000. https://doi.org/10.1177/0011000010374881

Boykin, A. W. (1986). The triple quandary and the schooling of Afro-American children. In U. Neisser (Ed.), *The school achievement of minority children*. Hillsdale, NJ: Lawrence Erlbaum.

Burkett, K., Morris, E., Manning-Courtney, P., Anthony, J., & Shambley-Ebron, D. (2015). African American families on autism diagnosis and treatment: The influence of culture. *Journal of Autism and Developmental Disorders*, *45*(10), 3244–3254. https://doi.org/10.1007/s10803-015-2482-x

Clauss-Ehlers, C. S., Chiriboga, D. A., Hunter, S. J., Roysircar, G., & Tummala-Narra, P. (2019). APA Multicultural Guidelines executive summary: Ecological approach to context, identity, and intersectionality. *American Psychologist*, *74*(2), 232.

DeGruy-Leary, J. (2017). *Post-traumatic Slave Syndrome: America's legacy of enduring injury*. Portland, OR: Joy DeGruy Publications Inc.

Faye, A. G. (2005). Stigma: Barrier to mental health care among ethnic minorities. *Issues in Mental Health Nursing*, *26*(10), 979–999. https://doi.org/10.1080/01612840500280638

Felitti, V. J., Anda, R. F., Nordenberg, D., Williamson, D. F., Spitz, A. M., Edwards, V., & Marks, J. S. (1998). Relationship of childhood abuse and household dysfunction to many of the leading causes of death in adults: The adverse childhood experiences (ACE) study. *American Journal of Preventive Medicine*, *14*(4), 245–258. https://doi.org/10.1016/s0749-3797(98)00017-8

Fong, E. H., Catagnus, R. M., Brodhead, M. T., Quigley, S., & Field, S. (2016). Developing the cultural awareness skills of behavior analysts. *Behavior Analysis in Practice*, *9*(1), 84–94. https://doi.org/10.1007/s40617-016-0111-6

Fong, E. H., Ficklin, S., & Lee, H. Y. (2017). Increasing cultural understanding and diversity in applied behavior analysis. *Behavior Analysis: Research and Practice*, *17*(2), 103–113. http://doi.org/10/1037/bar00000076

Gilliam, W. S., Maupin, A. N., Reyes, C. R., Accavitti, M., & Shic, F. (2016). *Do early educators' implicit biases regarding sex and race relate to behavior expectations and recommendations of preschool expulsions and suspensions*. Research Study Brief. Yale University, Yale Child Study Center, New Haven, CT.

Gregory, A., Skiba, R. J., & Noguera, P. A. (2010). The achievement gap and the discipline gap: Two sides of the same coin?. *Educational Researcher*, *39*(1), 59–68. https://doi.org/10.3102/0013189X09357621

Kashima, Y. (2014). How can you capture cultural dynamics?. *Frontiers in Psychology*, *5*, 995. https://doi.org/10.3389/fpsyg.2014.00995

Kauffman, J. M., Conroy, M., Gardner, R., III, & Oswald, D. (2008). Cultural sensitivity in the application of behavior principles to education. *Education and Treatment of Children*, *31*(2), 239–262. https://doi.org/10.1353/etc.0.0019.

Marques, L. (2016). *The United States and the transatlantic slave trade to the Americas, 1776–1867.* New Haven, CT: Yale University Press.

Milner, H. (2007). Race, culture, and researcher positionality: Working through dangers seen, unseen, and unforeseen. *Educational Researcher: A Publication of the American Educational Research Association, 36*(7), 388–400. https://doi.org/10.3102/0013189X07309471

Myers, L. J. (1987). The deep structure of culture: Relevance of traditional African culture in contemporary life. *Journal of Black Studies, 18*(1), 72–85. https://doi.org/10.1177/002193478701800105

Robertson, R. (2016). Effectiveness and acceptability of parent-interventions for children with autism in three African American families. *Education and Training in Autism and Developmental Disabilities, 51*(2), 107–121.

Roche, M. J., Bush, H. H., & D'Angelo, E. D. (2018). The assessment of treatment of Autism Spectrum Disorder: A cultural examination. *Practice Innovations, 3*(2), 107–122. https://doi.org/10.1037/pri00000067

Rosenwasser, B., & Axelrod, S. (2001). The contributions of Applied Behavior Analysis to the education of people with autism. *Behavior Modification, 25*(5), 671–677. https://doi.org/10.1177/0145445501255001

Sellers, R. M., Smith. M. A., Shelton, J. N., Rowley, S. A., & Chavous, T. M. (1998). Multidimensional model of racial identity: A reconceptualization of African American racial identity. *Personality and Social Psychology Review, 2*(1), 18–39. https://doi.org/10.1207/S15327957psrpr0201_2

Skinner, B. F. (1981). Selection by consequences. *Science, 213*(4507), 501–504. https://doi.org/10.1126/science.7244649

Sue, D. W., Sue, D., Neville, H. A., & Smith, L. (2019). *Counseling the culturally diverse: Theory and practice.* Hoboken, NJ: John Wiley & Sons.

Tatum, B. D. (2017a). *Why are all the Black kids sitting together in the cafeteria?: And other conversations about race.* New York, NY: Basic Books.

Tatum, D. C. (2017b). Donald Trump and the legacy of Bacon's rebellion. *Journal of Black Studies, 48*(7), 651–674. https://doi.org/10.1177%2F0021934717713758

Thomas, S. B., & Casper, E. (2019). The burdens of race and history on black people's health 400 years after Jamestown. *American Journal of Public Health, 109*(10), 1346–1347 https://doi.org/10.2105/AJPH.2019.305290

Wade, R., Shea, J. A., Rubin, D., & Wood, J. (2014). Adverse childhood experiences of low income urban youth. *Pediatrics, 134*(1), e13–e20. https://doi.org/10.1542/peds.2013-2475

Wilson, C. P., Wilson, S. A., & Thou, M. (2015). Perceptions of African American police officers on racial profiling in small agencies. *Journal of Black Studies, 46*(5), 482–505. https://doi.org/10.1177/0021934715583596

Wilson, E. (2014). Diversity, culture and the glass ceiling. *Journal of Cultural Diversity, 21*(3), 83–89.

Zilber, D. M., & Niven, J. (2000). Elite use of racial labels: Ideology and preference for African American or Black. *Howard Journal of Communication, 11*(4), 267–277. https://doi.org/10.1080/10646170050

5

Latinos in Applied Behavior Analysis

We Have a Long Way to Go

Isaac L. Bermudez and Jose D. Rios

Learning Objectives

■ Readers will be able to pinpoint the disparity in the provision of behavioral services for Latino individuals.

■ Readers will identify the potential impact of continued disparity in services to Latino individuals with developmental disabilities and providers of ABA services.

■ Readers will gain an increased understanding of ethical issues that impact the delivery of services provided to a Latino individual with developmental disabilities.

■ Readers will review a case study that exemplifies the potential issues a Latino individual with developmental disabilities and their family may face in securing the proper behavior intervention.

Introduction

A scientific analysis of human behavior enables us to better understand and address many global cultural and diversity conditions, needs, and issues. A major and onerous constraint existed in the authors' development of this chapter, that is, how to even begin addressing the myriad complexities, methodological and conceptual issues, needs, and challenges involved in social and cultural diversity related to Latinos and applied behavior analysis (ABA), and how to do so in a single chapter.

Therefore, given the significant role that ABA practitioners play in the services to individuals with autism spectrum disorder (ASD) and developmental disabilities, the focus here is on treatment disparity – more specifically, the imbalance in services received by Latino children, adolescents, and adults with autism when compared to white individuals with similar diagnoses.

Practical Considerations and Implications in ABA Delivery

In general, there is a significant disparity in the provision of health and behavioral services for Latinos with developmental disabilities (Flores, Abreu, Olivar, & Kastner, 1998; Iland, Weiner, & Murawski, 2012). Disparities in service levels have also been shown across other ethnic groups, socioeconomic levels, and a variety of health, medical and behavioral service needs (Cohen & Northridge, 2008; Cook et al. (2018); Link, Northridge, Phelan, & Ganz, 1998; Orsi, Margellos-Anast, & Whitman, 2010).

This treatment variance illustrates the need for service providers to actively address and close the gaps in standards of care to ensure that all individuals receive equitable levels of treatment and services (Iland et al., 2012; Parish, Magaña, Rose, & Timberlake, 2012; Singh & Bunyak, 2018; Zuckerman et al., 2014).

As behavior analysts, we may ask ourselves, "What role do I or my agency play in understanding and addressing disparities in treatment?" A follow-up question may be, "Does the issue of inequitable treatment impact the services that I or my agency provide?"

Depending on several factors (e.g., one's geographical location), a behavior analyst who works in the field of developmental disabilities will likely work with children, adolescents, adults, and families from a Latino background. The Pew Research Center indicated that in 2016 the Latino population in the United States reached 58 million. This growth has been the principal driver in overall demographic growth in the United States, accounting for half of the national population growth (Flores, 2017). For example, in 2013, Latino children and adults with autism were the largest ethnic group receiving services from California's Department of Developmental Services (Angell, Frank, & Solomon, 2016; Leigh, Grosse, Cassady, Melnikow, & Hertz-Picciotto, 2016). Given this, unequal access to services for this population should not be seen as a concern only to those practitioners who work in heavily Latino communities (Zuckerman et al., 2014). In addition, it is a given that an agency's ability to serve a larger array of individuals and families increases in an agency's service impact and profitability.

Research on the prevalence of developmental disabilities suggest discrepancies in rates between Latinos and non-Latino white children, with some showing lower rates of autism in Latinos while others have reported higher rates (Chaidez, Hansen, & Hertz-Picciotto, 2012; Fountain, King, & Bearman, 2011; Goyat, Vyas, & Sambamoorthi, 2016; Iland et al., 2012). There currently does not exist conclusive evidence for this disparity. In addition to socio-economic status, research has identified several possible additional factors. There has been a reported difference between the age at which Latino and non-Latino children are diagnosed. In a study by Mandell, Listerud, Levy, and Pinto-Martin (2002), the authors reported that non-Latino white children received a diagnosis at the average age of 6.3 years, while Latino children were diagnosed approximately one year later, at the age of 7.4 years. Studies also suggest that Latino families often report less milder forms of ASD compared to non-Latino white families (Rogers & Vismara, 2008; Vismara & Rogers, 2010). Studies have shown that communication barriers between primary Spanish-speaking Latino families and their health care providers impact the ability of providers to adequately assess cognitive delays and/or a diagnosis of autism (Brewis & Schmidt, 2003; Weinick & Krauss, 2000). One possible contributing factor to the discrepancy of autism rates is an existing disparity in access to and use of health care, in part because Latino families are much more likely to not have health insurance compared to non-Latino white families (Flores & Tomany-Korman, 2008).

A study by Iland et al. (2012) of 96 Latina mothers of children with autism provides preliminary evidence about the substantial level of unmet service needs faced by these mothers and describes the harmful barriers faced by Latina families in obtaining a diagnosis, advocating for their child, and addressing the onerous demands of care. Four barriers were experienced by 70% or more of participants and included difficulty understanding how the special education or school system works (86%); understanding how the medical and social service systems work (84%); dealing with complicated paperwork (79.3%); and finding a medical or other professional to make the diagnosis (70.8%).

Studies have shown significant discrepancies in the timing of a diagnosis of autism between Latino and non-Latino whites, with Latino children being diagnosed at a later age (Singh & Bunyak, 2018; Zuckerman et al., 2014; Zuckerman et al., 2013). Mandell and colleagues (2009) noted that the pattern of delayed and missed diagnosis may be exacerbated among underserved ethnic and racial minorities. For example, Fountain et al. (2011) found in their analysis of 10 birth cohorts of California children with autism that certain socioeconomic factors (i.e., parental education, race, and maternal immigrant status) influenced the age of diagnosis for autism. In this study, researchers showed that socioeconomic status was a stronger predictor than even the severity of symptom expression at the point of diagnosis and that children with more educated parents are diagnosed earlier. Similarly, other researchers have reported that African-American and Hispanic children are less likely to be diagnosed with autism, they often receive an initial diagnosis at a later age, and their families face difficulties in accessing needed services in comparison to other groups (Keller-Bell, 2017; Jarquin, Wiggins, Schieve, & Van Naarden-Braun, 2011).

The early identification of autism in children can have a significant impact on outcomes for children and their families. Additionally, early detection of a developmental disability may help with diagnosis, monitoring for associated developmental and medical disorders, and the provision of behavioral, educational, rehabilitative, medical, and psychiatric services (Hebbeler et al., 2007). The early detection of a developmental disability also leads to increased and more intense ABA interventions (Orinstein et al., 2014).

Magaña, Parish, Rose, Timberlake, and Swaine (2012) analyzed disparities in the quality of ABA services and compared black and Latino children to white children. The authors found racial and ethnic disparities on five of six quality outcomes. These quality indicators included that the provider (1) listened carefully to the parent, (2) gave needed information, (3) helped parents feel like partners, (4) spent enough time with the child, and (5) was sensitive to the family's values and customs. Others have also found disparities in the quality of services as well as significantly lower spending levels for Latino populations (Leigh et al., 2016; Magaña, Parish, & Son, 2015). One study by Zuckerman and colleagues (2017) found that Latino families who had limited English proficiency were less likely to receive social skills training and lesser amounts of ABA services. These authors found that compared with white children, Latino families with limited English proficiency were more likely to have less than one or no hours of weekly therapy versus 11 or more weekly therapy hours for white children. In an earlier study looking at the perspective that Latino families have related to services for their children with autism, the authors noted that the "diagnostic process itself was slow, inconvenient, confusing, and uncomfortable for the child. These factors led many parents to normalize their child's early behaviors, deny that a problem existed, and [to] lose trust in the medical system" (Zuckerman et al., 2014, pp. 1–2).

Ethical and Professional Issues

There are many ethical issues that impact the Latino population related to the treatment of autism and developmental disabilities. In response to the previously asked questions, "What role do I or my agency play in understanding and addressing disparities in treatment?" and "Does the issue of inequitable treatment impact the services that I or my agency provide?" as behavior analytic providers it should be an ethical and humane practice to ensure that all individuals served are provided with the service level and quality of care commensurate to those available for other populations. A hallmark of behavior analysis is that our assessment and treatment protocols are specific to the individual.

Behavior analysts should understand that many Latino parents operate in an environment poor in information on autism. They often face contradictory information on normal versus autistic-related behavior. Furthermore, they face the stigma attached to disability and mental health issues (Zuckerman et al., 2014). Under the Behavior Analyst Certification Board's® (BACB®, 2019) *Professional and Ethical Compliance Code for Behavior Analysts*, behavior analysts are expected to provide services in a competent manner and to practice within the scope of our professional competencies. A critical and complex question is, "How do we define and measure cultural competence in behavior analysis?" This is a critical question that as a field we must answer in order to best measure our growth in the area of social and cultural competence and diversity. Cultural competence may be defined as the ability of a practitioner to effectively deliver services that meet the social, cultural, educational, and linguistic needs of the individual and his or her family. However, as of yet, there is no specific measurement to determine cultural competence in behavior analytic practice.

In the BACB's® (2019) *Professional and Ethical Compliance Code for Behavior Analysts*, code 1.02 states that behavior analysts must provide service, teach or conduct research only within our boundaries of competence. What if the behavior analyst has not been trained to work with

Latino clients or families? Should such a practitioner not provide service, as this would fall outside of their cultural competence, and who would decide if the practitioner has met some vague measurement of social and cultural competence? Related to code 1.02, a practitioner's ability to navigate cultural issues that will permeate treatment is critical to the behavior analyst's success working with a Latino family and may impact progress. Should there be training in cultural competence to the various subcultures in our country? According to code 1.03, we are expected to maintain competence through professional development activities such as reading literature, attending conferences, participating in workshops, or taking additional coursework.

Additionally, codes 3.03, 3.04, and 4.06 bring up another possible ethical dilemma when providing service to Latino families. These codes discuss the practice of attaining behavior analytic consent, being able to explain the assessment results, and discuss behavior-change programs and objectives. These areas are important aspects in service delivery. It is critical that our services be explained in the language of those giving consent and that intake and assessment forms be translated into Spanish. Informed consent is difficult to obtain from a parent/guardian who does not fully understand what may be involved.

In addition, code 3.04 explicitly requires behavior analysts to share assessment results using language that is understandable to the client. This should include explaining and even translating the report to Spanish. While this is a noteworthy recommendation, often the authorized hours that behavior analysts receive for an assessment may result in too few hours to conduct such an assessment and effectively translate the documents into the appropriate language for the parent/guardian. This gap exists in our service and is one that behavior analysts should work with funders (e.g., insurance companies) to address as we strive to close the cultural gaps in our field. The final ethical consideration is code 5.01, which mandates that behavior analysts supervise only in their area of competence. This refers to behavior analysts receiving training and support to understand how to develop a level of cultural competency to offer assessment, treatment and consultation services to Latino families. This is especially critical when services need to be delivered in Spanish so that there is clear consent and understanding of treatment plans. Training to develop cultural competence can also minimize issues such as provider bias, which has been shown to affect the results of identifying a child's diagnosis.

Conclusion

As previously stated, there is a growing population of Latinos in the United States, and consequently an increased population of children, adults, and families who require ABA services. It would be erroneous for behavior analysis to oversimplify the complexities of working with an individual and their family in an overly simplistic manner. As service providers, behavior analysts must recognize that the Latino population of the United States encompasses a wide range of individuals who differ on language, place of origin, degree of assimilation, education, religion/spirituality, and socioeconomic status. Cardemil and La Roche (2017) and Ollendick, Lewis, and Fraire (2010) expressed that practitioners may erroneously surmise that members of an ethnic or cultural group are an unvaried, homogenous, and monolithic entity and therefore develop simplistic means to address an ethnic group. For example, working with a two-parent, third-generation Mexican, English-dominant family with a child with autism will likely significantly differ than the approaches used when working with a less assimilated, more recently immigrated Spanish-dominant single mother.

A growing body of research has identified a large gap in treatment provision and standard of care between Latinos and non-Latino whites. Increasingly practitioners, including ABA practitioners, are addressing social, ethnic and cultural issues, practices, and methodologies with the aim of closing the gaps and eliminating disparities in treatment and to increase parity in services. Only through an assertive push to improve service provision can this long overdue need be addressed. This includes increasing diversity of ABA graduate and undergraduate programs, developing mentorship models, increasing professional association leadership diversity, and recognizing the need for ABA practitioners to be more aware, involved, and trained on cultural and linguistic issues. The field of behavior analysis is in the infancy stage of addressing the many factors involved in cultural diversity. A nagging question is "Who will be the ones who define the complexities of cultural competency for our field?"

Currently, there are special interests groups (SIG) such as the Association for Behavior Analysis International's (ABAI) Multicultural SIG: Multicultural Alliance of Behavior Analysts, whose mission is to connect behavior analysts with an interest in serving multicultural and minority populations and create a network of professionals. In addition to ABAI's SIG, there is also the Latino Association for Behavior Analysis (LABA), an organization that promotes inclusion for all members regardless of race, color, national origin, age, gender, religion, sexual orientation, and gender identity. LABA's mission is to train, support, and mentor the next generation of behavior analysts to serve underrepresented populations and to increase diversity in all facets of the field of behavior analysis. There are opportunities for professionals through the LABA FastTrack intense mentorship project that focuses on mentorship and support for Latinos and others. In addition, behavioral venues are beginning to delve into cultural diversity, as can be seen by the increased number of invited talks, symposiums, continuing education webinars, and conference panels related to cultural diversity issues. Although there is still a long way to go in our field, it appears that the topic of cultural diversity is finally coming to grips with this long overdue topic.

CASE STUDY

Andres is an 8-year-old male who received a diagnosis of autism at the age of 6. He resides with his mother in a small one-bedroom apartment along with an elderly aunt who assists in his care. Andres's mother speaks minimal English and his aunt only speaks and understands Spanish. Andres's mother indicated that she did not have a clear understanding of autism spectrum disorder and it was clear that she also was not provided with a prognosis of this disorder. Andres is obese, and his aunt often provides him with snacks to keep him happy and in an effort to prevent

(continued)

(continued)

problem behavior. Andres was displaying atypical behaviors, a lack of verbalizations, various mild forms of stereotypy, and occasional bouts of self-injurious facial striking (the self-injury began at approximately the age of 2), but his mother had not initially sought out assistance and was unaware of autism. A year after being diagnosed, Andres began exhibiting more frequent tantrum behaviors including an escalation of his self-injurious behavior. While Andres's case manager was aware of the increased problem behaviors, she had not offered Andres's mother supportive services such as in-home behavior intervention. When this family eventually was referred for behavioral services, Andres was placed on a waiting list until the agency could find a Spanish-speaking practitioner. After several months of increased problem behavior, the agency was pressured to send out someone to do the initial functional assessment, although the individual who conducted the parent interview had only a passing understanding of Spanish. While Andres's aunt often cares for him when his mother is at work, she was not included in the assessment process because of the language barrier. Andres's mother was handed a series of surveys (e.g., an ABC analysis form, a FAST), with the idea that she would compete the applicable forms as problem behavior occurred. While Andres's self-striking was referred to in the functional assessment and plan, his mother felt that too much attention was being given to his weight issue by the assessor, and she wanted more advice on his problem behavior, language delays, and other skill deficits.

Multiple factors in the primary care setting may contribute to delayed identification for Latinos. Promoting language-appropriate screening, disseminating culturally appropriate autism materials to Latino families, improving the specialist workforce, and providing support in screening and referral of Latino children may be important ways to reduce racial and ethnic disparities in the level and timing of service provision.

DISCUSSION QUESTIONS

1. As a provider of ABA services, how do you begin to prepare yourself to provide service to a diverse clientele, in particular to Spanish-speaking clients and their families?

2. Are your forms, tools, assessments, and reports translated into Spanish so informed consent can be achieved by a Spanish-speaking client?

3. Have you participated in or attended continuing education coursework to increase your understanding of working with a diverse population – in this case, working with Spanish-speaking individuals with developmental disabilities and their families?

4. Have you joined (and/or encouraged by staff to join) associations that will prepare you and them to enrich your understanding of issues impacting Spanish-speaking clients and their families?

5. What BACB® ethical guidelines may impact you when working with Spanish-speaking clients and their families?

References

Angell, A. M., Frank, G., & Solomon, O. (2016). Latino families' experiences with autism services: Disparities, capabilities, and occupational justice. *Occupational Therapy Journal of Research, 16*(4), 195–203. https://doi.org/10.1177/1539449216666062

Behavior Analyst Certification Board. (2019). *Professional and ethical compliance code for behavior analysts.* Retrieved from www.bacb.com/wp-content/uploads/BACB-Compliance-Code-english_190318.pdf.

Brewis, A., & Schmidt, K. (2003). Gender variation in the identification of Mexican children's psychiatric symptoms. *Medical Anthropology Quarterly, 17*(3), 376–393. https://doi.org/10.1525/maq.2003.17.3.376

Cardemil, E., & La Roche, M. (2017). Introduction to special issue on evidence-based treatments with Latinas/os: Attending to heterogeneity. *Journal of Latina/o Psychology, 5*(4), 243–247. https://doi.org/10.1037/lat0000103

Chaidez, V., Hansen, R. L., & Hertz-Picciotto, I. (2012). Autism spectrum disorders in Hispanics and non-Hispanics. *Autism, 16*, 381–397. https://doi.org/10.1177/1362361311434787

Cohen, H. W., & Northridge, M. E. (2008). Getting political: Racism and urban health. *American Journal of Public Health, 98*(9), S17–S19. https://doi.org/10.2105/AJPH.98.Supplement_1.S17

Cook, B. L., Hou, S. S.-Y., Lee-Tauler, S. Y., Progovac, A. M., Samson, F., & Sanchez, M. J. (2018). A review of mental health and mental health care disparities research: 2011–2014. *Medical Care Research and Review.* https://doi.org/10.1177/1077558718780592

Flores, A. (2017, September 18). *How the U.S. Hispanic population is changing.* Retrieved from www.pewresearch.org/fact-tank/2017/09/18/how-the-u-s-hispanic-population-is-changing/

Flores, G., Abreu, M., Olivar, M. A., & Kastner, B. (1998). Access barriers to health care for Latino children. *Archives of Pediatrics and Adolescent Medicine, 152*(11), 1119–1125. https://doi.org/10.1001/archpedi.152.11.1119

Flores, G., & Tomany-Korman, S. C. (2008). Racial and ethnic disparities in medical and dental health, access to care, and use of services in US children. *Pediatrics, 121*, e286–e298.

Fountain, C., King, M., & Bearman, P. (2011). Age of diagnosis for autism: Individual and community factors across 10 birth cohorts. *Journal of Epidemiology & Community Health, 65*(6), 503–510. https://doi.org/10.1136/jech.2009.104588

Goyat, R., Vyas, A., & Sambamoorthi, U. (2016). Racial/ethnic disparities in disability prevalence. *Journal of Racial and Ethnic Health Disparities, 3*(4), 635–645. https://doi.org/10.1007/s40615-015-0182-z

Hebbeler, K., Spiker, D., Bailey, D., Scarborough, A., Malik, S., Simeonsson, R. J. . . . Nelson, L. (2007). *Early intervention for infants and toddlers with disabilities and their families: Participants, services, and outcomes.* Menlo Park, CA: SRI International.

Iland, E. D., Weiner, I., & Murawski, W. W. (2012). Obstacles faced by Latina mothers of children with autism. *Californian Journal of Health Promotion, 10*, 25–36. https://doi.org/10.32398/cjhp.v10iSI-Latino.1480

Jarquin, V. G., Wiggins, L. D., Schieve, L. A., & Van Naarden-Braun, K. (2011). Racial disparities in community identification of autism spectrum disorders over time; Metropolitan Atlanta, Georgia, 2000–2006. *Journal of Developmental and Behavioral Pediatric, 32*(2), 179–187. https://doi.org/10.1097/DBP.0b013e31820b4260

Keller-Bell, Y. D. (2017). Disparities in the identification and diagnosis of autism spectrum disorder in culturally and linguistically diverse populations. *Perspectives of the ASHA Special Interest Groups*, *2*(14), 68–81.

Leigh, J. P., Grosse, S. D., Cassady, D., Melnikow, J., & Hertz-Picciotto, I. (2016). Spending by California's department of developmental services for persons with autism across demographic and expenditure categories. *PLoS One*, *11*(3), 1–23. https://doi.org/10.1371/journal.pone.0151970

Link, B. G., Northridge, M. E., Phelan, J. C., & Ganz, M. L. (1998). Social epidemiology and the fundamental cause concept: On the structuring of effective cancer screens by socioeconomic status. *The Milbank Quarterly*, *76*(3), 375–305. https://doi.org/10.1111/1468–0009.00096

Magaña, S., Parish, S. L., Rose, R. A., Timberlake, M., & Swaine, J. G. (2012). Racial and ethnic disparities in quality of health care among children with autism and other developmental disabilities. *Intellectual Developmental Disabilities*, *50*(4), 287–299. https://doi.org/10.1352/1934–9556–50.4.287

Magaña, S., Parish, S. L., & Son, E. (2015). Have racial and ethnic disparities in the quality of health care relationships changed for children with developmental disabilities and ASD? *American Journal on Intellectual and Developmental Disabilities*, *120*(6), 504–513. https://doi.org/10.1352/1944-7558-120.6.504

Mandell, D. S., Listerud, J., Levy, S. E., & Pinto-Martin, J. A. (2002). Race differences in the age at diagnosis among Medicaid-eligible children with autism. *Journal of the American Academy of Child & Adolescent Psychiatry*, *41*(12), 1447–1453. https://doi.org/10.1097/00004583-200212000-00016

Mandell, D. S., Wiggins, L. D., Carpenter, L. A., Daniels, J., DiGuiseppi, C., Durkin, M. S. . . . Kirby, R. S. (2009). Racial/ethnic disparities in the identification of children with autism spectrum disorders. *American Journal of Public Health*, *99*(3), 492–498. https://doi.org/10.2105/AJPH.2007.131243

Noe-Bustamante, L. (2017). *Key facts about U.S. Hispanics and their diverse heritage*. Retrieved from www.pewresearch.org/fact-tank/2019/09/16/key-facts-about-u-s-hispanics/.

Ollendick, T., Lewis, K., & Fraire, M. G. (2010). Cultural adaptations to empirically supported treatments: The challenge before us. *The Scientific Review of Mental Health Practice*, *7*, 22–25.

Orinstein, A. J., Helt, M., Troyb, E., Tyson, K. E., Barton, M. L., Eigsti, I. M. . . . Fein, D. A. (2014). Intervention for optimal outcome in children and adolescents with a history of autism. *Journal of Developmental & Behavioral Pediatrics*, *35*(4), 247–256. https://doi.org/10.1097/DBP.0000000000000037

Orsi, J. M., Margellos-Anast, H., & Whitman, S. (2010). Black-White health disparities in the United States and Chicago: A 15-year progress analysis. *American Journal of Public Health*, *100*(2), 349–356. https://doi.org/10.2105/AJPH.2009.165407

Parish, S., Magaña, S., Rose, R., Timberlake, M., & Swaine, J. G. (2012). Health care of Latino children with autism and other developmental disabilities: Quality of provider interaction mediates utilization. *American Journal on Intellectual and Developmental Disabilities*, *117*(4), 304–315. https://doi.org/10.1352/1944-7558-117.4.304

Rogers, S., & Vismara, L. (2008). Evidence-based comprehensive treatments for early autism. *Journal of Clinical Child & Adolescent Psychology*, *37*(1), 8–38. https://doi.org/10.1080/15374410701817808

Singh, J. S., & Bunyak, G. (2018). Autism disparities: A systemic review and meta-ethnography of qualitative research. *Qualitative Health Research*, *29*(6), 796–808. https://doi.org/10.1177/1049732318808245

Vismara, L., & Rogers, S. (2010). Behavioral treatments in autism spectrum disorder: What do we know? *Annual Review of Clinical Psychology*, *6*(1), 447–468. https://doi.org/10.1146/annurev.clinpsy.121208.131151

Weinick, R. M., & Krauss, N. A. (2000). Racial/ethnic differences in children's access to care. *American Journal of Public Health*, *90*(11), 1771–1774. https://doi.org/10.2105/ajph.90.11.177

Zuckerman, K. E., Lindly, O. J., Reyes, N. M., Chavez, A. E., Macias, K., Smith, K. N, & Reynolds, A. (2017). Disparities in diagnosis and treatment of autism in Latino and non-Latino white families. *Pediatrics*, *139*(5), e20163010. https://doi.org/10.1542/peds.2016–3010

Zuckerman, K. E., Mattox, K., Donelan, K., Batbayar, O., Baghaee, A., & Bathell, C. (2013). Pediatrician identification of Latino children at risk for autism spectrum disorder. *Pediatrics*, *132*(3), 445–453. https://doi.org/10.1542/peds.2013-0383

Zuckerman, K. E., Sinche, B., Cobian, M., Cervantes, M., Mejia, A., Becker, T., & Nicolaidis, C. (2014). Conceptualization of autism in the Latino community and its relationship with early diagnosis. *Journal of Developmental and Behavioral Pediatrics*, *35*(8), 522–532. https://doi.org/10.1097/DBP.0000000000000091

Zuckerman, Z. E., Sinche, B., Mejia, A. Corbian, M., Becker, T., & Nicolaidis, C. (2014). Latino parents' perspectives of barriers to autism diagnosis. *Academic Pediatrics*, *14*(3), 301–308. https://doi.org/10.1016/j.acap.2013.12.004

6

Applied Behavior Analysis With Indigenous Populations

Kristine Melroe and Joanne Robbins

Learning Objectives

- To increase one's knowledge of the history, periods of education, and current conditions of US Indigenous people.
- To examine how the history of Indigenous people relates to intra-generational trauma.
- To flesh out the difference between cultural appreciation and cultural appropriation.
- To learn how to be responsive as a behavior analyst when working with Indigenous populations.

Introduction

To be an effective and ethical behavior analyst, one must diligently work at developing and improving personal and cultural awareness skills. One's own biases, norms, and values can either be detrimental or beneficial to understanding other perspectives. Learning to combine the science of behavior analysis with the knowledge of another's culture and histories is challenging and complex. This chapter presents examples of challenges one could face when doing this work.

Developing sensitivity to cultural differences requires dedication and self-reflection. Take a moment to evaluate your own bias and knowledge about Indigenous people. What images come to mind when you hear the word "Indian"? Did you conjure up images of marauding Indians murdering settlers, alcoholics, or powwow dancers? These types of images have been systematically taught and reproduced in movies, books, and sports images (e.g., Washington Redskins, Cleveland Indians). Now, try these questions (the answers are on page 67):

1. How many Native Americans currently live in the United States? How many lived here pre-contact?

2.   What year did Native Americans gain the right to vote?

3.   How many tribes are federally recognized?

4.   Who was a slave trader of Natives, killed 250,000 of them, and was declared a hero in 1937?

5.   Which president said: "I don't go so far as to think that the only good Indians are dead Indians, but I believe nine out of ten are, and I shouldn't like to inquire too closely into the case of the tenth."

Some Basics

There is no single, all-encompassing term used to describe the first people of North America. The term "Indian" originated from Columbus's mistaken belief that he had landed in India. The terms "Native American" and "Indigenous" emerged out of the civil rights activism starting in the 1970s. This chapter uses the words Indigenous and Native American interchangeably.

The realities of Indigenous life in the United States are harsh. Reservation and urban Natives have high unemployment rates and live closer to the poverty line than any other group. One of the poorest areas in the United States is the Pine Ridge Reservation (Data-U.S.). Indigenous health statistics are dismal when compared to other US groups (e.g., highest rates of diabetes, tuberculosis, alcoholism, and teen suicide); all are factors that lead to a life expectancy of 66.8 years (Dunbar-Ortiz, 2016). If an individual has lived predominantly in an urban area, away from tribal culture and family, the loss of tribal connections brings about a different set of conditions to consider. The loss of community, personal history, knowledge of ancestors, and unmooring from the land are contributing factors to mental and physical health issues that must be considered.

Culture can be defined as "the extent to which a group of individuals engage in overt and verbal behavior reflecting shared behavioral learning histories, serving to differentiate the group from others" (Sugai, O'Keeffe, & Fallon, 2012, p. 12). There is not one Indigenous culture but hundreds of cultural variations with different languages, norms, and histories. These cultures are alive, even though they seem invisible to mainstream society. Roxanne Dunbar-Ortiz, a noted historian, provides a rich resource in *All the Real Indians Died Off and 20 Other Myths About Native Americans*. This title succinctly captures the dismal state of non-Native understanding and refutes the assumption that Native Americans are a vanishing population.

Some tribes have had European contact for 500 years and others for 200 years. Some Indigenous people may be physically identifiable and others may not. Many tribes have few remaining fluent speakers while others have a vibrant language base. "Losing languages is a grave concern, it is a race against the clock and we are in the 59th minute of the last hour," stated Ryan Wilson, member of the National Indian Education Board (Frosch, 2008). Until the 1960s, most Native Americans lived on reservations, but today 71% live in urban areas (Urban Indian Health Institute, 2018). Each Tribal Nation has different rules regarding needed blood quantum for enrollment. Enrollment is complicated for individuals who come from multiple tribes. Each Nation has its own tribal government, elected Tribal Chair, court system, and police force. However, all health care services fall under one national system, the Indian Health Service. Jurisdiction is complex and beyond the scope of this paper.

Brief Historical Overview

History is a record of events that establishes the current conditions of any group. Most non-Natives know little about the history between Indigenous Nations and European invaders, therefore learning the history is an essential first step. Since the final version of history is written from the perspective of the winners, most of the Indigenous perspective has been expunged. John McCain summed it up this way: "Europeans coming to this country created a clash of two civilizations . . . and the least mature suffered the loss" (Adams, 1995, p. 87).

While figures vary, there is agreement that the pre-invasion population of North America ranged between 50 and 70 million people. There were multiple failed attempts to form settlements before the first permanent colony was established at Plymouth Rock. These unsuccessful attempts at colonization (European term) or invasion (Indigenous term) had horrific ramifications. Approximately one-third of the population died from diseases (e.g., smallpox) due to these settlements. The reduced population set up conditions for the invasion to continue and thrive (Zinn, 2015). The Constitution allows the president, with the Advice and Consent of the Senate, to make treaties between nations. The United States made 376 such Treaties with native nations.

The United States replaced the nation-to-nation treaty policy with military force, whose goal was genocide (Adams, 1995). The United States needed the land and resources in order to fulfill its manifest destiny. Using force was more profitable and efficient than negotiations and peace. Propagating the view that individuals could own land was radically different than community-owned land. When laws were enacted to prevent community ownership, this altered social contingencies. The United States attacked this cultural norm through the Dawes Act (1887) and the Termination Act (1953), among other legislation (Dunbar-Ortiz, 2016).

Policymakers turned to educational institutions as a way to handle the "Indian problem." The goal of education was to qualitatively alter the behavior of natives by restricting their languages and everyday way of life. As one policy maker succinctly stated,

> The kind of education they are in need of is one that will habituate them to the customs and advantages of civilized life . . . and at the same time cause them to look with feelings of repugnance on their native state.
>
> (Adams, 1995, p. 21)

Since the solution lay in the re-education of the Indigenous people, the question became what types of educational institutions would be most effective? Tribal Chair of the Cherokees

1778-1871	*Treaty 374 treaties made and broken*
1824	*Indian Affairs formed under War Department*
1810s -1840s	*Missionary School Movement*
1840s-1870s	*Indian Day School Movement*
1879-1910s	*New Boarding School Movement*
1887	*Dawes Act - land allotted to individuals*
1910s-1990s	*Off Reservation Boarding School Movement*
1924	*Citizenship Act – Right to vote*
1934	*Indian Reorganization Act*
1953	*Termination Act (attempted to end Tribal funding)*
1973	*Wounded Knee Occupation*

FIGURE 6.1 Historical Timeline of Events

Wilma Mankiller stated it this way, "Whoever controls the education of our children, controls our future" (Hill, 1999).

The following is a brief summary of Adams's research from *Education of Extinction*.

1. *Missionary School Movement* (early 1800s) was developed by a coalition of Christian church groups who were critical of the government's corrupt economic treatment of the tribes. They divided the reservations among themselves and only educated the youngest children. Leupp, Education Commissioner, stated, "Our main hope lies with the youthful generations who are still measurable and plastic. The bright-eyed children are not yet savages with hideously painted faces" (Adams, 1995, p. 23). The system failed because parents began hiding their children at the site of missionary wagons.

2. *Indian Day School Movement* (mid-1800s) created permanent day schools for children located close to various military forts. Forty-eight church day schools were established during the 1860s. However, there was a major flaw with this movement. The Native camps seasonally migrated and therefore the school structures were left empty. Floyd Red Crow, an American Indian Movement musician, wrote the popular song with the poignant refrain, "Missionaries go and leave us all alone. Take your white god to your white men, we've a way of our own" (Henhouse Studios, 2008).

3. *New Boarding Schools* began in 1879 by liberal philanthropists (e.g., Boston Indian Citizenship Association and Women's National Indian Association (including abolitionist Harriet Beecher Stowe), among others. They funded armies of teachers who were instructed to teach only in English, thereby undermining Native families' influence. Students were not allowed to return home until summertime. Often, 12-foot fences were built around the boarding schools as a way to "keep out the bad influences."

4. *Off-Reservation Boarding School* continued through the 1990s, traumatizing thousands by taking children against parents' wishes and placing them in large dorms. Corporal punishment was commonly employed. Native languages, dress, ceremonies, and traditional long hair were outlawed. The head of the infamous Carlisle Industrial School popularized his educational goal of "kill the Indian and save the man" (Adams, 1995). Multiple

generations were traumatized by this experience that severely restricted available alternatives. Dennis Banks, American Indian Movement (AIM) leader, said:

> I was taken at four . . . 3,000 miles away from my parents and forced to stay there for six years. The beatings began immediately. They kept my mom's letters away from me . . . so I thought I was abandoned, it completely destroyed my relationship with my mother.
> (Goodman, 2012, October 28)

A documentary called *The Indian Schools, the Survivors' Story* gives further personal accounts.

5. *Current Tribal Schools* are either controlled through the Bureau of Indian Education or are contracted or grant schools operated by tribal governments. Power shifted from the government to Native control. However, for those students who reside (off-reservation) in a city, very few social service assistance programs exist (www.bie.ed). Basic needs of health often take precedence over time in the classroom. The Pierre Indian Learning Center in South Dakota is a tribal-run off-reservation boarding school for 160 students who have been removed from their families by Tribal Courts. These students required 184 orthodontic, primary care, and orthopedic appointments from 9/2018 to 2/2019.
(personal communication, Dr. Mobley, 2019)

The history of Native education fraught with corruption has ultimately led to the destruction of the fabric of the family. The network of aunties, grandparents, and relatives who took much of the responsibility for teaching children was completed disrupted or destroyed. This is the legacy of intergenerational trauma, a field of study in and of itself examining the disproportionate rates of psychiatric distress (Urban Indian Health Institute, 2018). Behavior analysts, as psychologists, could certainly contribute to the research and application of effective support services.

Conditions Facing Educators

Given these conditions, it is not surprising that Indigenous students enter school lacking readiness skills for classroom success. The Hart and Risley (1995) observations of in-home word type and word frequency usage found significant differences depending upon socioeconomic status (SES). Suskind's (2015) research and parent training attempted to address these disparities, however, the parent and child training in word type and conversational turn-types were not observed post-intervention 4 months later. Distinguishing between the function of language at home and at school might better be served with an asset-based (Flores & Rosa, 2015) or constructional approach (Goldiamond, 1974).

Designing instruction with the specific objective of building common classroom language includes the need for frequency-based fluency measures alongside accuracy measures (Johnson & Street, 2012; Johnson & Layng, 1996). Building language repertoires requires the learner to gain vocabulary skills and have automatic access to receptive and expressive usage.

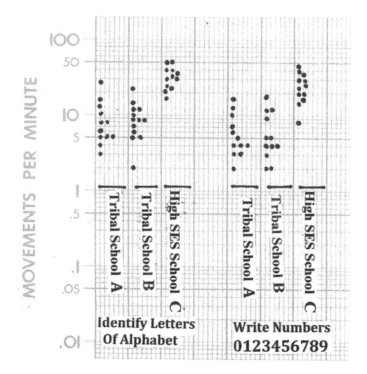

FIGURE 6.2 Data on Skill Acquisition

To this end, Melroe collected pre-intervention data from two tribal schools where the student population was 90% eligible for free and reduced lunch (FRL). Their assessment data was compared to that of a high socioeconomic (SES) school with 4% eligible FRL. Data were collected on kindergarten students in the fall. All their correct responses were recorded on a Standard Celeration Chart (see Figure 6.2), the only data display that depicts the accuracy of behavior in real time. Each dot represents an individual with one column showing the behavior of the group.

First, 12 students were presented with a series of letters and asked to orally name them for a duration of 1 minute. The range for Tribal School A's range was from 4 to 29 correct and Tribal School B's range was from 2 to 21 correct. The high SES school's range was from 8 to 45 correct. Second, students were asked to write digits (0 through 9) in rows for 1 minute. Tribal School A's range was from 2 to 18 and Tribal School B's range was from 2 to 19. The high SES school's range was from 8 to 47. The data clearly show the discrepancy in the entering repertoires and highlights the difficult task teachers face in raising the accuracy and fluency rates (Melroe, 2009).

When Tribal School A examined their data, they concluded that lowering expectations was not an option and instead selected procedures to accelerate learning. The plan included teacher training on new curriculum, using positive reinforcement, employing fluency-building procedures, and relying on elders to add cultural stories. Their gap was reduced because research-based practices were combined with activities that sustained and supported the culture with inclusion of "home language" phrases and "awards" based upon traditional values and well-known people.

Lessons in Application

The development and implementation of effective instruction for any culturally diverse groups must consider both the group's or individual's behavioral history in conjunction with the principles of behavior analysis. The following are suggestions and insights for improving one's skills when working across the cultural divide.

Lesson 1: Utilize The Successes From Applied Behavior Analysis

The first step in any interaction is acquiring knowledge of what has been already applied and proven successful by behavior analysts in our field. Two particular methodologies based on behavioral principles can be studied in numerous publications. The first, the Morningside Model of Generative Instruction (MMGI), founded by Dr. Kent Johnson, is a complex blend of technologies including direct instruction, precision teaching, curriculum-based measurement, talk aloud problem solving, behaviorally based classroom management procedures, and discovery learning through adduction (Johnson & Street, 2012).

The second is School-Wide Positive Behavioral Support (SWPBS), which is a comprehensive behavioral approach that arranges the contingencies to promote safer schools, reduce problem behavior, and improve student behavior. "SWPBS is firmly rooted in an applied behavior analytic tradition and in a solid body of research" (Sugai & Horner, 2006, p. 245).

These systems offer a way to introduce the science of behavior analysis and the principles and the language that guide the procedures and what underpins the carefully selected curricula. Redefining everyday terms can change the way educators talk about what they see and what they want or need to change and shape. For example, the word "behavior" (from its often used shorthand for "bad behavior") can be redefined such that there is a shared understanding that all behavior makes sense. Learning how to observe and describe the topography of the behavior leads to asking what the student is gaining from that specific behavior. Determining if a behavior stems from either a "can't do" or a "won't do" standpoint helps develop a teacher's analytical skills. While this may appear to be simplistic in learning about the function of behavior, examining the consequences of classroom interactions sets one on the road to using the science of human behavior.

Lesson 2: Use Culturally Appropriate Language

The popularization of corrupted names and meaning instead of the intended names and meaning exemplifies a skewed perspective and lack of sensitivity. When referring to a specific tribe, it is respectful to use the tribe's original name (e.g., Dene vs. Navajo, Lakota vs. Sioux).

For example, the intended meaning of Lakota is "friends that unite", however French trappers chose to use "Sioux" instead. Sioux means "the rattling sound a snake makes before it bites" (Oehler, 1959). Use of appropriate terminology is vital. If one is unsure, then ask. If this is glossed over, it can create a permanent gulf.

Lesson 3: Take Into Account How Local Conditions Impact Application

Research-based intervention will have limited effectiveness if the historical and social conditions are not taken into account. Collaboration with all the stakeholders prevents mistakes and creates buy-in. A case in point occurred on the Pine Ridge Reservation when an intervention called "walk to reading" was implemented. Data on the students' entering repertoires was collected, and then students were homogeneously grouped based on similar skills and needs. Homogeneous grouping intervention increases instructional time. A meta-analysis of 43 studies demonstrated that homogeneous grouping significantly increases student achievement and has an average effect size of .35, or about 12% (Kulik, 2004).

When the consultants mistakenly created class lists without input from staff about relevant community dynamics, there was uproar from parents and staff. While the events of 1973 may seem to have come and gone, the 71-day occupation at Wounded Knee on this reservation deeply affected people's trust and ability to work together. This act of resistance was a fight over who controlled the sale of resources. The Tribal Chair, US military, and the FBI tried to contain the activists using armed tanks and helicopters. Many tribal members were hurt, two were killed, and schools were closed (Akwesasne Notes, 1974). Years later, these scars were still raw. Changes were rearranged to take into account both the social contingencies and the students' academic needs.

Another example occurred with a presentation delivered to parents on expanding support of their child's reading. A presentation, which had previously received rave reviews, was used without considering the reservation setting. As the presentation proceeded, the parents were polite, silent, and not engaged. Finally, one parent asked if we realized that there are NO public libraries on any reservations. After apologizing, the discussion switched to a group brainstorming on ways to functionally support reading. One such idea for beginner readers was searching for letters and words on food containers in the store or at home.

Lesson 4: Establish Rapport and Collaborative Relationships

Setting aside the time to develop individual connections and trust is an integral part of building rapport. This process must be done step by step involving listening and openly sharing "the good, the bad, and the ugly" experiences.

As behavior analysts apply these principles to organizations, application must be inclusive and involve listening and brainstorming with all the stakeholders to determine a comprehensive intervention plan. In one case, it was determined that the students had a deficit in sequential recall of story events and low vocabulary skills. The recommendation called for adding a "retelling procedure." However, the school's schedule was too tight. The consultant requested a staff and administration problem-solving meeting at which the group was shown student data and learned about the research and the implementation procedures. After an in-depth discussion, the cultural teacher stepped forward and agreed to learn the new procedure if she could apply it with tribal stories and myths so it would be familiar and relevant to the cultural practices.

Lesson 5: Understand Role That Native Languages Play in Maintaining Culture

Language is a key component of any group's ability to maintain its culture. Natives view their language as essential because it can better express their values and norms and helps maintain the community. Transmitting cultural knowledge is weakened when it is only transmitted through English. This continues to be a struggle for Natives both on and off the reservations (Dunbar-Ortiz, 2016).

Since many Native languages are on the brink of extinction, tribes are requiring inclusion of language and/or cultural school plans. These range from native language classes to immersion programs. As a behavior analyst, making the attempt to learn some of the language is a sign of respect and demonstrates a commitment to being culturally aware. Assessing the level of language used in the school is a crucial step to implementation before engaging with staff. Learning the commonly used indigenous classroom words increases the accuracy of observational data since the environment does not need to be altered when a consultant is present. An example of an error was made while collecting classroom management data (ratio between specific praise, non-specific praise, and negative statements) to determine what training was needed. The outcome data revealed a high rate of negative statements due to misinterpretation of an Indigenous phrase. Once this was cleaned up, the training took a different course. Publicly acknowledging the mistake led to teasing, laughter, and an offer for personal language lessons.

In a Hawaiian kindergarten classroom, the teacher taught body parts and directional words in English and Hawaiian by inserting Hawaiian while using the direct instruction program *Language for Learning*. What more powerful way to learn vocabulary than applying the concept of two-way associations – for example, see body part/say word; hear word/point to body part (Tiemann & Markle, 1991). Applauding this effort was a concrete way of supporting the mandate to improve Hawaiian language skills. Encouraging students to teach the consultant their language is an amazing exchange.

Lesson 6: Observe and Evaluate One's Own Behavior

As the speaker, one needs to be aware of how one's interactions impact the listener. Identifying the differences in rates of speech, duration of pauses, physical boundaries, body language, and eye contact is critical. Evaluating and accommodating these differences is all part of being culturally aware. We know that even differences in accents require changing the pace, and articulating requires attention.

An essential element developing of socially sensitive cultural skills is to continually be reflective and open to changing one's own behavior. Learning is not complete as a result of reading a few articles or attending a presentation on cultural sensitivity. Making a commitment to self-evaluation and even public acknowledgment of mistakes is all part of the process.

Lesson 7: Be Aware of Current Conditions: Indigenous Women Issues

Traditional women's roles have also been displaced and changed over time. A major concern is the high numbers of Indigenous women who have been murdered or are missing. Sex trafficking affects women of all ages, including young girls. It is safe to say that there is not a family on or off the reservation that hasn't had someone affected by this issue. In 2016, the Urban Indian Health Institute researched and collected data from 71 cities. They identified 506 cases of murdered or missing Indigenous. The 2013 Women Against Violence Act (WAVA) didn't address the fact that Indigenous women had no legal recourse if a non-Native attacked a Native woman on a reservation. Neither the tribal nor state courts had legal jurisdiction in this situation. While it is unconscionable that this loophole existed at all, a rider to WAVA was later passed that gave Indigenous women recourse.

On or off the reservation, it is a guarantee that the vast majority of individuals, teachers, or students will be affected by the loss of a member of their family. Without a more in-depth understanding of these issues in combination with cultural healing norms, behavior analysts unintentionally could provide ineffective services to individuals seeking counseling.

Cultural Appreciation Versus Cultural Appropriation

When working with Native Americans, the distinction between appreciation and appropriation is absolutely critical. Appreciation is the action of honoring the culture by learning about behavioral histories before interacting with that group. It is not the Indigenous person's responsibility to "inform" the analyst about their culture. Only after rapport is established can questions and comparing experiences begin in earnest.

Non-Natives appear to have an insatiable appetite to appropriate and mimic Native cultures and, in particular, religious ceremonies. Identifying appropriation occurs when another group wears Pocahontas costumes for Halloween or when sports fans do the "tomahawk chop" or pray to the four directions. These types of cultural appropriation are not harmless; they are demeaning. Dunbar-Ortiz stated that appropriation occurs "when people from outside a particular culture take elements or another culture in a way that is objectionable and I might add without permission" (Dunbar-Ortiz, 2016, p. 82).

When working as a consultant on the Lakota reservation, an administrator invited Melroe to a ceremonial sweat, which is a sacred ritual held in a natural structure for purification. The invitation was declined because the author sought to maintain a professional relationship. Previous experience of the administrator was that typically white people were highly reinforced by attending ceremonies. A more open and respectful rapport developed due to the consultant's response. Interacting with the community by attending community events (e.g., games, fairs) can set the occasion for positive interactions.

Conclusions

Does behavior analysis have anything to offer Indigenous populations? The answer is a resounding "Yes." All organisms are subject to the same principles that govern behavior; clearly, the application of our science is meaningful to this population as well. As behavior analysts, our contribution is to help arrange the contingencies that will maintain the behavior of the students, teachers, administrators, and the families of the students while sustaining Indigenous culture. The task behavior analysts face is how to acquire culturally appropriate communication skills and to align behavior analysis with the goals of the Indigenous population.

The sooner the field of behavior analysis recognizes the necessity to include cultural awareness skills training in undergraduate and graduate programs, the more likely the quality of services for diverse populations will improve. The contingencies of reinforcement that define cultural practices should be routinely incorporated in course work along with offerings for continuing educational credits.

A challenge we face is how to develop pathways for Indigenous people to become involved in behavior analysis. How many Native Americans have a BCBA®, and what do we need to do to change that? How can current graduate and undergraduate programs coordinate with over 120 tribal colleges?

Education opens new possibilities and opportunities; however, for Native Americans this poses a different set of problems. Since few businesses are willing to move to the reservation, Native Americans need to move to urban areas for employment. The urban environment changes the relationship to the land, extended families, norms, language, and religious tradition. "Skinner called for bringing scientific principles of behavior to bear on the design of cultural practices that are likely to enhance the survival of a culture" (Glenn, 2001, p. 14). This reality begs the question of how to support the retention of Indigenous culture. Behavior analysts' response or lack thereof to the crisis that Native Americans face today says much about our understanding of social responsibility.

Answers to Questions at Beginning of Chapter

Answers: (1) 2010 census = 5.2 million; 50–70 million; (2) 1924; (3) recognized tribes = 573; unrecognized tribes = 250; (4) Christopher Columbus; (5) Teddy Roosevelt.

DISCUSSION QUESTIONS

1. What effects does the current educational system have on preserving or destroying Native culture? How can a behavior analyst avoid historical mistakes?

2. How will you prepare yourself to be culturally aware? What evaluation procedures will you employ?

3. What actions can be taken to attract Native Americans to behavior analysis?

4. How might specific services be provided to urban populations?

References

Adams, D. W. (1995). *Education for extinction: American Indians and the boarding school experience.* Lawrence, KA: University Press of Kansas.

Akwesasne Notes (Eds.). (1974). *Voices from Wounded Knee, 1973.* Rooseveltown, NY: Akwesasne Notes.

Dunbar-Ortiz, R. (2016). *All the real Indians died off: And 20 other myths about Native Americans.* Boston, MA: Beacon.

Flores, N., & Rosa, J. (2015, December). Undoing appropriateness: Raciolinguistic ideologies and language diversity in education. *Harvard Educational Review, 85*(2), 149–171.

Frosch, D. (2008, October 16). Is native tongue facing extinction, Arapaho tribe teaches the young. *New York Times.* Retrieved from www.nytimes.com/2008/10/17/us/17arapaho.html

Glenn, S. S., Dinsmoor, J. A., Balcazar, F. E., Geller, E. S., Thyer, B. A., Lamal, P. A. . . . Wyatt, W. J. (2001). Commentaries on "The Design of Cultures." *Behavior and Social Issues, 11,* 14–30.

Goldiamond, I. (1974). Toward a constructional approach to social problems: Ethical and constitutional issues raised by applied behavior analysis. *Behaviorism, 2*(1), 1–84.

Goodman, A. (2012, October 28). *Native American Leader Dennis Banks on overlooked tragedy of Indian boarding schools.* Radio Interview (War and Peace Report). New York, NY: Pacifica Radio.

Hart, B., & Risley, T. R. (1995). *Meaningful differences in the everyday experience of young American children.* Baltimore, MD: Paul H. Brookes Publishing Company.

Hill Jr, N. S. (Ed.). (1999). *Words of power: Voices from Indian America.* Golden, CO: Fulcrum Publishing.

Johnson, K. R., & Layng, T. V. (1996). On terms and procedures: Fluency. *The Behavior Analyst, 19*(2), 281–288.

Johnson, K. R., & Street, E. M. (2012). From the laboratory to the field and back again: Morningside Academy's 32 years of improving students' academic performance. *The Behavior Analyst Today, 13*(1), 20–40. http://doi.org/10.1037/h0100715

Kulik, J. A. (2004). Grouping, tracking, and de-tracking: Conclusions from experimental, correlational, and ethnographic research. In H. Walberg, A. Reynolds, & M. Wang (Eds.), *Can unlike students learn together?: Grade retention, tracking, and grouping,* (pp. 157–182). Charlotte, NC: Information Age Publishing Inc.

Melroe, K. (2009, May). *Language: Its role in indigenous education.* Presented at Symposium #479, Annual 2009 Association for Behavioral Analysis, Phoenix, AZ.

Sugai, G., & Horner, R. R. (2006). A promising approach for expanding and sustaining school-wide positive behavior support. *School Psychology Review, 35*(2), 245–259.

Sugai, G., O'Keeffe, B. V., & Fallon, L. M. (2012). A contextual consideration of culture and positive behavior support. *Journal of Positive Behavioral Support, 14*(4), 197–208. https://doi.org/10.1177/1098300711426334

Suskind, D. (2015). *Thirty million words: Building a child's brain.* New York, NY: Dutton/Penguin Books.

Tiemann, P. W., & Markle, S. M. (1991). *Analyzing instructional content.* Seattle, WA: Morningside Press.

Urban Indian Health Institute. (2018). *Missing and murdered indigenous women and girls: A snapshot of data from 71 urban cities.* Abigail Echo-Hawk. Retrieved from info@uihi.org

Zinn, H. (2015). *A people's history of the United States: 1492-present.* New York: HarperCollins.

7

Culturally Tailored ABA Treatments for Asian American Clients and Families

Kwang-Sun Cho Blair, James Donggeun Lee, Kozue Matsuda, and Ashley Knochel

Learning Objectives

- Describe the need for culturally sensitive behavior analysts.
- Identify barriers and obstacles to receiving ABA treatments in Asian American individuals with disabilities and their families.
- Describe a basic approach to adapting ABA treatment to culturally and linguistically diverse clients and families.
- Provide examples of strategies for use by behavior analysts to deliver culturally tailored ABA treatments to Asian American clients and families.

Need for Culturally Sensitive Behavior Analysts

Researchers and professionals in education, health, and psychology have pointed out the cultural misapplication in their fields (Krahn, Walker, & Correa-De-Araujo, 2015; Lee & Richardson, 1991), indicating that current behavioral interventions for cultural and ethnic minority groups may be inadequate given the lack of integration of culturally tailored services (Kim et al., 2019). The current literature on evidence-based behavioral interventions (EBIs) has been predominantly derived from research in the United States and other high-income countries (Khan et al., 2012; Zhang & Bennett, 2003). Thus, ethical and professional considerations are warranted for providing services to clients who are members of ethnic minority groups. The *Professional and Ethical Compliance Code for Behavior Analysts* (Behavior Analyst Certification Board® [BACB®], 2014), guideline 1.03, indicates that behavior analysts should maintain competence in the skills they use by furthering their knowledge through appropriate means. Therefore, a basic understanding of cultural practices and values is essential for behavior analysts to provide effective and ethical services to cultural and ethnic minority populations (Barrerra, Castro, Strycker, & Toobert, 2013; Fong, Catagnus, Broadhead, Quigley, & Field, 2016). However, despite the ethical urgency to increase cultural competence among behavior analysts, many argue that behavior analyst preparation programs lack the provision of training on cultural awareness and diversity (Beaulieu, Addington, & Almeida, 2019; Conners, Johnson, Duarte, Murriky, & Marks, 2019).

Needs of individuals with disabilities from ethnocultural groups. Individuals with disabilities in the United States represent a large segment of the population and in general they experience a variety of health disparities, which reflects social inequalities (Krahn et al., 2015; Weinstein, Geller, Negussie, & Baciu, 2017). Recent reports revealed that individuals with autism spectrum disorder (ASD) have shown increased morbidity and early mortality compared to those without ASD (Croen et al., 2015; Hill, Pérez-Stable, Anderson, & Bernard, 2015). This indicates that these disparities are likely exacerbated when the individuals are members of cultural and ethnic minority groups. Evidence suggests that children with ASD who have heightened risk factors due to racial, ethnic, and socioeconomic disadvantages are less likely to receive a timely ASD diagnosis (Mazumdar, Winter, Liu, & Bearman, 2013) and more likely to receive limited ASD treatment services, resulting in poor health and developmental outcomes (Ennis-Cole, Durodoye, & Harris, 2013; Nguyen, Krakowiak, Hansen, Hertz-Picciotto, & Angkustsiri, 2016). These health disparities reflect the need for culturally appropriate treatments in addition to adequate treatments for individuals with disabilities from ethnocultural groups (Butler et al., 2016).

Limited access and lack of culturally appropriate ABA treatment. Bishop-Fitzpatrick and Kind (2017) indicated that parents of African American and Latino children with ASD reported having health service providers who were not sensitive to family values and customs, did not value partnerships with parents, and did not provide sufficient information. This suggests that even though families can be valuable partners who collaborate and contribute in making accurate diagnoses and designing treatment plans, it is likely that ethnically and culturally diverse children with disabilities may not have access to culturally appropriate services. In providing ABA services, cultural conflict can emerge with respect to the use of behavioral techniques in working with parents of children with disabilities, given that parenting goals, values, and practices vary from culture to culture (Bornstein & Cote, 2006).

For example, delivering contingent praise has been recognized as an effective and powerful social reinforcer in promoting appropriate behavior in children. However, Asian parents often practice strict control and their parenting involves low expressions of affection, whereas American parenting styles typically involve praising and physical affection (Park, Kim, Chiang, & Ju, 2010; Huntsinger, Jose, Rudden, Luo, & Krieg, 2002). In a qualitative study with Korean American parents who participated in the standardized Incredible Years parenting program (Kim, Hong, & Rockett, 2016), the parents expressed that the specific behavioral techniques taught in the program, such as praising, encouragement, using sticker charts, and ignoring, were foreign to them and that although the program was effective, it was based on Western parenting strategies. These findings highlight the need for recognizing and incorporating culturally based values into ABA treatment as well as actively involving parents in designing treatments. However, our field may lack conscientious behavior analysts who are aware of their own cultural background, experiences, and biases that might influence their ability to assist clients from ethnocultural groups to provide fair, appropriate, and respectful treatments (Fong et al., 2016).

Growing Asian Population in the United States

Based on recent statistics, there are more than 20 million Asian Americans (Pew Research Center, 2017). Asian Americans account for 5.8% of the US population and are one of the fastest growing populations in this country. Based on a projection by Pew Research Center (2015), Asian Americans are projected to be the largest immigrant group by 2055 and will account for up to 14% of the US population. These numbers are based on the current immigration trend from more than 20 nations in different parts of Asia, which is responsible for the diversity among the Asian population in the United States. Among these groups, Chinese Americans account for the largest population with nearly 5 million people, followed by Indian Americans (3.9 million), Filipino Americans (3.8 million), Vietnamese Americans (1.9 million) and Korean Americans (1.8 million).

Many Asian Americans who reside in the United States are foreign born and experience high levels of immigration-related stressors. For example, it is estimated that of the 1.8 million Korean Americans who reside in the United States, more than 1 million are foreign born and experience immigration-related stressors such as separation from family members, income loss, cultural shock, discrimination, deficiencies in community support, and general adjustment difficulties such as language, acculturation stress, and employment (Mui & Kang, 2006; Noh & Kaspar, 2003). In spite of their needs, evidence shows that many immigrants do not receive proper treatment (Abe-Kim et al., 2007).

Needs of Asian American Individuals With Disabilities

The needs of Asian American individuals with disabilities are increasing significantly. The US Census Bureau (2018) reported that among the Asian American population, an estimated 11.1% of children and 20.1% of adults live with at least one type of disability. The current status of ABA services for Asian American individuals is difficult to estimate due to limited relevant statistics. However, with increasing access to ABA treatment services via the public health infrastructure (e.g., Medicaid, state-mandated private insurance coverage), it is presumed that more and more Asian Americans have access to ABA services. However, due to the lack of relevant literature, little is known about how to maintain clinical integrity while adapting interventions and practices to be culturally sensitive for this population. Fong and colleagues (2016) provided some insight about how behavior analysts should cultivate cultural awareness of the individuals who receive services, as well as the behavior analysts themselves, including (1) identifying an individual or a unit that is responsible for ensuring cultural awareness, (2) incorporating cultural awareness in individual clinical supervision, and (3) incorporating cultural awareness into clinical supervision and training.

Barriers and Obstacles to Receiving ABA Treatment Among the Asian American Population

There are some barriers and obstacles to receiving ABA treatment in the Asian American community. First, families who are relatively new immigrants may not be familiar with the services that are available to them and may struggle to navigate the system to access those services. In an ethnographic study, Jegatheesan, Fowler, and Miller (2010) reported that new Asian immigrant parents of children with disabilities expressed their frustration with trying to understand what to do after being diagnosed in the United States. Conventional resources (e.g., support groups) that were available to mainstream American parents were not familiar to these families, and they reported limited knowledge of their rights and options. Second, there appears to be a gap in professional standards for adapting ABA practices to meet the needs of culturally and linguistically diverse families. Because ABA treatment is built on the foundation of assessment, programming, intervention, and evaluation, cultural considerations and adaptations must occur in all phases of treatment. Prejudicial perceptions and misguided beliefs of ABA treatment may also hinder active participation of stakeholders.

Another potential area for cultural barriers is the family's limited involvement. Individualized treatment is a defining feature and integral component of ABA. All aspects of intervention must be customized to the strengths, needs, preferences, and environmental circumstances of each individual client and their family members. However, immigrant parents are less likely to be directly involved with their children's care and education, even though they express the desires for their children to do well in school (Siu & Feldman, 1996). Although the parents can offer insight into the cultural adequacy of the treatment plan, barriers related to linguistic diversity may impact the ability or willingness of Asian American parents to be involved with the implementation process (Wang & West, 2016).

Adapting ABA Treatment to Asian American Clients and Families

Although the majority of the literature on culturally adapted EBIs provides insufficient details on the methods used to adapt the interventions to diverse ethnocultural groups, thereby hindering replication efforts (Soto, Smith, Griner, Rodriguez, & Bernal, 2018), the field of clinical psychology has suggested several cultural adaptation models and frameworks (e.g., Bernal & Adames, 2017; Domenech Rodriguez & Bernal, 2012). These models and frameworks may be used to guide the adaptation of ABA treatment for the Asian American population, given that the field of ABA has yet to propose a model for the systematic adaptation of ABA treatment that is both technically adequate and culturally responsive.

Basic Approach to Cultural Adaptation of Treatments

Bernal and Adames (2017) proposed a set of guidelines for cultural adaptations of psychological treatments, including the following recommendations: (1) use a conceptual adaptation framework to identify key elements in the adaptation, (2) carefully document all adaptations, (3) evaluate outcomes of the culturally adapted treatment, (4) evaluate the integrity of the original treatment model vis-à-vis the adapted version, and (5) reevaluate outcomes of the adapted evidence-based treatment. Beyond these general stages in cultural adaptation, Lau (2006) suggested that the intervention must be contextualized by altering the intervention content (procedures), and that the engagement of participants must be enhanced to ensure social validity when adapting an EBI. Bernal and colleagues (1995) suggested that the following eight dimensions should be adapted to contextualize content and enhance participant engagement: language, persons, metaphors, content, concepts, goals, methods, and context. As a general strategy of adapting an EBI, Castro, Barrera, and Steiker (2010) also suggested identifying specific sources of intervention-consumer mismatch and introducing specific adaptive activities to resolve each mismatched source to enhance relevance and fit. The authors indicated that possible sources of mismatch would be group characteristics, program delivery staff, and administrative and community factors.

Based on the suggested approach of Castro and colleagues (2010), Table 7.1 illustrates potential sources of cultural mismatch that may impact the effectiveness of ABA treatment for Asian American population.

The most basic form of cultural adaptation is linguistic adaptation that involves translating the intervention into the first language of the current consumer group for individuals who lack proficiency in English. This linguistic adaptation may be necessary to promote parental involvement and comprehension of intervention elements. When sources of cultural mismatch are identified amid ethnic or context differences, the level of cultural adaptation may be more complex. It would be necessary for behavior analysts to possess extensive cultural sensitivity skills and establish a comprehensive understanding of the client's culture prior to initiating adaptations related to cultural values and traditions. Given that the development of such skills may not be viable due to resource and time constraints, behavior analysts must consider alternative ways for ensuring cultural adequacy of ABA treatment plans.

For instance, parental involvement throughout the assessment and intervention process may be critical for developing effective and meaningful adaptations related to cultural differences in belief systems, experiences, and perceptions (Theara & Abott, 2015). The cultural adaptation frameworks often only focus on intervention content rather than on practitioners delivering the interventions, and that cultural competence and clinical skills of the practitioners should be considered in designing culturally appropriate treatment plans (Castro et al., 2010). Methods for developing the cultural awareness skills of behavior analysts have been

TABLE 7.1 Potential Sources of Cultural Mismatch in Western-Derived EBIs

	Source of Mismatch	Original Validation Group(s)	Current Consumer Group	Actual or Potential Mismatch Effect
Group Characteristics	Language	English	Mandarin, Japanese, Korean, Lao, Thai, Vietnamese, etc.	Inability to understand assessment reports and content of intervention plan that may hinder parental involvement
	Country of Origin/ Race/ Ethnicity	American descent/ white/ non-minority	Immigrant families/ ethnic minority	Difference in cultural values and traditions, support systems, socioeconomic status, resource constraints
	Cultural Context	Western	Non-Western (East, South, and Southeast Asians)	Conflicts in belief systems, different family systems, understanding parental perspectives
Program Delivery Practitioners	Type of Practitioners	Certified Behavior Analysts	Registered Behavior Technician	Lesser or different program delivery skills and perspectives
	Practitioner Cultural Sensitivity	Culturally sensitive or incentive behavior analysts	Culturally insensitive or sensitive registered behavior technician	Insensitivity to cultural issues, referring to missing cultural elements or criticizing culturally insensitive treatment plan
Community Factors	Community Consultation and Readiness	Consulted with community in treatment plan design, moderate readiness	Not consulted with community, low readiness	Absence of community buy-in, absence of infrastructure and organization

discussed (Fong et al., 2016), and a small but emerging body of literature has shed light on the critical need for culturally competent practitioners in behavior analysis (Conners et al., 2019). However, due to distinct social contingencies that impact human behavior among different cultures, it is unlikely that behavior analysts will ever establish true *cultural competency*. Rather, behavior analysts should aim to be *culturally informed* or *culturally sensitive* when working with clients and families outside of the dominant culture through which the science of behavior analysis was derived. In addition, it is essential for behavior analysts to become self-aware of how one's own culture impacts service delivery and treatment effectiveness (Beaulieu et al., 2018).

Strategies for Designing Culturally Tailored ABA Treatment

The BACB® (2017) has provided clinical guidelines about using ABA as a treatment for ASD. Within the guidelines, the following four areas are discussed as core characteristics of ABA treatment: (1) an objective assessment and analysis of the client's conditions; (2) understanding the context of the behavior and the behavior's values to the individual, the family, and the community; (3) utilization of the principles and procedures of behavior analysis; and (4) consistent, ongoing, objective assessment and data analysis (p. 10). Based on these core characteristics of ABA treatment and the critical features of a treatment plan for service authorization, which is suggested in the guidelines, we provide examples of strategies for designing and providing culturally tailored ABA treatments to Asian American clients and families.

Step 1: Gathering the Client's Background Information

It is essential that behavior analysts collect information about client demographics, reason for referral, family background, diagnoses, and services received previously when initiating an ABA treatment. Out of fear of being discriminated against and feelings of "family shame" due to the diagnosis, Asian families may avoid sharing information with service providers if they perceive a risk of disclosure and embarrassment (Kang-Yi et al., 2018; Yan, Accordino, Boutin, & Wilson, 2014). To help reduce difficulty or reluctance of sharing personal information, bilingual, bicultural staff should help parents in the process of information gathering and should explain to them that correct information leads to effective intervention (Jegatheesan et al., 2010; Pondé & Rousseau, 2013). Most importantly, staff should have an open mind and be willing to ask questions about the child and family, viewing the child through the cultural context. As discussed earlier, many Asian Americans are first-generation immigrants who have had negative experiences receiving services and communicating with their children's service providers because of language barriers and their limited knowledge of American education and other service systems (Cooc & Yang, 2017). Thus behavior analysts should provide general information about services that families may benefit from within their knowledge.

Step 2: Conducting Assessment

During the assessment phase, behavior analysts conduct both indirect and direct assessments including interviews and observations. Although other family members are encouraged to participate in this process, behavior analysts should also take into account the "face-saving" nature of Asian parents' likely reactions (Tsai-Chae & Nagata, 2008). When discussing the child's target behaviors, the behavior analyst should address social validity of the target behaviors (i.e., treatment goals; Wolf, 1978) by identifying the behaviors with input from the families.

Behavior analysts may need to encourage parents to voice their opinions and to create a more collaborative dialogue that emphasizes their input in making decisions (Cooc & Yang, 2017).

Asian families may object to what they perceive as professional-driven, condescending remarks about their home environment and family interaction styles, or when professionals use an authoritative tone of voice, or insist on using behavioral jargons that the families question (Jegatheesan et al., 2010). Because conducting a functional analysis (FA) of the problem behavior may not be well received in Asian cultures – as the procedure provokes problem behavior a family tries to hide – behavior analysts should select the most effective and acceptable approach when conducting an FA. For example, the Interview Informed Synthesized Contingency Analysis (IISCA; Hanley, Jin, Vanselow, & Hanratty, 2014) and precursor FA (Heath & Smith, 2019) both involve less provocation of problem behavior.

Step 3: Designing a Treatment Plan

The behavior analyst should explain the treatment plan – which has been designed based on the assessment results – while adapting treatment goals and objectives, behavioral techniques, data collection procedures, and the generalization plan to Asian families. The behavior techniques and procedures included in the treatment plan should represent their cultural context. Considering that using physical punishment is often accepted in Asian family homes (Choi, Kim, Kim, & Park, 2013), the legality of corporal punishment and alternative ways of reducing problem behavior should be discussed with the Asian families. In addition, a family may feel that the therapist's interventions with them are "cold", which may present as very straightforward and time-conscious (Jegatheesan et al., 2010). Additionally, when employing an extinction procedure, the behavior analyst should explain the function of the child's problem behavior and the rationale for such procedure. Asian families may also view the therapist's provision of tangible reinforcement as frivolous, similar to how some Asian parents object to what they perceive as overuse of verbal praise (Kim & Hong, 2007). Thus, the definition and effectiveness of reinforcement procedures should be explicitly explained to Asian American families within the family cultural context. Furthermore, a generalization plan should be discussed prior to starting the intervention, as extended family members (e.g., grandparents) live together with nuclear families in Asian cultures (Wang & Casillas, 2013).

Step 4: Parent/Caregiver Training

Parent and caregiver training is an integral part of ABA treatment, thus, the plan must include specific parent training and data collection procedures for monitoring treatment integrity. Given that language barriers may discourage parents from implementing behavioral interventions, behavior analysts should respond to both the strengths and challenges they face. Effective parent training procedures (e.g., behavioral skills training, in vivo coaching, performance feedback, problem solving) should be used to help parents become competent in implementing interventions at home (Robertson, Wehby, & King, 2013). If language presents an issue, a bilingual behavior analyst should be involved in parent training to support parents with achieving treatment goals.

Step 5: Coordinating Care and Planning for Transition, Discharge, and Crisis

Because individuals with disabilities often receive multidisciplinary services, coordinating care and services with other service providers is critical to achieve treatment goals. The behavior analysts are to coordinate the treatment and care with other professionals and assist the families in communicating between the parents and professionals in various environments and settings (e.g., school, outpatient hospitals, community health centers) to maximize treatment outcomes. To prevent confusion about discharging the client and to better prepare the client and their family, transition and discharge planning should be gradual and initiated at least a few months prior to discharge. ABA treatment should also be systematically faded out and planned in collaboration with family members as treatment goals are achieved. Procedures should also be in place to maintain the safety of family members in the event of a behavioral or other emergency situation; risk management and safety plans should be developed and adjusted if necessary, and they should reflect the cultural context of the family. To make the discharge plan successful, the plan should focus on strengths of the client, and family support should be provided during the process of implementing the discharge plan, including providing resources, assessing for barriers, problem-solving, and follow-up actions if problems arise.

Conclusion

A growing body of research supports culturally tailored ABA treatment for ethnically and culturally diverse clients and their families. As the Asian American population grows in the United States, there is a critical need for behavior analysts who can tailor evidence-based ABA treatment to this population. Designing culturally appropriate and culturally tailored ABA treatment for this population requires behavior analysts to understand their unique needs and their barriers and obstacles to receiving ABA treatment. This also requires behavior analysts to be culturally sensitive, value partnerships with families, and have knowledge and skills on using the basic approach to cultural adaptation of treatments and the strategies for designing culturally tailored ABA treatment plans. Therefore, behavior analysts who work with various populations including cultural and ethnic minority groups in the United States must consider the diversity of their clientele as well as the importance of culturally tailored ABA treatments to enhance the treatment outcomes and clients' quality of life. Behavior analysts must establish a comprehensive understanding of their clients' cultures prior to initiating adaptations of ABA treatments, recognizing the limits of their competencies and expertise. Future research should examine attempts of culturally tailored ABA treatments and the effectiveness of such treatments for ethnic, linguistic, and culturally diverse populations.

CASE STUDY

When Mina first learned that her 4-year-old son, Gene, had ASD, she feared that she and her husband would not be able to navigate the educational and treatment service systems to find the right services for their child. As a first-generation immigrant, Mina learned very early that both she and her husband were frequently misunderstood due to their limited proficiency in English and often had difficulty completing various legal documents. She had to take her son Gene to a neighborhood preschool program at a public school due to her and her husband's employment. She was the more responsible parent for Gene's education, but taking time off from work to participate in meetings to develop an individualized education plan (IEP) for Gene was not easy. Moreover, it was difficult for Mina to understand the professional jargon at the IEP meetings. She felt excluded due to her language barrier and cultural differences. She also felt that her child was not receiving appropriate services at school. Gene engaged in physical aggression toward his peers and classroom staff, verbal stereotypy, and elopement. Mina and her husband were concerned that Gene's problem behaviors were not adequately addressed because the levels of the problem behaviors persisted, and at the end of the first semester, he continued to have difficulty communicating with others and engaging in learning activities. Mina was introduced to ABA therapy through her church, and Gene started receiving ABA therapy at home in the evenings. After 5 months of ABA therapy, both Mina and her husband were pleased to see improvement in Gene's behavior and his initiation of communication; however, Gene was still having difficulty engaging in family routines (e.g., mealtime, bedtime), and his problems at school persisted.

DISCUSSION QUESTIONS

1.   What are the unique barriers and obstacles to receiving educational and ABA treatment services experienced by Gene and his parents?

2.   It appears that Gene's parents have difficulty participating in their son's IEP meetings, and his IEP has not been effective. What strategy should a behavior analyst use to address Gene's problem behavior at school?

3.   What procedures or steps should a behavior analyst follow when working with Gene's parents to design a culturally tailored ABA treatment?

4.   What cultural factors should be considered to improve Gene's behavior within family routines, given that he still has difficulty engaging in family routines even after 5 months of ABA therapy?

5.   If Gene continues to have difficulty engaging in family routines and continues to display problem behavior, what strategies could a behavior analyst use to resolve the issue?

References

Abe-Kim, J., Takeuchi, D., Hong, S., Zane, N., Sue, S., Spencer, M. S. . . . Alegria, M. (2007). Use of mental health-related services among immigrant and US-born Asian Americans: Results from the national Latino and Asian American study. *American Journal of Public Health, 97*, 91–98. https://doi.org/10.2105/AJPH.2006.098541

Barrera, M., Jr., Castro, F. G., Strycker, L. A., & Toobert, D. J. (2013). Cultural adaptations of behavioral health interventions: A progress report. *Journal of Consulting and Clinical Psychology, 81*(2), 196–205. https://doi.org/10.1037/a0027085

Beaulieu, L., Addington, J., & Almeida, D. (2019). Behavior analysts' training and practices regarding cultural diversity: The case for culturally competent care. *Behavior Analysis in Practice, 12*, 557–575. https://doi.org/10.1007/s40617-018-00313-6

Behavior Analyst Certification Board. (2014). *Professional and ethical compliance code for behavior analysts*. Retrieved from www.bacb.com/wp-content/uploads/BACB-Compliance-Code-english_190318.pdf

Behavior Analyst Certification Board. (2017). *Applied behavior analysis treatment of autism spectrum disorder: Practice guidelines for healthcare funders and managers*. Retrieved from www.bacb.com/wp-content/uploads/2017/09/ABA_Guidelines_for_ASD.pdf

Bernal, G., Bonilla, J., & Bellido, C. (1995). Ecological validity and cultural sensitivity for outcome research: Issues for cultural adaptation and development of psychosocial treatments with Hispanics. *Journal of Abnormal Child Psychology, 23*, 67–82. http://dx.doi.org/10.1007/BF01447045

Bernal, G., & Adames, C. (2017). Cultural adaptations: Conceptual, ethical, contextual, and methodological issues for working with ethnocultural and majority-world populations. *Prevention Science, 18*(6), 681–688. https://doi.org/10.1007/s11121-017-0806-0

Bishop-Fitzpatrick, L., & Kind, A. J. (2017). A scoping review of health disparities in autism spectrum disorder. *Journal of Autism and Developmental Disorders, 47*(11), 3380–3391. https://doi.org/10.1007/s10803-017-3251-9

Bornstein, M. H., & Cote, L. R. (2006). Parenting cognitions and practices in the acculturative process. In M. H. Bornstein & L. R Cote (Eds.), *Acculturation and parent-child relationships: Measurement and development* (pp. 173–196). Mahwah, NJ: Lawrence Erlbaum Associates Publishers.

Butler, M., McCreedy, E., Schwer, N., Burgess., D, Call., K., Przedworski, J., Rosser, S. . . . Kane, R. L. (2016). *Improving cultural competence to reduce health disparities*. Rockville, MD: Agency for Healthcare Research and Quality (AHRQ). Retrieved from www.effectivehealthcare.ahrq.gov/ehc/products/573/2206/cultural-competence-report-160327.pdf

Castro, F. G., Barrera, M., & Steiker, L. K. (2010). Issues and challenges in the design of culturally adapted evidence-based interventions. *Annual Review of Clinical Psychology, 6*, 213–239. https://doi.org/10.1146/annurev-clinpsy-033109-132032

Choi, Y., Kim, Y. S., Kim, S. Y., & Park, I. J. (2013). Is Asian American parenting controlling and harsh? Empirical testing of relationships between Korean American and Western parenting measures. *Asian American Journal of Psychology, 4*(1), 19–29. https://doi.org/10.1037/a0031220

Conners, B., Johnson, A., Duarte, J., Murriky, R., & Marks, R. (2019). Future directions of training and fieldwork in diversity issues in applied behavior analysis. *Behavior Analysis in Practice, 12*, 767–776. https://doi.org/10.1007/s40617-019-00349-2

Cooc, N., & Yang, M. (2017). Underrepresented and overlooked: A review of Asian American children with disabilities. *Multiple Voices for Ethnically Diverse Exceptional Learners*, *17*(1), 3–19. https://doi.org/10.5555/1547-1888.17.1.3

Croen, L. A., Zerbo, O., Qian, Y., Massolo, M. L., Rich, S., Sidney, S., & Kripke, C. (2015). The health status of adults on the autism spectrum. *Autism*, *19*(7), 814–823. https://doi.org/10.1177/1362361315577517.

Domenech Rodríguez, M. M., & Bernal, G. (2012). Frameworks, models, and guidelines for cultural adaptation. In G. Bernal & M. M. Domenech Rodríguez (Eds.), *Cultural adaptations: Tools for evidence-based practice with diverse populations* (pp. 23–44). Washington, DC: American Psychological Association.

Ennis-Cole, D., Durodoye, B. A., & Harris, H. L. (2013). The impact of culture on autism diagnosis and treatment: Considerations for counselors and other professionals. *The Family Journal*, *21*(3), 279–287. https://doi.org/10.1177/1066480713476834

Fong, E. H., Catagnus, R. M., Brodhead, M. T., Quigley, S., & Field, S. (2016). Developing the cultural awareness skills of behavior analysts. *Behavior Analysis in Practice*, *9*, 84–94. https://doi.org/10.1007/s40617-016-0111-6

Hanley, G. P., Jin, C. S., Vanselow, N. R., & Hanratty, L. A. (2014). Producing meaningful improvements in problem behavior of children with autism via synthesized analyses and treatments. *Journal of Applied Behavior Analysis*, *47*(1), 16–36. https://doi.org/10.1002/jaba.106

Heath, H., & Smith, R. G. (2019). Precursor behavior and functional analysis: A brief review. *Journal of Applied Behavior Analysis*, *52*(3), 804–810. https://doi.org/10.1002/jaba.571

Hill, C. V., Pérez-Stable, E. J., Anderson, N. A., Bernard, M. A. (2015). The National Institute on Aging health disparities research framework. *Ethnicity & Disease*, *25*(3), 245–254. https://doi.org/10.18865/ed.25.3.245

Huntsinger, C. S., Jose, P. E., Rudden, D., Luo, Z., & Krieg, D. B. (2002). Cultural differences in interactions around mathematics tasks in Chinese American and European American families. In C. C. Park, A. L. Goodwin, & S. J. Lee (Eds.), *Research on the education of Asian Pacific Americans* (pp. 75–103). Greenwich, CT: Information Age Publishing.

Jegatheesan, B., Fowler, S., & Miller, P. J. (2010). From symptom recognition to services: How South Asian Muslim immigrant families navigate autism. *Disability & Society*, *25*(7), 797–811. http://doi.org/10.1080/09687599.2010.520894

Kang-Yi, C. D., Grinker, R. R., Beidas, R., Agha, A., Russell, R., Shah, S. B. . . . Mandell, D. S. (2018). Influence of community-level cultural beliefs about autism on families' and professionals' care for children. *Transcultural Psychiatry*, *55*(5), 623–647. https://doi.org/10.1177/1363461518779831

Khan, N. Z., Gallo, L. A., Arghir, A., Budisteanu, B., Budisteanu, M., Dobrescu, I. . . . Elsabbagh, M. (2012). Autism and the grand challenges in global mental health. *Autism Research*, *5*(3), 156–159. https://doi.org/10.1002/aur.1239

Kim, E., & Hong, S. (2006). First-generation Korean-American parents' perceptions of discipline. *Journal of Professional Nursing*, *23*(1), 60–68. https://doi.org/10.1016/j.profnurs.2006.12.002

Kim, E., Hong, S., & Rockett, C. M. (2016). Korean American parents' perceptions of effective parenting strategies in the United States. *Journal of Cultural Diversity*, *23*(1), 12–20.

Kim, M. T., Han, H. R., Song, H. J., Lee, J. E., Kim, J., Ryu, J. P., & Kim, K. B. (2019). A community-based, culturally tailored behavioral intervention for Korean Americans with type 2 diabetes. *The Diabetes Educator*, *35*(6), 986–994. https://doi.org/10.1177/0145721709345774

Krahn, G. L., Walker, D. K., & Correa-De-Araujo, R. (2015). Persons with disabilities as an unrecognized health disparity population. *American Journal of Public Health, 105*(S2), S198–S206. https://doi.org/10.2105/AJPH.2014.302182.

Lau, A. (2006). Making the case for selective and directed cultural adaptations of evidence-based treatments: Examples from parent training. *Clinical Psychology Science and Practice, 13*(4), 295–310. https://doi.org/10.1111/j.1468-2850.2006.00042.x

Lee, C. C., & Richardson, B. L. (1991). Promise and pitfalls of multicultural counseling. In C. C. Lee & B. L. Richardson (Eds.), *Multicultural issues in counseling: New approaches to diversity* (pp. 79–90). Alexandria, VA: American Association for Counseling and Development.

Mazumdar, S., Winter, A., Liu, K. Y., & Bearman, P. (2013). Spatial clusters of autism births and diagnoses point to contextual drivers of increased prevalence. *Social Science & Medicine, 95*, 87–96. https://doi.org/10.1016/j.socscimed.2012.11.032

Mui, A. C., & Kang, S. Y. (2006). Acculturation stress and depression among Asian immigrant elders. *Social Work, 51*(3), 243–255.

Nguyen, C. T., Krakowiak, P. K., Hansen, R., Hertz-Picciotto, I., & Angkustsiri, K. (2016). Sociodemographic disparities in intervention service utilization in families of children with autism spectrum disorder. *Journal of Autism and Developmental Disorders, 46*(12), 3729–3738. https://doi.org/10.1007/s10803-016-2913-3

Noh, S., & Kaspar, V. (2003). Perceived discrimination and depression: Moderating effects of coping, acculturation, and ethnic support. *American Journal of Public Health, 93*(2), 232–238. https://doi.org/10.2105/ajph.93.2.232

Park, Y. S., Kim, B. S., Chiang, J., & Ju, C. M. (2010). Acculturation, enculturation, parental adherence to Asian cultural values, parenting styles, and family conflict among Asian American college students. *Asian American Journal of Psychology, 1*(1), 67–79. https://doi.org/10.1037/a0018961

Pew Research Center. (2015). *Modern immigration wave brings 59 million to U.S., driving population growth and change through 2065: Views of immigration's impact on U.S. society mixed.* Washington, DC: Author. http://www.pewresearch.org/Hispanic/wp-content/uploads/sites/5/2015/09/2015-09-28_modern-immigration-wave_REPORT.pdf.

Pew Research Center. (2017). *Key facts about Asian Americans, a diverse and growing population.* Washington, DC: Author. https://www.pewresearch.org/fact-tank/2017/09/08/key-facts-about-asian-americans/

Pondé, M. P., & Rousseau, C. (2013). Immigrant children with autism spectrum disorder: The relationship between the perspective of the professionals and the parents' point of view. *Journal of the Canadian Academy of Child and Adolescent Psychiatry, 22*(2), 131–138. https://doi.org/10.1007/s00787-013-0377-y

Robertson, R., Wehby, J. H., & King, S. (2013). Increased parent reinforcement of spontaneous requests in children with autism spectrum disorder: Effects on problem behavior. *Research in Developmental Disabilities, 34*(3), 1069–1082. https://doi.org/10.1016/j.ridd.2012.12.011

Siu, S. F. W., & Feldman, J. A. (1996). *Patterns of Chinese American family involvement in young children's education.* Boston, MA: School of Education: Center on Families, Communities, Schools & Children's Learning.

Soto, A., Smith, T. B., Griner, D., Rodriguez, M. D., & Bernal, G. (2018). Cultural competence and therapist multicultural competence: Two meta-analytic reviews. *Journal of Clinical Psychology, 74*, 1907–1923. https://doi.org/10.1002/jclp.22679

Theara, G., & Abott, D.W.F. (2015). Understanding the experiences of South Asian parents who have a child with autism. *Educational and Child Psychology*, *32*(2), 47–56.

Tsai-Chae, A. H., & Nagata, D. K. (2008). Asian values and perceptions of intergenerational family conflict among Asian American students. *Cultural Diversity and Ethnic Minority Psychology*, *14*(3), 205.

U.S. Census Bureau. (2018). *Americans with disabilities: 2014. Household economic studies.* Retrieved from www.census.gov/content/dam/Census/library/publications/2018/demo/p70-152.pdf

Wang, H. T., & Casillas, N. (2013). Asian American parents' experiences of raising children with autism: Multicultural family perspective. *Journal of Asian and African Studies*, *48*(5), 594–606. https://doi.org/10.1177/0021909612467421

Wang, H., & West, E. A. (2016). Asian American immigrant parents supporting children with autism: Perceptions of fathers and mothers. *International Journal of Whole Schooling*, *12*(1), 1–21.

Weinstein, J. N., Geller, A., Negussie, Y., & Baciu, A. (2017). *Communities in action: Pathways to equity.* Washington, DC: The National Academies Press. Retrieved from www.ncbi.nlm.nih.gov/books/NBK425848/pdf/Bookshelf_NBK425848.pdf

Wolf, M. M. (1978). Social validity: The case for subjective measurement or how Applied Behavior Analysis is finding its heart. *Journal of Applied Behavior Analysis*, *11*(2), 203–214. https://doi.org/10.1901/jaba.1978.11–203

Yan, K. K., Accordino, M. P., Boutin, D. L., & Wilson, K. B. (2014). Disability and the Asian Culture. *Journal of Applied Rehabilitation Counseling*, *45*(2), 4–8.

Zhang, C., & Bennett, T. (2003). Facilitating the meaningful participation of culturally and linguistically diverse families in the IFSP and IEP process. *Focus on Autism and Other Developmental Disabilities*, *18*(1), 51–59. https://doi.org/10.1177/108835760301800107

8

Applied Behavior Analysis With Arab-Muslim Populations

The Importance of Cultural Awareness

Pamela M. Olsen and Michelle P. Kelly

Learning Objectives

- To describe key aspects of Arab-Muslim culture.
- To identify some potential challenges faced by behavior analysts working with Arab-Muslim populations.
- To describe practice considerations for ABA professionals working with Arab-Muslim populations.
- To outline some potential ethical and professional issues associated with working with Arab-Muslim populations.

Introduction

The challenge of effective, international practice of applied behavior analysis (ABA) is intensified given the wide range of stimulus and response classes that occur across different cultures including religion, race, nationality, socioeconomic class, age, sexual orientation, and disability (Kelly, Martin, Dillenberger, Kelly, & Miller, 2019). The field of ABA has recently shown an increased interest in cultural considerations in service delivery (Fong, Ficklin, & Lee, 2017; Fong & Tanaka, 2013). Adapting behavior analytic service delivery and supervision to accommodate cultural factors is a requirement of culturally responsive and culturally sensitive practice. This attention to culture is important not only when we are working abroad but also when working in our home country with individuals from diverse backgrounds (Olsen, Bailey, & Gould, 2018).

To ensure culturally competent practice, behavior analysts need to be aware of their own cultural influences in addition to those of their clients (Fong, Catagnus, Brodhead, Quigley, &

Field, 2016). Cultural awareness and adaptation is increasingly at the forefront of our service delivery, supervision of others, and professional development. In this chapter, we focus on the culture of Arab-Muslim individuals around the world and include specific observations from our experience providing behavior analytic services in the Middle East for more than a decade. We present information that will be of general relevance to behavior analysts working with Arab-Muslim individuals outside the Middle East.

A Review of Arab-Muslim Culture

Culture is one of three levels of selection described by Skinner (1981), yet until recently behavior analysts paid little attention to the role of cultural factors. One theory for this may be that behavior analysts focus on the individual and shy away from generalizations about groups of individuals. Yet there is no denying that cultural differences do exist and that descriptions of culture may provide valuable heuristics.

There are many definitions of culture, but the most useful for behavior analysts is one that focuses on the fact that cultural variables influence behavior. From a behavior analytic perspective, culture is a collection of the contingencies of reinforcement into which individuals are born and to which they are exposed throughout their lives (Skinner, 1971). As a result of differences in learning histories, the behavioral norms that are common among one cultural group may be very different from those that are common among another cultural group. These intergroup differences have the potential to cause conflict and misunderstanding when behavioral norms and expectations are not met, and thus an understanding of cultural norms is important to behavior analysts who are practicing outside their own cultural groups.

Numerous models for defining and characterizing cultures have been developed (Hall, 1976; Lewis, 1996; Trompennars, 1994). One well-known, data-based model is presented by Hofstede (Hofstede, 2011; Hofstede, Hofstede, & Minkov, 2010). This model can serve as a framework for examining cultural factors that can be expected to affect behavior analytic service delivery. Hofstede (2011, p. 8) identified six dimensions that describe different cultures:

1. Power distance

2. Uncertainty avoidance

3. Individualism versus collectivism

4. Masculinity versus femininity

5. Long-term versus short-term orientation

6. Indulgence versus restraint.

Hofstede et al. (2010) define *power distance* as the extent to which less powerful members of a culture accept an unequal distribution of power. In a culture with large power distance there may be a more or less rigid hierarchy of power in political systems and in the family; elders are treated with respect and obedience; there is a teacher-centered education system, and a reliance upon authority. Cultures that are characterized by large power distance may also be described as having paternalistic attitudes (Aycan, 2006). Discrimination against some individuals or groups may be a side effect of large power difference (Ourfali, 2015).

Uncertainty avoidance relates to how the members of a culture feel about ambiguous situations and the future. A high degree of uncertainty avoidance correlates with characteristics such as strict rule-governed behavior and an intolerance of deviations from the norm. Uncertainty may be avoided through reliance on religion, government, and other institutions that provide stability in individual lives and in society (Livermore, 2015).

The behavior of an individual can be profoundly impacted by whether that individual is a member of an *individualist or a collectivist* culture. Members of an individualist culture are more likely to be concerned with themselves and their immediate family, whereas members of a collectivist culture have a greater focus on, and loyalty to, the group as a whole (Darwish & Huber, 2003). The group in a collectivist culture may be defined at several levels; for example, it may comprise the extended family, the tribe, or even all members of the same religion.

Hofstede et al. (2010) define the *masculinity-femininity* dimension as the extent to which a culture values "competition, achievement and success" (masculine orientation) over "caring for others and . . . where quality of life is the sign of success" (feminine orientation). This dimension exemplifies how some important social reinforcers may be bound up in culture. Arab-Muslim culture is considered to be relatively neutral with respect to this dimension (Hofstede et al., 2010).

Long-term versus short-term orientation, also referred to as the *pragmatism* dimension (Harb, 2016), defines the extent to which a culture relies on historical traditions and norms and resists change versus adopting a future-oriented, pragmatic approach to preparing for change. Arab-Muslim culture is generally regarded as having a more traditional orientation, however modern Arab-Muslim countries vary widely on this dimension (Hofstede et al., 2010).

The final dimension, *indulgence versus restraint*, should be of special interest to behavior analysts practicing in a multicultural context. This dimension relates to how young children are raised and the subsequent degree to which they "try to control their desires and impulses" (Hofstede et al., 2010, p. 281). Arab-Muslim culture is considered to be more restrained than indulgent. Again, however, this is a generalization that may vary considerably, even from family to family. Histories of reinforcement that derive from different degrees of indulgence versus restraint will likely have significant implications for behavioral interventions (e.g., a child who is frequently indulged by parents may have more difficulty when denied access to desired items in school).

In Hofstede and colleagues' (2010) analysis and others that followed (Harb, 2016; Najm, 2015), Arab culture was characterized as having (1) large power distance; (2) strong uncertainty avoidance; (3) collectivist tendencies; (4) relatively neutral masculine-feminine orientation; (5) more traditional rather than pragmatic orientation; and (6) more restrained than indulgent orientation. Although these characteristics have been attributed to Arab culture as a whole, it is important to note that they are generalizations and there may be important differences among Arab countries and tribes, reflecting the "unity and diversity" of Arab culture (Harb, 2016).

Specific Cultural Influences Relevant to Arab-Muslim Populations

Several additional behaviors that are selected at the cultural level are relevant to behavior analysts practicing with Arab-Muslim clients. These include cultural influences on communication; behaviors related to time; the role of the family and personal relationships; gender roles; and generosity, hospitality, and gift giving (Greaves, 2012; Harb, 2016; Williams, 2008). Each of these areas will be discussed further in the subsequent sections.

Cultural Influences on Communication

One of the most important concepts for understanding cultural influences on communication is the dimension referred to as context (Vaughn, 2010). In a high-context (HC) culture, speakers rely heavily on implicit meaning and contextual cues. The listener is expected to be able to "read the air" or "read between the lines" and understand the meaning of the communication as it relates to individual and interpersonal context based on shared histories and references (Meyer, 2014; Nishimura, Nevgi, & Tella, 2009). As a result, less of the communication is explicitly and overtly verbal and there is an emphasis on indirectness, politeness, and ambiguity (The Conference Board of Canada, n.d.). In a HC culture, more of the meaning of communication will be conveyed through non-verbal means. Most Arab cultures are characterized as being HC. In contrast, in a low-context (LC) culture communication is much more direct, linear, and relies more heavily on verbal communication. The message is explicitly conveyed and the listener is not expected to add additional interpretation (Nishimura et al., 2009). Communication in a LC culture, such as the United States, is characterized by directness, clarity, and confrontation.

As an example, in our admission screening interviews with Arab-Muslim parents we often hear, "She used to do that in the past" when we ask about a challenging behavior the child emits such as stereotypy. We have come to understand that in the context of these interviews, the statement frequently means that the behavior is a current concern as evidenced by later observation. Parents from LC cultures are more likely to be direct and explicitly state their concerns to the behavior analyst.

Behaviors Related to Time

Behaviors related to time can vary significantly across cultures. In the United States and other time-bound cultures, time is treated precisely. When an appointment or meeting is arranged, it is expected that the precise time of the appointment will be adhered to. In contrast, with many non-Western cultures, including Arab culture, time is treated much more loosely (Vaughn, 2010). This may cause conflict when, for example, an American behavior analyst expects a call from an Arab colleague to say she will be 10 minutes late for a meeting, but the Arab colleague does not consider 10 minutes to be late and therefore would be unlikely to communicate so. The Arab colleague may consider that it is not the scheduled time that is important, but rather *timing* that is important; that is, there is an appropriate moment for communication (Williams, 2008).

Another indication of the Arab culture's flexibility with time is frequent omission of a precise time for a meeting or an appointment. One may hear, "I will see you tomorrow, *insha'Allah*" (God willing) or "I will see you after prayers this afternoon, *insha'Allah*". In both of these cases, the communication would seem ambiguous to a time-bound American. One who recognizes the cultural context for this communication, however, will understand that the meeting will take place, although the exact time may be flexible, and there is a chance that it could be postponed due to competing priorities, such as family obligations (Williams, 2008).

Role of the Family and Personal Relationships

The extended family plays a central role in Arab culture as it does in most collectivist cultures (Harb, 2016). In a collectivist culture, one's identity is interdependent with family, friends, and other in-group members (Vaughn, 2010). Family obligations frequently take precedence over all other obligations, including meetings and appointments that would be considered higher priorities by members of more individualistic cultures (Williams, 2008). Family members often accompany one another to appointments, even including job interviews. In our experience, it is not uncommon for an employee to be called away from work due to a visit from a distant cousin or to be away for weeks at a time due to extended family travel obligations.

Personal relationships are highly valued in Arab culture (Greaves, 2012; Williams, 2008). This is of particular relevance to behavior analysts due to their frequent, close contact with clients and families (Witts, Brodhead, Adlington, & Barron, 2018). The Arab culture's behavior toward personal relationships also has implications for the way in which they may behave during meetings, appointments, treatment sessions, and other formal situations (Livermore, 2015). A phone call from a family member or friend will not be ignored; it will be readily accepted during the meeting with no excuse or apology. Such interruptions are normal and to be expected. Similarly, a meeting in a family home is almost certain to be interrupted by children, who will not be turned away by the parent. During treatment sessions and observations, it is not uncommon for siblings to come and go from the room; during parent meetings it is not uncommon for another child to come and sit on the mother's lap or to take her attention away from the meeting at hand. In the former case, the interruption may be helpful in promoting a more naturalistic learning environment. In the latter, the behavior analyst must be patient and tolerant of the inevitable interruption.

Gender Roles

Gender roles inside and outside the family home are changing rapidly in Arab-Muslim society, however, many groups remain strongly traditional and patriarchal. In many Arab-Muslim communities, women are expected to cover their head while in public or when in the presence of a male other than a close family member. In some Arab-Muslim countries or cultural communities, girls and boys may be educated separately. Further, parents may follow strict rules regarding the gender of the behavior analyst who is treating their child, entering their house, or attending a face-to-face meeting. Many Arab-Muslim women do not shake the hand of men who are not relatives. Male behavior analysts should refrain from offering a handshake unless the Arab-Muslim woman initiates.

Generosity, Hospitality, and Gift Giving

Generosity, hospitality, and honoring the guest are important values in Arab culture and in the Islamic religion (Greaves, 2012). Hospitality is one of the deepest-rooted values in Arab-Muslim culture and is codified in the concept of *zakat* (the giving of alms), one of the five pillars of Islam (Faruqi, 2007). Arab hospitality is also rooted in the historical practicalities of desert life (Greaves, 2012). Visitors to an Arab home will be presented with food and drinks that are impossible to refuse, and in some cases, the visitor may be offered other items such as perfumes or other gifts. The giving and receiving of gifts is a complex matter in Arab culture, and has implications for behavior analysts that will be discussed further below.

Practice Considerations and Implications for Service Delivery

In this section we present some general practice considerations as well as some specific considerations related to Arab-Muslim culture. These include a need to (1) develop awareness of the principles of Islamic religion; (2) develop awareness of family dynamics; (3) develop awareness of high context communication; (4) develop awareness of cultural formalities; (5) find a "cultural insider"; (6) be flexible; (7) establish personal relationships; and (8) respect gender roles and cultural norms.

It is important to note that Arab-Muslim culture is not monolithic, therefore, behavior analysts should be sensitive to local variations. Even within a country there will be variations from family to family, so the behavior analyst must learn about their individual clients' culture-related practices. Further, behavior analysts must be aware of the effects of their own personal values and beliefs, understanding that they have been influenced by their cultural upbringing and socialization.

Develop Awareness of Islamic Religion

When working with Arab-Muslim clients, behavior analysts should develop a basic understanding of the principles of the Islamic religion. Behavior analysts should familiarize themselves with cultural and societal norms, values, and mores that dictate what is and what is not appropriate when working within Arab-Muslim culture. As an example, during the holy month of Ramadan, behavior analysts should be aware of religious norms that dictate the behavior of Muslims and how this might affect non-Muslims as well. For example, a non-Muslim behavior analyst can show respect by avoiding eating, drinking, or listening to music in the presence of their Muslim client. Behavioral interventions that rely on primary reinforcers, such as food and drinks, might require modification during Ramadan, although Islam gives special consideration to children and those with special needs. Behavior analysts should also remain sensitive to the fact that more time may be spent praying and reflecting on the practices of Islam during Ramadan, which may result in less time for treatment sessions and meetings. Further, behavior analysts who are supervisors may observe changes in the behavior of their staff members who are fasting during Ramadan.

Develop Awareness of Family Dynamics

Aspects of collectivism and large power distance that are characteristic of Arab-Muslim culture may be seen in family structure and the central role of family in daily life. Because of the importance of extended family, parents may defer to elders regarding treatment decisions. Behavior analysts may improve their effectiveness by utilizing interventions that are acceptable to and supported by the extended family. Training of family members in evidence-based practice should go beyond parents to include extended family members. Additionally, behavior analysts may consider planning clinical and educational review meetings to include extended family members as opposed to just parents.

In a high power distance culture, parents may defer to elders but may also view the behavior analyst as an authority figure with whom they might never disagree. In this case, the parents are highly unlikely to overtly disagree with a behavior analyst's recommendations even though they have no intention of following them. Behavior analysts must develop an understanding of the real meaning of communications or lack thereof, that is, they must learn to "read the air" (Meyer, 2014). Similar to other cultures, treatment compliance may be the best indicator of the Arab-Muslim parents' acceptance of recommendations. When the behavior analyst sees that recommendations are not being followed, she should consider whether the treatment has elements that may not be acceptable to the parents. Over time, as the behavior analyst develops a more personal relationship with the parents, they are more likely to be forthcoming with their opinions.

Develop Awareness of High Context Communication

One aspect of Arab-Muslim culture is a dislike for disappointing others or giving bad news (Williams, 2008). Bad news may be communicated indirectly or ambiguously. Disabilities can be highly stigmatized in the Middle East region, and a family can face social repercussions for having a child with special needs (Kelly et al., 2016). These stigmas can be caused by cultural standards, parents' lack of understanding, and misinformation given by doctors and therefore, behavior analysts need to be sensitive when discussing the client's diagnosis, if applicable (Al-Kandari, 2006).

Furthermore, we have frequently experienced parents speaking about their child's problem behaviors that "occurred in the past but no longer occur," even though in reality the behavior is still a concern that should be carefully attended to. This example of HC communication could be easily overlooked by Western behavior analysts who expect parents to be direct and forthcoming about their concerns. Behavior analysts also need to be aware of cultural influences on non-verbal communication. For example, in Arab-Muslim culture unrelated women and men often avoid eye contact, showing the sole of one's foot is considered highly offensive, and a man does not extend his hand to shake that of a woman unless the woman extends her hand first.

Develop Awareness of Cultural Formalities

Behavior analysts should also be sensitive to formalities that exist and may be more prevalent in HC cultures. For example, HC cultures may focus more on formalities when speaking with others (e.g., use of formal names, acknowledging the eldest male or highest-ranking individual in the room first) (Vaughn, 2010). Additionally, there may be formalities related to meetings, for example, the authority sits at the head of the table, men often do not sit next to women, and the speaker may orient toward a specific person even when speaking to the entire group.

Find a "Cultural Insider"

One way to facilitate learning about and navigating a new culture is through the use of a "cultural insider," a member of the target culture who can share knowledge about the norms and behaviors and may also serve as a language translator for the behavior analyst. However, even with the assistance of a cultural insider or translator, the behavior analyst must be prepared to use simple language and avoid the use of *behavior speak* that may become confused in translation (Kelly et al., 2019; Rolider & Axelrod, 2005). Written documents such as consent forms and program materials should be translated to the client's language. Backward and forward translation should be used whenever possible to ensure that the meaning of the original document does not get lost during the translation process (Poder, Carrier, Mead, & Stevens, 2018). This is particularly important when documents include content or concepts that might not translate in a direct manner.

Be Flexible

Practice considerations related to time orientation involve the need for behavior analysts to remain flexible to a culture that is considerably less time bound than Western cultures (Livermore, 2015). Scheduling meetings or appointments far in advance will almost certainly result in a last minute postponement or cancellation. Arriving 5 to 10 minutes after the scheduled start of a meeting may not be viewed as late. Meetings are frequently scheduled with the caveat *insha'Allah*, which leaves a degree of uncertainty about whether the meeting will actually take place. Once the meeting does begin, behavior analysts should be prepared for a period of small talk and many deviations from the agenda (Williams, 2008). The importance of this small talk cannot be overemphasized as it is the basis for forming personal relationships.

Establish Personal Relationships

Personal relationships have an extremely important role in Arab-Muslim culture. Behavior analysts should strive to achieve a balance between personal relationships that remain within the boundaries of their professional code of conduct while also meeting cultural expectations. In our experience, it is not uncommon to be publicly asked about topics that, as Westerners, we consider highly personal. Establishing a personal relationship with an Arab-Muslim colleague may help the behavior analyst to learn more about their culture. Alternatively, behavior analysts may enlist the support of a family elder (e.g., grandmother or grandfather) to function as a cultural insider (Earley, Ang, & Tan, 2006). However, the behavior analyst must proceed with caution to avoid creating an inappropriate dual relationship.

Respect Gender Roles and Cultural Norms

In practice, behavior analysts should familiarize themselves with expectations related to gender roles and norms within their client's family. Gender roles and norms in some Arab-Muslim cultural communities may be entrenched from birth and may be quite different from the behavior analyst's Western culture (Vaughn, 2010). Segregation of genders typically begins in childhood or early adolescence and thus may have an impact on delivery of services. In some situations, it may not be appropriate for male behavior analysts to interact with females in the family home, therefore, they may need to enlist the support of a female colleague or male member of the household. Behavior analysts should also be aware of and adhere to other norms when interacting with members of a different gender. For example, there may be expectations regarding shaking hands with members of a different gender, making eye contact, or even being alone in a room with a member of a different gender. All of these norms and expectations related to gender roles have the potential to impact on practice.

Arab-Muslim hospitality includes the previously mentioned relationship building, small talk in meetings, and a generosity toward others inherent in their cultural upbringing. The generosity almost always includes offers of food and drinks and may include gift giving that can create a conflict for behavior analysts. Once again, behavior analysts must achieve a balance between adhering to the code and respecting the cultural norms and expectations of their clients. This is one of many important topics for ethical and professional consideration, which we turn to next.

Ethical and Professional Issues

The Behavior Analyst Certification Board's® (BACB[i], 2014) *Professional and Ethical Compliance Code for Behavior Analysts* ("the Code") explicitly cites the behavior analyst's responsibility for ensuring cultural competence:

> Where differences of age, gender, race, culture, ethnicity, national origin, religion . . . significantly affect behavior analysts' work . . . behavior analysts obtain the training, experience, consultation, and/or supervision necessary to ensure the competence of their services, or they make appropriate referrals.

(p. 5)

In addition to the general competence requirement that touches on many areas of practice, we have previously alluded to a number of potential ethical and professional considerations when working with diverse cultures. We will expand on a few of these.

The language of communication between behavior analyst and client is a major consideration (Critchfield & Doepke, 2018). Code 1.05 (BACB®, 2014) requires that behavior analysts "use language that is fully understandable to the recipient of those services while remaining conceptually systematic" (p. 5). This places a special burden on ensuring appropriate translation of not only the specific content, but also the concept described by the content. In other words, simply translating the word "reinforcement" from English to Arabic may fail to communicate the concept of a behavior increase following an environmental change. Whenever possible, translation should be conducted by an individual who is bilingual and is also knowledgeable about principles of behavior analysis.

According to code 4.02, behavior analysts are obligated to "involve the client in the planning" for the treatment program (BACB®, 2014, p. 12). Given the paternalistic orientation of Arab-Muslim culture, parents may be reluctant to make recommendations or offer opinions about their child's treatment, preferring to rely on the authority of the behavior analyst. One way to avoid this problem is to survey multiple cultural insiders to identify their treatment priorities. Treatment goals that are identified in this way may have a greater chance of being socially valid (Wolf, 1978). Olsen (2015) reported that the treatment priorities of Arab-Muslim mothers of children with autism included many of the same priorities as non-Muslim mothers, but also included culture-specific goals such as learning religious rituals, behavior in the mosque, and learning to dress in traditional clothing (Olsen et al., 2018).

Parents may also wish to incorporate culture-specific treatments into their child's behavior-change program. As per code 2.09, clients have the right to scientifically supported, most-effective behavioral procedures. Therefore, it is the responsibility of the behavior analyst to educate themselves and the parents/clients about the evidence-base of culture-specific interventions, such as Epsom salt baths and *hijama*, a complementary and alternative treatment that involves detoxifying the blood through the process of wet cupping (AlBedah, Khalil, Elolemy, Elsubai, & Khalil, 2011; Kelly et al., 2016; Kelly, Tennant, & Al-Hassan, 2016).

As previously discussed, personal relationships are particularly important in Arab-Muslim culture. Behavior analysts often work closely with parents and may deliver services in the family home. This potentially creates a situation in which multiple relationships may develop (see code 1.06). Additionally, during a home visit a parent is highly likely to offer food, drinks, or even small gifts to the behavior analyst. As with the issue of personal relationships, this can create conflict for behavior analysts who are ethically bound to avoid accepting gifts (see code 1.06d). In these situations, the behavior analyst must attend closely to professional and ethical responsibilities while simultaneously balancing cultural expectations so as not to damage the relationship with the parent. The BACB® provides some very useful clarifications and guidance with respect to gifts in a newsletter (BACB®, 2015). The BACB® suggests an antecedent approach, specifically, at the outset of the professional relationship providing clients with a gift policy. If a gift is offered despite the policy, the BACB® suggests that the behavior analyst consider the intention of the gift and the likely effect that accepting or refusing may have on the professional relationship, that is, the *context* within which the gift is offered is relevant (pp. 2–3). Thus, although the ethical code appears quite black-and-white with respect to gifts, the BACB® acknowledges that factors such as the client's cultural background may play a role in ethical decision making. Although the cultural context in which a gift is offered is important, it is still the responsibility of the individual behavior analyst to judge the appropriate response in a given situation.

Conclusion

This chapter examined key aspects of multiculturalism and diversity issues related to practicing ABA with Arab-Muslim populations, focusing on Hofstede's (2011) six-dimensional framework for examining cultural factors. Challenges related to cultural influences on communication, behaviors related to time, the role of the family and personal relationships, gender roles and generosity, hospitality, and gift giving were outlined. Practice considerations and implications for service delivery were suggested to help future ABA professionals understand this particular culture and included the need to have awareness of Islam, family dynamics, high context communication, and cultural formalities. It was also recommended that the reader find a "cultural insider," be flexible, establish personal relationships, and respect gender roles and cultural norms. Finally, potential ethical and professional issues associated with working with Arab-Muslim populations were discussed, including the use of fully understandable language; client involvement in the planning of programs; the right to effective, culturally acceptable treatment; the creation of multiple relationships; and the acceptance of gifts.

CASE STUDY

1. You are a behavior analyst working in an educational setting with an Arab-Muslim family in the United States. During a meeting to discuss your client's individualized education plan, the parents ask what changes they should expect with their child's behavior change program during the holy month of Ramadan. How do you respond?

Sample Response to Case Study 1

First, it is recommended that you familiarize yourself with the rituals of Ramadan and how the family observes them. Families may differ in their practices, for example, some will stay up much of the night in prayer or in family gatherings and will sleep during the day while others will maintain their normal schedule. You should ask the parents about expectations for the client during Ramadan, including:

■ If the client will be fasting from dawn to sunset

■ The client's new sleep routine during Ramadan

■ Events that the client may be expected to attend

■ Skills related to Ramadan that might be a focus of teaching during treatment sessions (e.g. prayers specific to Ramadan).

You could then help prepare the client for these changes in routine using behavioral interventions such as visual supports (activity schedules, first-then boards, etc.), social stories, and task analyses. It might also be necessary to change the frequency, duration, or schedule of sessions or to modify expectations for the client's behavior during sessions, considering that she might have had no food or water during daylight hours and little sleep the night before. If the client is fasting and sessions are conducted during daylight hours, edible reinforcers will not be available, so you will need to ensure that alternative reinforcers are available. Finally, once Ramadan ends you will need to help prepare the client for a return to non-Ramadan routines.

2. You are a behavior analyst working with an Arab-Muslim client with special needs in a home setting. During an informal meeting, the father mentions that they wish to try hijama with their son. He explains that this is a treatment that is culturally popular in their home country. How do you respond?

Sample Response to Case Study 2

This is a situation that may involve deeply held spiritual and religious beliefs and therefore it must be handled with the utmost sensitivity and respect so as not to damage the client-therapist relationship. First, it is recommended that you thank the father for letting you know that they are considering this treatment. If you are unfamiliar with the suggested treatment (hijama in this case), you should respectfully ask that the parents do not begin implementing the treatment until you have researched the evidence base for the proposed intervention. You should remind the parents that while you appreciate that hijama is popular within their culture, interventions without scientific evidence may not be effective and may have a negative impact on the goals of their child's behavior-change program.

DISCUSSION QUESTIONS

1. Define culture. Give five examples of your own cultural norms.

2. Name and briefly define the six cultural dimensions outlined by Hofstede et al. (2010).

3. Name three important practice considerations for behavior analysts working with Arab-Muslim populations.

4. Behavior analysts cannot possibly learn every aspect of every culture. How can you avoid engaging in culturally insensitive behavior when working with clients from cultural backgrounds different from your own?

5. You are working with an Arab-Muslim family who has recently moved to your country. The family has never heard of ABA. How might you introduce them to ABA?

References

AlBedah, A., Khalil, M., Elolemy, A., Elsubai, I., & Khalil, A. (2011). Hijama (cupping): A review of the evidence. *Focus on Alternative and Complementary Therapies, 16*(1), 12–16. https://doi.org/10.1111/j.2042-7166.2010.01060.x

Al-Kandari, M. T. (2006). *Parenting an autistic child in Kuwait: Kuwaiti mothers' voice and experiences with children labeled autistic.* Doctoral dissertation, School of Syracuse University, New York.

Aycan, Z. (2006). Paternalism: Towards conceptual refinement and operationalization. In U. Kim, K.-S. Yang, & K.-K. Hwang (Eds.), *Indigenous and cultural psychology: Understanding people in context* (pp. 445–466). New York, NY: Springer.

Behavior Analyst Certification Board. (2014). *Professional and ethical compliance code for behavior analysts.* Littleton, CO: Author.

Behavior Analyst Certification Board. (2015). *The professional and ethical compliance code for behavior analysts: An update.* Retrieved from www.bacb.com/wp-content/uploads/BACB_Newsletter_05-15.pdf.

The Conference Board of Canada. (n.d.). *Communicating across cultures.* Retrieved from http://highered.mcgraw-hill.com/sites/dl/free/0070958262/462504/loc958262_module03.pdf

Critchfield, T. S., & Doepke, K. J. (2018). Emotional overtones of behavior analysis terms in English and five other languages. *Behavior Analysis in Practice, 11*(2), 97–105. https://doi.org/10.1007/s40617-018-0222-3

Darwish, A.-F. E., & Huber, G. L. (2003). Individualism vs collectivism in different cultures: A cross-cultural study. *Intercultural Education, 14*(1), 47–55. https://doi.org/10.1080/1467598032000044647

Earley, P., Ang, S., & Tan, J. (2006). *Developing cultural intelligence at work.* Palo Alto, CA: Stanford Business Books.

Faruqi, Y. M. (2007). Islamic view of nature and values: Could these be the answer to building bridges between modern science and Islamic science. *International Education Journal, 8*(2), 461–469.

Fong, E. H., Catagnus, R. M., Brodhead, M. T., Quigley, S., & Field, S. (2016). Developing the cultural awareness skills of behaviour analysts. *Behavior Analysis in Practice, 9*(1), 84–94. https://doi.org/10.1007/s40617-016-0111-6

Fong, E. H., Ficklin, S., & Lee, H. Y. (2017). Increasing cultural understanding and diversity in applied behavior analysis. *Behavior Analysis: Research and Practice, 17*(2), 103–113. http://doi.org/10.1037/bar0000076

Fong, E. H., & Tanaka, S. (2013). Multicultural alliance of behaviour analysis standards for culture competence in behaviour analysis. *International Journal of Behavioral Consultation and Therapy, 8*(2), 17–19. https://doi.org/10.1037/h0100970

Greaves, S. (2012). A primer of Middle Eastern leadership culture. *Journal of Strategic Security, 5*(4), 99–118. https://doi.org/10.5038/1944-0472.5.4.7

Hall, E. (1976). *Beyond culture.* New York: Doubleday.

Harb, C. (2016). The Arab region: Cultures, values, and identities. In M. Amer & G. Awad (Eds.), *Handbook of Arab, American psychology* (pp. 3–18). New York: Routledge.

Hofstede, G. (2011). Dimensionalizing cultures: The Hofstede model in context. *Online Readings in Psychology and Culture, 2*(1), 1–26. http://doi.org/10.9707/2307-0919.1014

Hofstede, G., Hofstede, G. J., & Minkov, M. (2010). *Cultures and organizations: Software of the mind.* New York: McGraw Hill.

Kelly, M. P., Alireza, I., Busch, H. E., Northrop, S., Al-Attrash, M., Ainsleigh, S., & Bhuptani, N. (2016). An overview of autism and applied behavior analysis in the Gulf Cooperation Council in the Middle East. *Review Journal of Autism and Developmental Disorders, 3*(2), 154–164. https://doi.org/10.1007/s40489-016-0073-1

Kelly, M. P., Martin, N., Dillenberger, K., Kelly, A. N., & Miller, M. M. (2019). Spreading the news: History, successes, challenges and the ethics of effective dissemination. *Behavior Analysis in Practice, 12*(2), 440–451. https://doi.org/10.1007/s40617-018-0238-8

Kelly, M. P., Tennant, L., & Al-Hassan, S. (2016). Autism treatments used by parents in Abu Dhabi, United Arab Emirates. *Austin Journal of Autism & Related Disabilities, 2*(3), 1–6.

Lewis, R. (1996). *When cultures collide: Leading across cultures.* Boston, MA: Nicholas Brealey International.

Livermore, D. (2015). *Leading with cultural intelligence: The real secret to success* (2nd ed.). New York: Amacom.

Meyer, E. (2014). *The culture map: Breaking through the invisible boundaries of global business.* New York: PublicAffairs.

Najm, N. A. (2015). Arab culture dimensions in the international and Arab models. *American Journal of Business, Economics and Management, 3*(6), 423–431.

Nishimura, S., Nevgi, A., & Tella, S. (2009). *Communication style and cultural features in high/low context communication cultures: A case study of Finland, Japan, and India.* Retrieved from https://people.uwec.edu/degravjr/GEOG-ANTH%20351/Articles/NishimuraNevgiTella-highcontextlowcontext.pdf

Olsen, P. M. (2015). *Raising a child with autism: Perspectives from Arab-Muslim mothers* Unpublished doctoral dissertation, The Chicago School of Professional Psychology, Illinois.

Olsen, P. M., Bailey, L. S., & Gould, D. D. (2018). Using video modelling to teach culture-specific dressing skills. *European Journal of Behavior Analysis, 19*(2), 247–259. https://doi.org/10.1080/15021149.2018.1541205

Ourfali, E. (2015). Comparison between Western and Middle Eastern cultures: Research on why American expatriates struggle in the Middle East. *Otago Management Graduate Review, 13*, 33–43.

Poder, T. G., Carrier, N., Mead, H., & Stevens, K. J. (2018). Canadian French translation and linguistic validation of the child health utility 9D (CHU9D). *Health and Quality of Life Outcomes, 16*, 161–168. https://doi.org/10.1186/s12955-018-0998-4

Rolider, A., & Axelrod, S. (2005). The effects of "behavior speak" on public attitudes toward behavioral interventions: A cross-cultural argument for using conversational language to describe behavioral interventions to the general public. In W. L. Heward, T. E. Heron, N. A. Neef, S. M. Peterson, D. M. Sainato, G. Cartledge . . . J. C. Dardig (Eds.), *Focus on behavior analysis in education* (pp. 283–293). Upper Saddle River, NJ: Pearson/Merrill Prentice Hall.

Skinner, B. F. (1971). *Beyond freedom and dignity.* New York: Alfred A. Knopf/Random House.

Skinner, B. F. (1981). Selection by consequences. *Science, 213*(4507), 501–504. https://doi.org/10.1126/science.7244649

Trompennars, F. (1994). *Riding the waves of culture: Understanding diversity in global business.* New York: Professional Publishing.

Vaughn, L. M. (2010). *Psychology and culture: Thinking, feeling and behaving in a global context.* New York: Psychology Press. https://doi.org/10.4324/9780203852965

Williams, J. (2008). *Don't they know it's Friday? Cross cultural considerations for business and life in the Gulf.* Dubai: Motivate Publishing.

Witts, B. N., Brodhead, M. T., Adlington, L., C., & Barron, D. K. (2018). Behavior analysts accept gifts during practice: So now what? *Behavior Analysis: Research and Practice* [Advance online publication]. https://doi.org/10.1037/bar0000117

Wolf, M. M. (1978). Social validity: The case for subjective measurement or how Applied Behavior Analysis is finding its heart. *Journal of Applied Behavior Analysis, 11*(2), 203–214. https://doi.org/10.1901/jaba.1978.11-203

9

Clinical Competence and Social Validity

Special Issues in Serving LGBTQIA Clients and Their Allies

Worner Leland and August Stockwell

Clinical Competence and Social Validity: Special Issues in Serving LGBTQIA Clients and Their Allies

Because LGBTQIA individuals are members of a stigmatized class, it is crucial for helping professionals who serve this population to address the additional barriers to care that may be faced by these clients. These challenges include but are not limited to arranging the environment to affirm disclosed identities, addressing intolerance from peers or other people in the client's community, addressing clinician personal bias, and increasing access to care for this typically underinsured population.

While often grouped together as an acronym, it is important to distinguish between the functions of terminology used to describe the LGBTQIA community. The terms *lesbian, gay*, and *bisexual* (LGB) all refer to sexual or romantic attraction based on others' gender(s). The term *transgender* (T) refers to one's own gender. The terms *queer* and *questioning* (Q) can refer to sexual or romantic attraction or can refer to gender identity. The term *intersex* (I) refers to a naturally occurring difference of sex characteristic development. The terms *asexual* and *aromantic* (A) refer to sexual attraction variability and romantic attraction variability based on context or internal factors.

Review of Terminology

The following section provides a review of the terminology related to sex, gender, and sexuality.

Sex

Sex refers to a person's biological makeup, including chromosomes, hormones, and internal and external sex organs. While individuals are often assigned a binary sex at birth, typically male or female, this assignment is usually made based on appearance of external genitalia alone and fails to account for the wide amount of variability sex characteristic development. An estimated 1%–2% of all people have some difference of sex development (DSD), also known as intersex traits, and many people are unaware of their own DSD (Ainsworth, 2015). Sex development is a matter of phylogenic selection and is different than gender identity development. Intersex individuals may be cisgender or may be transgender, or may use other terms entirely to describe their gender. One does not necessitate the other.

Gender

In addition to being assigned a binary sex at birth, people are often assumed to be of a correlating binary *gender*. Gender refers to a person's experience of themselves as male, female, or something else entirely, such as a nonbinary or agender identity. For some people, their assigned gender at birth (AGAB) is congruent with their experience of themselves. When one's AGAB is aligned with one's actual experienced gender, a person can be said to be *cisgender*, (American Psychological Association [APA], 2015). Cisgender is a descriptive term with a Latin prefix, "cis" meaning "on the same side of" or in alignment with. For other people, their AGAB is incongruent with their experience of themselves. People with this experience typically use the term *transgender* to describe this experience (APA, 2015; James et al., 2016). Transgender is a descriptive term with a Latin prefix, "trans" meaning "on another side of" or not in alignment with. Some individuals may instead prefer to use the term *transsexual*, noting that their gender had always felt consistent and that it is their biology that feels incongruent. All individuals have a different learning history of relational responding, and it is important to honor whatever term resonates for the individual.

For transgender individuals, some identify with a binary gender and may choose to refer to themselves as transgender men or transgender women, or simply as men and women. Many other transgender individuals however have identities that are *nonbinary*. Nonbinary means that one's identity does not fit neatly into a male-or-female distinction. Nonbinary individuals may use a wide variety of terms to describe their gender, such as *genderqueer, agender,* or *gender nonconforming* (APA, 2015; James et al., 2016). Also, many individuals experience a fluctuation in their experience of gender over time and may use terms such as *genderflux* or *genderfluid* to describe this experience (APA, 2015).

Additionally, it is important to note that concepts of binary gender are directly related to colonization. Many cultures have long histories of more than two genders being a part of their cultural norms. Some culturally specific identities such as *two-spirit* or *third gender* may be used to directly describe a specific cultural gender identity (Slater & Yarbrough, 2012; Chiang & Arondekar, 2019). It is important to note that individuals who have culturally significant gender identities may identify with the term transgender or nonbinary, or they may reject these terms and solely identify with language rooted in their own culture or language.

There are many theories of how an individual's sense of gender develops, including cognitive and biological theories (Bancroft, 2002; Martin, Ruble, & Szkrybalo, 2002); however, none of these theories provides an account for the behavior-environment relations that impact gender-based categorizations. When examining gender categorization, we can also think about gendered traits as mentalistic labels attributed to one's category and gender roles as behavioral expectations based on one's category. While individuals are assigned a sex at birth by a medical professional and typically socialized as a correlating binary gender by family, friends, and others in their environment, the only person who can truly identify one's gender and accurately assign any of the aforementioned gender labels is the individual themselves. For individuals who are cisgender, because the labels assigned to them at birth are accurate ones, there may be little consideration of or exploration around gender labels. For individuals who are not cisgender, however, it may be more challenging to find terminology that accurately describes their experience and may require more language exploration.

Sexuality

Although gender terminology is useful for tacting one's experience of one's own identity, *sexuality* describes one's attraction to others and the impact of gender on this attraction. *Heterosexual* (or *straight*) is a term typically used by people who have a binary gender to describe an attraction to the opposite binary gender (regardless of if either of the individuals are cisgender or transgender). *Homosexual* (or *gay* or *lesbian*) is a term typically used by people who have a binary gender to describe an attraction to the same binary gender (regardless of whether either individual is cisgender or transgender). Men who are attracted to men are the predominant users of the term gay, and women who are attracted to women are the predominant users of the term lesbian (Gay Lesbian & Straight Education Network [GLSEN], 2014). It is important to note that this describes common use, and not exclusive use, of these terms. For many reasons (such as ease of explaining one's identity to a stranger, ease of finding community, affinity for a term as one's identity shifts, affinity for a term as a political identity as much as a sexuality or gender identity, etc.) a person may use a term outside of this common use. For example, gay is often seen as a catch-all term used by many in the LGBTQIA community, even if it does not specifically or precisely describe the nuance of one's identity.

Bisexual is a term used to describe experiencing attraction to someone of the same gender as well as attraction to someone of a different gender. Some may also use the term *pansexual* to describe an experience of attraction to all genders. Often the use of these two terms overlap, and historical and political use over time may impact the specific language one chooses to use to describe their attraction (GLSEN, 2014).

It is also important to note that sexuality terminology is often used as a catch-all to describe both one's sexual attraction and one's romantic attraction, but that these may not always covary. A little over 1% of the population are estimated to not experience sexual attraction (Bogaert, 2004). *Asexual* is a term describing for describing this lack of experiencing sexual attraction. Comparably, *aromantic* is a term describing a lack of experiencing romantic attraction. And while some asexual individuals are also aromantic, an individual may be asexual but still experience romantic attraction, or may be aromantic but still experience sexual attraction. In all of these contexts, one's attraction to others can still be influenced by gender. Asexual and aromantic experiences and histories vary widely, and individuals may or may not choose to engage in sexual or romantic behavior irrespective of physiological attraction experienced (Carrigan, 2011; Gupta, 2017).

Gender, Sexuality, and Verbal Behavior

Relational frame theory (RFT) provides an account of language as operant behavior, with antecedent stimuli and consequence stimuli impacting verbal behavior (Hayes, Barnes-Holmes, & Roche, 2001). One principle of RFT, derived relational responding, exemplifies how behavior may be altered without direct behavioral training. If a relation between two stimuli is directly trained and an individual then responds based on the untrained reverse relation (mutual entailment), or makes an untrained response based on two other directly trained relations (combinatorial entailment), these can be thought of as types of derived relational responses (Hayes et al., 2001; Torneke, 2010). Through the process of derived relational responding we may see assumptions about gender occurring in the absence of direct training. For example, through a verbal community's training of concepts like "football is for boys" and "I am not a boy," we may see a derived belief that "football is not for me" even if this is never directly trained or stated. Or through the training of concepts like "women are supposed to be emotional" and "I am not a woman" we may see a derived belief that "I am not supposed to be emotional" (Brown & Stockwell, 2015). This may also account for the phenomenon of internalized self-stigmatization, even in the absence of direct training. For example, through community training or education that heavily teaches that "women being attracted to men is healthy and normal" and internal verbal behavior "I am a woman and am not attracted to men" we may see a derived belief that "I am unhealthy and not normal" even in the absence of direct homophobia or acephobia within a verbal community.

Operant conditioning by one's verbal community provides a theoretical rationale for the development of gender categorization and gender beliefs (Brown & Stockwell, 2015). In addition to derived relational responding, behaviors that align with gender relations are labeled as "good" and often immediately followed by praise or social approval, leading to an increase in the future frequency of that behavior in that context. Behavior that does not align with gender relations, however, is labeled as "bad" and often is immediately followed by correction or social disapproval, leading to decreases in the future frequency of that behavior in environments where the behavior has contacted those specified consequences (Brown & Stockwell, 2015). This punishment can range from the highly aversive, such as ridicule, oppression, exclusion, and violence, to the minimally aversive, such as corrective feedback in the form of statements or rules for governing behavior like "girls don't do yucky things like that," or "you can only shop in the boys' section" (Leland, 2016; Skinner, 1969). It is important to recognize that even with knowledge of common-use of LGBTQIA terminology, that language is constantly shifting and evolving, and that a term may function for one individual in an entirely different way than it does for another individual.

LGBTQIA History and the Helping Professions

Rooted in early religious ideology and a moral model of sexuality, homosexuality was pathologized within the medical and early psychological community (Drescher, 2015). In 1952 when the original *Diagnostic and Statistical Manual of Mental Disorders* (DSM) was published, LGBTQIA identities and behavior were characterized as a "sociopathic personality disturbance." A diagnosis of sexual deviation included "pathologic behavior, such as homosexuality, transvestism, pedophilia, fetishism, and sexual sadism" (APA, 1952). This persisted in the DSM-II until an APA position paper noted clinician observations that some individuals experienced and expressed distress at their homosexuality, whereas others experience no distress (APA, 1973). Future DSM printings and editions would go on to shift the classification of homosexuality and recommended courses of action; however, the prior scientific weight given to the pathologization of gender variance and sexuality variance was deeply damaging and aided in the further stigmatization of LGBTQIA individuals (Baughey-Gill, 2011). Additionally, gender identity and sexuality were conflated throughout much of the early psychological literature, and while shifts in perceptions of homosexuality were occurring in the 1970s, it would take far longer for gender identity to receive the same steps toward depathologization (APA, 1952, 1968, 1980, 1994, 2013). Complicating the issue of depathologization, however, access to gender affirming medical care such as hormone replacement therapy and gender-affirming surgery throughout time has been contingent on the ability to prove a pathologized transgender identity or experiences of gender dysphoria. While the language around this gatekeeping of medical care has shifted over time, it is still common to see gender affirming medical care contingent on a diagnosis letter from a mental health professional instead of being solely contingent on the informed consent of the transgender patient (Cavanaugh, Hopwood, & Lambert, 2016; Deutsch, 2012).

Behavior analysis was also utilized in harmful and stigmatizing ways during this time. Throughout the 1970s, multiple studies were published that attempted to use behavioral procedures to shape, punish, or recondition operant and respondent "deviant" patterns of homosexual or transsexual behavior (e.g. Barlow & Agras, 1973; Barlow, Reynolds, & Agras, 1973;

Quinn, Harbison, & McAllister, 1970; Rekers & Lovaas, 1974). Perhaps the most infamous of these studies is "Behavioral Treatment of Deviant Sex-Role Behaviors in a Male Child" published in the *Journal of Applied Behavior Analysis* (Rekers & Lovaas, 1974). This study was presented at the time as a successful reinforcement control over feminine behaviors, utilizing a token economy and extinction procedures for feminine behaviors, and reinforcement for masculine behaviors. They also noted that beyond the single subject described in the study, they also were treating other children with similar therapy outcomes in clinic. Atypical of most studies in the field of behavior analysis, long-term outcomes and social validity were made available when the family of the study's sole participant reported after his death that this study had harmful effects on the participant and hypothesize that it contributed to his ultimate suicide (Bronstein & Joseph, 2011).

At the time, others in the field of behavior analysis were critical of the goals of the study; however, these criticisms were rooted predominantly in methodological soundness (Nordyke, Baer, Etzel, & LeBlanc, 1977; Winkler, 1977). Winkler (1977) noted that the study goal of preventing "future sexual deviance: transsexualism, transvestism and some forms of homosexuality and the predicted need for treatment of these behaviors" (p. 550) relied on the authors' ability to predict future sex-role behavior based on childhood behavior in a way that over-extrapolated from available data at the time, and also presumed that the persistence of these behaviors would be harmful to the participant, which available data could not predict, especially in the face of shifting social norms. Winkler (1977) also noted that the study goal of reducing "current aversiveness of the child's behavior to the parents and the child's peers" (p. 550) was rooted in value judgments based on sex-typing and sex-roles that may not be realistic or optimal for the participant. Nordyke et al. (1977) echoed these sentiments; however, much of the response focused far less on the appropriateness of attempting to eliminate homosexuality and far more on the methodology of doing so, suggesting alternatives for shifting these behaviors in healthier and more gender neutral ways, such as "teaching self defense, cooperation, independence, and even throwing and catching a ball" (p. 556) as well as "modifying behaviors that are considered inappropriate for either males or females, i.e., the boy's extreme fears, excessive crying, avoidance of his brother, or avoidance of certain types of play activities," (p. 566). Rekers (1977) published a response to these criticisms that reaffirmed the belief that the original study was an ethical course of action.

Russell and Winkler (1977) also published a study that year that attempted to increase homosexual quality of life and social functioning via behavioral training to increase assertiveness via outing oneself as a homosexual to others, instead of attempting to remove homosexual attraction. However, the data were inconclusive regarding overall improvement and showed minimal improvement differences between the control group and the training group. The authors noted that no homosexual individuals were involved in the design of the study or the selection of the dependent variables, and that while the primary concern had been that study tasks of outing oneself would be too easy, they may in fact have been too challenging, as indicated by an unwillingness to participate in all of the self-disclosure-related dependent variable measures by multiple participants.

Over time APA opinions shifted based on data and social validity, resulting in publications including the *Guidelines for Psychological Practice with Lesbian, Gay, and Bisexual Clients* (2012) and the *Guidelines for Psychological Practice with Transgender and Gender Nonconforming People* (2015). Core tenets of these guidelines include recognizing that sexual diversity and gender diversity represent normal human variation and are not mental illness, seeking to understand and address the impact of stigma for gender and sexual minorities, recognizing the harm and inefficacy of attempts at conversion therapy, and recognizing the research indicating increase in positive outcomes and decrease in negative outcomes for those receiving affirming care and social support (APA, 2012, 2015). To date, the governing bodies of the field of behavior analysis have no official guidelines or position statements on working with LGBTQIA clients, nor formal positions on engaging in conversion therapies and other non-socially valid or culturally informed behavior goals seen in past research. As such, it is important to look to broader ethical codes to guide current research and practice.

BACB® Ethical Codes

When considering current behavior analytic ethical best practice for working with gender and sexual minorities, it is crucial to examine the Professional and Ethical Compliance Code for Behavior Analysts. First and foremost, in their work behavior analysts do not engage in discrimination (1.05(d)) or behavior that is harassing or demeaning (1.05(e)), against individuals or groups based on a variety of factors, including gender and sexual orientation (BACB®, 2019). Although not directly addressed by the current code, the BACB® suggests an interpretation of "gender" that follows "the most inclusive definition available in the country where the behavior analyst practices" (M. R. Nosik, personal communication, March 11, 2017). As such, in the United States it may be meaningful to examine inclusive definitions of "gender" in the ethical best practice of comparable fields, which include factors such as gender identity and gender expression (APA, 2017; National Association of Social Workers [NASW], 2017). Outside of the USA, comparable organizational ethics codes should be sought out to inform interpretations of the BACB® code. It is important to consider that discrimination based on gender or sexuality may be obvious and include things like refusal of care, exclusion, harassment, and violence, but that it may also include more subtle things such as restricting expression or presentation, or targeting behaviors for decrease because they do not conform to stereotypical gender roles or heterosexual norms.

Additionally, behavior analysts are careful to consider cultural humility. When differences including, but not limited to, gender and sexuality significantly impact one's work, behavior analysts seek training, experience, consultation, and supervision to provide competent services, or they make referrals to providers who are competent (1.05(c)). Identifying personal biases and the impact of those biases on behavior is an important component of providing affirming care. Additionally, behavior analysts uplift cultural humility with LGBTQIA clients and beyond by providing services, teaching, or conducting research only after the appropriate study, training, supervision, and consultation (1.02(b)) and maintain this competence through ongoing professional development (1.03) with the understanding that as a culture evolves, best practice will shift over time (BACB®, 2019).

Behavior analysts operate in the best interests of their clients, and for LGBTQIA clients this includes additional ethical considerations. When considering the ethical obligation to rely on scientific knowledge (1.01), this includes being conscientious consumers of LGBTQIA research and examining researcher bias, the soundness of the methodology, and the social validity of the study for affected parties.

Behavior analysts have a responsibility to all parties affected by services, but that responsibility exists in a hierarchy that centers and prioritizes a primary beneficiary of services (2.02) before the other parties (BACB®, 2019). When a primary client holds an LGBTQIA identity, their best interests or values may differ from the interests or values of other affected parties. It is a behavior analyst's responsibility to sit with the discomfort of navigating conflict between parties regarding gender identity and expression interests and sexuality interests of the primary client, and to protect client rights and center client values and goals. Finally, behavior analysts have a responsibility to create an environment that promotes truthful and honest behavior (1.04(a)) for themselves and for others (BACB®, 2019). Creating an environment in which LGBTQIA clients do not feel they have to hide or lie about their identities is a critical component of providing affirming services. If a client has not specifically shared information about their sexuality or gender, it is crucial that this information is not assumed to be aligned with a cisgender or heterosexual default.

Practice Considerations and Implications in Applied Behavior Analysis Service Delivery

From initial assessment to termination of services, behavior analysts can assess their own cultural competence as it pertains to gender affirmation and sexuality affirmation (Leland & Stockwell, 2019), can utilize behavior analytic methodologies to address skill building and fluency in areas where there is room for growth, and can arrange an environment that is supportive of LGBTQIA clients and their right to autonomy and self-determination. When considering business operations, behavior analysts can take care to have an affirming and inclusive policy for hiring as well as for providing services that is clearly displayed in print or on a company website, and that directly states protections for LGBTQIA employees and clients. It is also crucial to build one's own commitment to affirmation by addressing the implicit and explicit biases to which helping professionals are not impervious (Sabin, Riskind, & Nosek, 2015). Clinicians can notice the impact of social stigma and prejudice against LGBTQIA people on one's own beliefs and behavior and utilize perspective-taking exercises to address one's own biases (McDowell, Berrahou, Goldhammer, Potter, & Keuroghlian, 2018). Clinicians can also utilize acceptance, mindfulness, and a commitment to value-aligned action and behavior to build compassion for LGBTQIA clients and to address the microaggressions and macroaggressions that may arise in the provision of services due to implicit or explicit bias and learning histories of cultural stigmatization (Lillis & Hayes, 2007; Skinta & Curtin, 2016).

In addition to an internal personal or organizational commitment to gender and sexuality affirmation, it is also valuable to maintain a referral list of helping professionals and medical professionals who are also committed to cultural humility and best practice in their field (American Medical Association, 2018; Daniel & Butkus, 2015) and to providing affirming services to LGBTQIA clients and patients. When considering the physical environment, utilizing gender-neutral washrooms provides a safe space for clients and employees of all genders. If gender-neutral washrooms are not possible, it can be meaningful to have a company policy that affirms the right of individuals to use the washroom of their choice. In spaces where there are not currently legal protections for affirming washroom access and in which affirming access is being denied to a client, it may be valuable to advocate for the client to have access to a wheelchair accessible, single-stall washroom.

When creating intake documents (see Figure 9.1), behavior analysts can use inclusive, non-gendered language (see Table 9.1) and use fill-in-the-blank options instead of check boxes for demographic information regarding gender.

Application for Services

Legal Name: _____   Preferred Name: _____

Date of Birth: __/__/____ SSN: _____ Gender: _____ Pronouns: _____

Guardian (if applicable): _____

Relationship to Guardian: _____ Diagnosis (if applicable): _____

Address: _____

FIGURE 9.1 An Example of Intake Paperwork Using Inclusive and Affirming Terminology and Design

TABLE 9.1 Brainstorm Gender-Neutral Options for the Terms Listed (Possible Answers Are Located at the End of the Chapter)

Instead of . . .	Try . . .
Boys and Girls	
Mom and Dad	
Grandma and Grandpa	
Brothers and Sisters	
Son and Daughter	
Boyfriends and Girlfriends	
Husband and Wife	
Ladies and Gentlemen	

For example, using neutral terms such as "parents or guardians" as opposed to "mother" and "father" not only avoids the assumption of heterosexual parenting, but also avoids the assumption that parents or guardians are binary males or females. For many transgender and gender nonconforming individuals, their legal name may not match their actual used name, and it may be distressing to have to disclose one's legal name. It is essential to provide a space on intake documents for a client's preferred name, to ensure that this name is utilized by all staff, and to ensure that no one has access to the client's legal name unless absolutely necessary.

When conducting intake assessments, it is important to include gender and sexual minority cultural identity in your analysis. Utilizing culturally aware language in one's intake assessment may be meaningful for client rapport and perception of services and may aid in identifying next steps, whether it be accepting the client, referring the client out, or building cultural knowledge or seeking supervision to best serve the client (Fong, Catagnus, Brodhead, Quigley, & Field, 2016) in the selection of affirming support systems and programs.

When conducting both preference assessments and skills assessments, be mindful of gender roles and cultural expectations, and take care not to limit your client's choices based on their gender. It is crucial to allow client values to drive goals and to support a client in identifying preferences and putative reinforcers. If a client discloses a non-cisgender or non-heterosexual identity or preference, it is important to believe them and to honor the language they are using for themselves. It is crucial to remember that there is no one physical presentation or topography for a gender identity or sexual identity, and that there may be many competing contingencies preventing a client from presenting or behaving in a way that aligns with cultural expectations, including cultural expectations for LGBTQIA identities.

When providing services for clients with LGBTQIA identities, there may be a conflict of values between the primary client and secondary clients (including guardians, family, staff, and communities) rooted in homophobia or transphobia. If this conflict arises, it may be the responsibility of the behavior analyst to provide secondary parties with data on the inefficacy and short- and long-term harms of conversion therapy (Scasta, Bialer, & American Psychiatric Association, 2013; Whitman, Glosoff, Kocet, & Tarvydas, 2006) as well as data on the protective factors of affirmation (Ryan, Russell, Huebner, Diaz, & Sanchez, 2010; Simons, Schrager, Clark, Belzer, & Olson, 2013), and to provide psychoeducation on how LGBTQIA affirmation aligns with primary client best interests and health outcomes.

When speaking about individuals in the third person, one often uses pronouns that are gendered, such as "he" and "his" or "she" and "hers," and people often assume which pronouns they should be using based on topographical assumptions of gender, such as clothing, appearance, and mannerisms. When utilizing topography assessment however, one runs the risk of incorrectly guessing someone's gender. Additionally, many individuals, an estimated nearly one-third of the transgender population (James et al., 2016) use gender-neutral pronouns "they" and "theirs" or neo-pronouns such as "ze" and "hirs." Misgendering can cause direct harm to others and it is beneficial to ask others for their names and pronouns instead of assuming one can guess based on presentation. If there has not yet been a chance to ask what pronouns a person uses, it may be meaningful to use gender-neutral pronouns until this information is learned. When asking what pronouns someone uses or when using gender-neutral pronouns, it is important to do this consistently for all individuals and not just individuals one assumes may be transgender or gender nonconforming based on topography.

While striving to be affirming, it is also important to be mindful of client and employee safety. Being out and open about one's gender or sexuality may be something that is helpful in some contexts and harmful in others (James et al., 2016; Williams Institute, 2019). If a client or employee discloses a gender or sexual minority identity, it is meaningful to follow up and ask how they would like to proceed. Some people, for example, may wish for support in asserting their identity in all spaces, whereas others may wish to use different signifiers in different spaces. As with everything, it is important to let the primary client's or employee's values drive what language is used for them and in which spaces.

When teaching all clients, regardless of gender identity or sexual orientation, it is valuable to utilize materials that accurately represent the normal variability that exists within humanity in both identity and behavior. It is imperative that teaching centers autonomy and identification of one's own values instead of propagating harmful stereotypes or myths with regard to sex, gender, sexuality, and experiences of attraction or desire. In this way we can create learning environments of safety and affirmation that promote truthful and honest behavior.

As with clients, an affirming workplace will attract and retain great employees, and there are several additional practices that create a culture of gender affirmation and sexuality affirmation for staff and other colleagues. First is the use of an inclusive dress code based on functional work responsibilities and consistent across all individuals rather than specific to gender; by questioning norms around what "business casual" clothing looks like, people of all genders are able to dress in the way that makes sense for their professional role and responsibilities rather than arbitrary gendered expectations. Second, employers and employees can include their personal pronouns in email signatures, during their in-person and remote introductions with others, and in everyday conversation. Because misgendering may happen, it is crucial that professionals are willing to correct each other, and be corrected, in the moment, to ensure that pronouns are honored for everyone involved, whether they are present in that interaction or not.

Conclusion

Mirroring the larger culture and comparable helping professions, behavior analysis has a history of harmful behavior toward portions of the LGBTQIA community. With increased understanding of sex, gender, sexuality, and desire, it is crucial that we acknowledge our collective history, while striving to realign our behavior with our values and ethical principles. LGBTQIA individuals face a variety of unique needs and barriers to care, many of which are directly tied to social oppression and marginalization. When we strive to increase our knowledge and shift our behavior to arrange affirming and supportive environments, we can better assist our LGBTQIA clients and colleagues in moving toward what they value. Professionals should continue to seek out training opportunities and conversations with colleagues specific to the ethics and social validity considerations related to working with LGBTQIA clients and continue to take steps to carry out research within their scope that is LGBTQIA affirming and inclusive, all from a standpoint of cultural humility

CASE STUDY

A 6-year-old first-grade client lives with his mother and father, his grandmother, and his 8-year-old sister with whom he shares a bedroom. The client identified a personal goal of being able to watch more TV in the morning before school and has agreed to work on a goal of dressing himself quickly and independently in the mornings, leaving more time for morning cartoons. The therapist and support staff have recently faded completely out of this routine and the client has been selecting his own clothes and getting dressed independently from start to finish. Within the past week, the client has consistently selected glittery outfits from his older sister's wardrobe and gotten dressed in them without any input or assistance. The therapist and support staff continue to praise and support this independent behavior. At the team meeting that week, the client's father is very upset. He tells you that he isn't going to raise a sissy, and that he is thinking about discontinuing services, because the all-female staff is negatively influencing his son. What actions would you take? What BACB codes are relevant here?

DISCUSSION QUESTIONS

1. Suppose you are working with a family who is resistant to a client's sexual orientation? What does it look like to maintain rapport with a family while still supporting client autonomy?

2. Why is it important for behavior analysts to be knowledgeable about the ways that behavioral procedures have been used in efforts to change gender and sexual identities in the past?

3. Why is it important to get feedback from clients regarding your LGBTQIA-affirming professional behaviors rather than only from colleagues or through self-reflection? What are some ways you can solicit client feedback, and how could you incorporate it in future sessions?

4. How would you respond to a coworker who states that LGBTQIA topics are irrelevant to behavior analysis, since "behavior is behavior"?

5. What history do you have with the topic of LGBTQIA identities? Why is it important to reflect on the ways that it may influence how you approach certain clinical or professional situations?

Possible Answers for Table 9.1

Instead of "Boys and Girls," try "children, kids, students, friends"

Instead of "Mom and Dad," try "parent, guardian"

Instead of "Grandma and Grandpa," try "grandparent"

Instead of "Brothers and Sisters," try "siblings"

Instead of "Son and Daughter," try "child, progeny"

Instead of "Boyfriends and Girlfriends," try "partner, significant other"

Instead of "Husband and Wife," try "spouse, partner"

Instead of "Ladies and Gentlemen," try "everyone, esteemed guests"

References

Ainsworth, C. (2015). Sex redefined. *Nature*. Retrieved from www.nature.com/news/sexredefined-1.16943

American Medical Association. (2018). *Health care needs of lesbian, gay, bisexual, transgender and queer populations H-160.991*. Retrieved from https://policysearch.amaassn.org/policyfinder/detail/transgender?uri=%2FAMADoc%2FHOD.xml-0-805.xml

American Psychiatric Association. (1952). *Diagnostic and statistical manual of mental disorders*. Washington, DC: American Psychiatric Association.

American Psychiatric Association. (1968). *Diagnostic and statistical manual of mental disorders* (2nd ed). Washington, DC: American Psychiatric Association.

American Psychiatric Association. (1973). *Homosexuality and sexual orientation disturbance: Proposed change in DSM-II, 6th printing, page 44, position statement (retired)*. Arlington, VA: American Psychiatric Association.

American Psychiatric Association. (1980). *Diagnostic and statistical manual of mental disorders* (3rd ed). Washington, DC: American Psychiatric Association.

American Psychiatric Association. (1994). *Diagnostic and statistical manual of mental disorders* (4th ed). Washington, DC: American Psychiatric Association.

American Psychiatric Association. (2013). *Diagnostic and statistical manual of mental disorders* (5th ed). Washington, DC: American Psychiatric Association.

American Psychological Association. (2012). Guidelines for psychological practice with lesbian, gay, and bisexual clients. *American Psychologist*, *67*(1), 10–42. https://doi.org/10.1037/a0039906

American Psychological Association. (2015). Guidelines for psychological practice with transgender and gender nonconforming people. *American Psychologist*, *70*(9), 832–864. https://doi.org/10.1037/a0039906

American Psychological Association. (2017). *Ethical principles of psychologists and code of conduct*. Retrieved from www.apa.org/ethics/code/

Bancroft, J. (2002). Biological factors in human sexuality. *Journal of Sex Research*, *39*(1), 15–21. https://doi.org/10.1080/00224490209552114

Barlow, D. H., & Agras, W. S. (1973). Fading to increase heterosexual responsiveness in homosexuals. *Journal of Applied Behavior Analysis*, *6*(3), 355–366. https://doi.org/10.1901/jaba.1973.6-355

Barlow, D. H., Reynolds, E. J., & Agras, W. S. (1973). Gender identity change in a transsexual. *Archives of General Psychiatry*, *28*(4), 569–576. https://doi.org/10.1001/archpsyc.1973.01750340089014

Baughey-Gill, S. (2011). When gay was not okay with the APA: A historical overview of homosexuality and its status as mental disorder. *Occam's Razor*, *1*(2). Retrieved from https://cedar.wwu.edu/orwwu/vol1/iss1/2

Behavior Analyst Certification Board (BACB). (2019). *Behavior Analyst Certification Board guidelines for responsible conduct for behavior analysts.* Retrieved from www.bacb.com/wp-content/uploads/170706r_compliance_code_english.pdf.

Bogaert, A. F. (2004). Asexuality: Its prevalence and associated factors in a national probability sample. *Journal of Sex Research*, *41*(3), 279–287. https://doi.org/10.1080/00224490409552235

Bronstein, S., & Joseph, J. (2011, June 10). Therapy to change "feminine" boy created a troubled man, family says. *CNN*. Retrieved from www.cnn.com

Brown, C., & Stockwell, F. (2015). Gender through a behavior analytic lens: Who you are, what you do, and why you do it. In B. McCormick (Chair), *Sexual Behavior SIG symposium: A behavior analytic perspective on gender and sexuality*. Symposium conducted at the Association for Behavior Analysis International Conference, San Antonio, TX.

Carrigan, M. (2011). There's more to life than sex? Difference and commonality within the asexual community. *Sexualities*, *14*(4), 462–478. https://doi.org/10.1177/1363460711406462

Cavanaugh, T., Hopwood, R., & Lambert, C. (2016). Informed consent in the medical care of transgender and gender-nonconforming patients. *AMA Journal of Ethics*, *18*(11), 1147–1155. https://doi.org/1001/journalofethics.2016.18.11.sect1–1611

Chiang, H., & Arondekar, A. (Eds.). (2019). *Global encyclopedia of lesbian, gay, bisexual, transgender, and queer (LGBTQ) history*. Farmington Hills, MI: Charles Scribner's Sons.

Daniel, H., & Butkus, R. (2015). Lesbian, gay, bisexual, and transgender health disparities: Executive summary of a policy position paper from the American College of Physicians. *Annals of Internal Medicine*, *163*(2), 135–137. https://doi.org/10.7326/M14–2482

Deutsch, M. (2012). Use of the informed consent model in the provision of cross-sex hormone therapy: A survey of the practices of selected clinics. *The International Journal of Transgenderism*, *13*(3), 140–140. https://doi.org/10.1080/15532739.2011.675233

Drescher, J. (2015). Out of DSM: Depathologizing homosexuality. *Behavioral Sciences*, *5*(4), 565–575. https://doi.org/10.3390/bs5040565

Fong, E. H., Catagnus, R. M., Brodhead, M. T., Quigley, S. P., & Field, S. (2016). Developing the cultural awareness skills of behavior analysts. *Behavior Analysis in Practice*, *9*(1), 84–94. https://doi.org/10.1007/s40617-016-0111-6

Gay, Lesbian & Straight Education Network. (2014). *Key concepts and terms*. New York: GLSEN. Retrieved from www.glsen.org/sites/default/files/GLSEN%20Terms%20and%20Concepts%20Thematic.pdf

Gupta, K. (2017). "And now I'm just different, but there's nothing actually wrong with me": Asexual marginalization and resistance. *Journal of Homosexuality*, *64*(8), 991–1013. https://doi.org/10.1080/00918369.2016.1236590

Hayes, S. C., Barnes-Holmes, D., & Roche, B. (Eds.). (2001). *Relational frame theory: A post-Skinnerian account of human language and cognition*. New York: Kluwer Academic/Plenum Publishers.

James, S. E., Herman, J. L., Rankin, S., Keisling, M., Mottet, L., & Anafi, M. (2016). *Executive summary of the report of the 2015 U.S. Transgender Survey*. Washington, DC: National Center for Transgender Equality.

Leland, W. (2016). Affirming atypical gender reinforcers and preferences. *Sexual Behavior: Research and Practice Newsletter, 9,* 5–7.

Leland, W., & Stockwell, A. (2019). A self-assessment tool for cultivating affirming practices with transgender and gender-nonconforming (TGNC) clients, supervisees, students, and colleagues. *Behavior Analysis in Practice, 12*(4), 816–825. https://doi.org/10.1007/s40617-019-00375-0

Lillis, J., & Hayes, S. C. (2007). Applying acceptance, mindfulness, and values to the reduction of prejudice: A pilot study. *Behavior Modification, 31*(4), 389–411. https://doi.org/10.1177/0145445506298413

Martin, C. L., Ruble, D. N., & Szkrybalo, J. (2002). Cognitive theories of early gender development. *Psychological Bulletin, 128*(6), 903–933. https://doi.org/10.1037/0033–2909.128.6.903

McDowell, M. J., Berrahou, I. K., Goldhammer, H., Potter, J., & Keuroghlian, A. S. (2018). *Learning to address implicit bias towards LGBTQ patients: Case scenarios.* National LGBT Health Education Center: Fenway Institute. Retrieved from www.lgbthealtheducation.org/wp-content/uploads/2018/10/Implicit-Bias-Guide-2018_Final.pdf

National Association of Social Workers. (2017). *NASW code of ethics.* Retrieved from www.socialworkers.org/About/Ethics/Code-of-Ethics/Code-of-Ethics-English

Nordyke, N. S., Baer, D. M., Etzel, B. C., & LeBlanc, J. M. (1977). Implications of the stereotyping and modification of sex role. *Journal of Applied Behavior Analysis, 10*(3), 553–557. https://doi.org/10.1901/jaba.1977.10-553

Quinn, J. T., Harbison, J., & McAllister, H. (1970). An attempt to shape penile responses. *Behavior Research and Therapy, 8*(2), 27–28. https://doi.org/10.1016/0005-7967(70)90095-1

Rekers, G. A. (1977). Atypical gender development and psychosocial adjustment. *Journal of Applied Behavior Analysis, 10*(3), 559–571. https://doi.org/10.1901/jaba.1977.10-559

Rekers, G. A., & Lovaas, O. (1974). Behavioral treatment of deviant sex-role behaviors in a male child. *Journal of Applied Behavior Analysis, 7*(2), 173–190. https://doi.org/10.1901/jaba.1974.7-173

Russell, A., & Winkler, R. (1977). Evaluation of assertive training and homosexual guidance service groups designed to improve homosexual functioning. *Journal of Consulting and Clinical Psychology, 45*(1), 1–13. https://doi.org/10.1037/h0045239

Ryan, C., Russell, S., Huebner, D., Diaz, R., & Sanchez, J. (2010). Family acceptance in adolescence and the health of LGBT young adults. *Journal of Child and Adolescent Psychiatric Nursing, 23*(4), 205–213. https://doi.org/10.1111/j.1744-6171.2010.00246.x

Sabin, J., Riskind, R., & Nosek, B. (2015). Health care providers' implicit and explicit attitudes toward lesbian women and gay men. *American Journal of Public Health, 105*(9), 1831–1841. https://doi.org/10.2105/AJPH.2015.302631

Scasta, D., Bialer, P., & American Psychiatric Association. (2013). *Position statement on issues related to homosexuality.* Arlington County: American Psychiatric Association. Retrieved from www.psychiatry.org/psychiatrists/search-directories-databases/policy-finder

Simons, L., Schrager, S. M., Clark, L. F., Belzer, M., & Olson, J. (2013). Parental support and mental health among transgender adolescents. *Journal of Adolescent Health, 53*(6), 791–793. https://doi.org/10.1016/j.jadohealth.2013.07.019

Skinner, B. F. (1969). An operant analysis of problem-solving. In B. F. Skinner (Ed.), *Contingencies of reinforcement: A theoretical analysis* (pp. 133–157). New York: Appleton-Century-Crofts.

Skinta, M., & Curtin, A. (2016). *Mindfulness and acceptance for gender and sexual minorities: A clinician's guide to fostering compassion, connection, and equality using contextual strategies* (The context press mindfulness and acceptance practice series). Reno: New Harbinger Publications.

Slater, S., & Yarbrough, F. A. (2012). *Gender and sexuality in indigenous North America, 1400–1850.* [N.p.]: University of South Carolina Press.

Torneke, N. (2010). *Learning RFT: An introduction to relational frame theory and its clinical applications.* Oakland, CA: New Harbinger Publications.

Whitman, J. S., Glosoff, H. L., Kocet, M. M., & Tarvydas, V. (2006). Exploring ethical issues related to conversion or reparative therapy. *Counseling Today, 49*(1), 14–15. retrieved from www.academia.edu/download/8061041/article_ethical_issues-and-reparativetherapy.doc

Williams Institute. (2019). *LGBT people in the U.S. not protected by state nondiscrimination statutes.* Retrieved from https://williamsinstitute.law.ucla.edu/wp-content/uploads/Equality-Act-March-2019.pdf

Winkler, R. C. (1977). What types of sex-role behavior should behavior modifiers promote? *Journal of Applied Behavior Analysis, 10*(3), 549–552. https://doi.org/10.1901/jaba.1977.10-549

10

Cultural Incompetency in Applied Behavior Analysis Service Delivery Models

Implications for Behavior Analysts

Paulina Luczaj, Fabiana Cacciaguerra-Decorato, and Brian M. Conners

---

Learning Objectives

- Identify the discrepancy between diverse behavior analysts and the population of clients with autism spectrum disorder.

- Describe how the lack of diverse behavior analysts can impact families of children with autism spectrum disorder with participation in treatment and access to services.

- Determine how cultural beliefs of autism spectrum disorder by families of various backgrounds can present barriers for behavior analysts in providing behavior analytic services.

- Identify components of cultural competency training that would be useful for behavior analysts to become culturally competent in providing services to individuals with autism spectrum disorder.

Walk into any event where the primary topic of conversation is about applied behavior analysis (ABA). As a behavior analyst, you naturally are very observant of what is occurring in your environment. You take a minute to observe the people you are surrounded by, and what do you notice? The individuals you are with are predominantly white females. Might this be a simple observation or coincidence? As data-driven professionals, let us examine the data. A study done by Conners, Johnson, Duarte, Murriky, and Marks (2019) surveyed behavior analysts across the nation to get a baseline of the different races that are represented in the field. The sample in the study showed that 82.61% of surveyed behavior analysts are white/Caucasian and 81.04% of those individuals are females. It looks like your observation might have been accurate! It can be speculated from this sample that the demographics of the population of behavior analysts may mirror the sample from this study, but the demographics are unknown in the field at this time.

You might be thinking "Okay, so what?" As we know, behavior analysts primarily work with individuals who have a diagnosis of autism spectrum disorders (ASD). We also know that ASD affects individuals from all cultural and ethnic backgrounds. So why do we not see a more culturally diverse population of behavior analysts? When comparing the data collected by Conners et al. (2019) to the demographic data on individuals with ASD from Autism Speaks (2014), we notice that the numbers of individuals from a minority background with a diagnosis of ASD are slightly higher than the individuals of that same minority background with a BCBA® (see Figure 10.1).

However, we also know that minority groups frequently get misdiagnosed or have a severe delay in diagnosis (Burkett, Morris, Manning-Courtney, Anthony, & Ebron, 2015; Zuckerman et al., 2014). The issue of under- and misdiagnosis of ASD in minority groups will be discussed later in this chapter.

Psychological research over the years reveals that data indicate having a shared identity between therapist and client in counseling leads to more effective, long-lasting changes. For example, someone who comes from a Polish cultural background may feel more comfortable disclosing and trusting a therapist who is also Polish. This shared identity may make rapport-building a smoother process. This could be possible due to various things, such as knowing a common language, cultural norms, traditions, and so forth. In addition, the therapeutic relationship may blossom at a quicker pace because the client will spend little to no time explaining different aspects of their culture in order for the therapist to understand the client's upbringing and cultural values. The same could hold true for ABA professionals in that clients receiving ABA services may be more likely to access and continue to retain services if the identity of the clients matches the ABA therapist. Although shared identity demonstrates

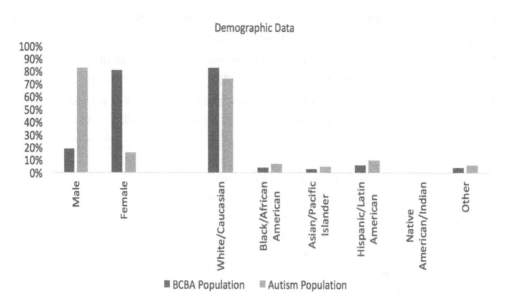

FIGURE 10.1 Demographics of BCBA® Population vs. Autism Population

great benefits, it is possible to reach the same result between a professional and client of different backgrounds. Dyches, Wilder, Sudweeks, Obiakor, and Algozzine (2004) found that a shared identity (i.e., sex, race, ethnicity) between students and their behavior analyst or Registered Behavior Technician™ (RBT®) is advantageous to their treatment. However, in order to understand culturally diverse clients, we must become culturally competent professionals.

The concept of understanding one's own culture, but also others', is beneficial to therapeutic relationships outside the field of psychology. This could be applied to everyday situations, but especially with the diverse clients and families we work with in the field of ABA. The importance of being a culturally competent behavior analyst is extremely important in order to provide treatment to a wide variety of clientele. Almost all graduate programs that are psychological in nature require students to take at least one class in multiculturalism in order to gain the knowledge necessary to be able to perform their job duty with culturally diverse clients. What about ABA? Why is learning about human beings and the cultures that shape their behavior not important enough to implement into behavior analytical training? This is an area of much-needed examination and one that the Behavior Analyst Certification Board® and the Association for Behavior Analysis International need to examine as part of training standards.

Not only do we have a lack of professional training in the area of cultural competence, but we also have a lack of diversity in the field. As we talked about in the beginning of the chapter, behavior analysts are primarily white females, as can be speculated from research samples (Conners et al., 2019). What are the chances that an Asian American family, who may have misconceptions about ASD, gets paired with an Asian BCBA® who is able to understand the family's concerns? Although it may be possible, based on the data thus far about demographics in the field, it could be argued that this may be difficult. This could also lead to concerns surrounding ethics given that behavior analysts do not receive training on multiculturalism and diversity issues and being able to provide culturally competent behavior analytic services.

As a behavior analyst, you may run into a scenario where it is no longer ethical to continue to provide services to a client. In this case, you must contact a provider who not only has the expertise in the client's needs, but also someone who may culturally or ethnically relate with that client and their family. Currently, there is a lack of diversity within the field that makes it incredibly challenging to match a client with a provider with these skills and shared identity. Whether it is the same gender or cultural beliefs, research has found that families are more likely to be a part of the therapeutic process when they feel connected to their provider (Dyches et al., 2004). Having a client's family be involved in the therapeutic process is essential in order to maintain consistency. Consistency between the behavior analyst, RBT®, and family members further promotes generalization of skills across other stimuli and environments. However, it is important to remember that parental buy-in from culturally diverse families will only become possible if the behavior analyst is culturally aware.

But before we can gain parental participation through cultural awareness, we must understand it. Skinner (1971) described culture as a collection of contingencies of reinforcement into which individuals are born and exposed throughout their lifetime. These contingencies are part of both the physical environment and private events that may serve as reinforcers, such as values and ideas that generate behavior. Furthermore, Sugai, O'Keefe, and Fallon (2012) described culture as common behaviors related by comparable learning histories, social and environmental contingencies, contexts, and stimuli. You might say, "What does this have to do with parental buy-in?" One area of behavior analysis involves behavior analysts going into homes and training parents or family and providing services there. The primary focus of the case would be the client; however, they might not have the cognitive awareness or ability to understand complex thoughts, such as identity. Or, they may not be concerned with sharing similar cultural beliefs with their behavior analyst or RBT®. However, behavior analysts frequently turn to the client's family (parents, guardians, etc.) to discuss their concerns and needs in programming/services. So if the client is not capable of building a relationship with the behavior analyst based on cultural identity, why should we care? However, this very mindset may be what is blocking ourselves as clinicians to relate to our culturally diverse clients. Self-awareness is the first, and most important, step to correcting the lack of cultural awareness the field may have of clients and families.

Fong, Catagnus, Brodhead, Quigley, and Field (2016) collected various strategies that previous researchers have suggested to gain cultural self-awareness for behavior analysts. One of the first suggests that behavior analysts discuss their diverse client interactions within the professional community, including group discussions, written forums, verbal feedback, and mentorship meetings (Tervalon & Murray-Garcia, 1998). Discussing our experiences with our colleagues may help us identify our own behavior and therefore may lead to change. Additionally, this may help us gain more insight from our colleagues' experiences with cultures we may not be familiar with (Tourinho, 2006). However, remember if you do use this strategy, keep your client and family anonymous, as disclosing personal information does not abide by our ethics code (Behavior Analyst Certification Board®, 2019).

In their article, Fong and colleagues (2016) shared various self-assessment tools the behavior analyst may consider using to discover their own cultural biases, values, and understanding. The *Diversity Self-Assessment* can help clinicians examine their own understanding of diversity by asking users to reflect on their own assumptions and biases by answering 11 questions (Montgomery, 2001). Additionally, Randall-David (1989) created the *How Do You Relate to Various Groups of People in Society?* self-test questionnaire, which asks respondents how they might respond to individuals of various cultural backgrounds. A final screening tool is the *Multicultural Sensitivity Scale*, which is a valid and reliable tool to measure multicultural sensitivity (Jibaja, Sebastian, Kingery, & Holcomb, 2000). Fong et al. (2016) suggests behavior analysts use these tools during the intake process to determine any cultural biases toward the client. They also suggest using the results to consider how their biases can affect treatment and if necessary, referring the client to another behavior analyst if there is a big discrepancy between the client's and the clinician's cultural beliefs.

The last strategy uncovers an area many behavior analysts are reluctant to discuss: private events. Skinner (1974) discussed radical behaviorism as a system of behavior that incorporates and seeks to understand all human behavior, including private events. Private events comprise all cognitions and emotions within one's skin as behavior (Skinner, 1974). Although we may not be able to observe the private events of our clients and their families, we can certainly acknowledge our own private events while observing them. To do this, it is suggested to use mindfulness when making these objective observations of the client's behaviors and interactions with their families. During our observations, we may automatically judge this interaction and attempt to resolve any issues that may arise due to the client's behavior. However, Hayes and Plumb (2007) and Vandenberghe (2008) suggest that professionals should not judge any private event that may come up while making these observations. Instead, being more aware and active throughout your observations, via mindfulness, may help reduce biases such as thoughts, feelings, and reactions to our culturally diverse clients (Lillis & Hayes, 2007). Therefore, the more you acknowledge your private events and not judge them, the more self-aware you will be!

Now that we have more insight on our self-awareness of our own culture, we must shift gears to understanding the culture of our client and their family. Are the parents participating in the treatment plan? Are they transparent with what they worked on? Or do they refuse to participate and believe that you, as the behavior analyst, are solely responsible for addressing the concerns? Although it may be frustrating not to have the key stakeholders involved in the client's treatment plan, there may be many factors as why they are not participating, such as high stress, socioeconomic status, education level, and lack of support (Bennett, 2012). Once we are able to consider these factors, there is one competency still missing: their culture. The next section will explore different perceptions of ASD from various cultural and minority groups.

Finding out that a child has been diagnosed with ASD has been historically a difficult thing to accept. Globally, this can be because of the misunderstandings, misconceptions, and myths about the diagnosis. Many families experience denial and even postpone seeking intervention due to lack of education. Understanding, accepting and intervening with ASD in a culturally diverse environment presents unique challenges. For example, in the Latino community, individuals with disabilities and/or mental health diagnoses are viewed as shameful or embarrassing (Zuckerman et al., 2014). This belief can indirectly harm a child by receiving minimal or no support from family members due to lack of psychoeducation. As culturally incompetent behavior analysts, we may assume that all individuals are well versed on ASD since there is so much information readily available to the public during this time period. Without any formal multicultural training, we may not think to provide education to families that come from culturally diverse backgrounds because we are not aware of how other cultures perceive the diagnosis. This could cause us to grow to become frustrated with families due to inconsistency in treatment or unwillingness to participate in treatment. Without having the knowledge about how this particular culture perceives ASD, we might assume that the family does not care about their child.

The Asian culture tends to view ASD as a cognitive deficit and individuals with this diagnosis are called "stupid" (Manghi, 2013). Having this viewpoint on the diagnosis may motivate a family to get academic services for their child rather than behavioral intervention. Manghi (2013) states that Asian families have a difficult time seeking services because, similar to Latino culture, it is considered shameful to have this diagnosis. This particular viewpoint and lack of education may hinder a child's opportunity to receive early intervention, for example. The Asian culture also believes that overt displays of emotion are considered shameful (Manghi, 2013). This is an example of a general Asian cultural belief that is not necessarily related to ASD. However, as we know, individuals with ASD may have a difficult time managing or expressing their emotions in a behaviorally appropriate manner. When this is an issue, we help individuals cope with their emotions in a way that is more behaviorally acceptable. Parents of a child from the Asian culture may not want their child to express any signs of emotion. Without any cultural training, we may perceive this to be a strange request due to our own cultural norms and beliefs. How would we know how to handle this situation in order to ensure the client's best interests?

Manghi (2013) provides several intervention tips when working with culturally diverse families of children with autism. First, it is important to gain an understanding of how the family defines autism. Upon assessing how they define and interpret autism, you should provide education of the disorder, including its diagnosis and treatment. Next, understand the family dynamic and if they feel they have a support system. Furthermore, if a support group is lacking, provide the family with information about local support groups that may be appropriate (i.e., church or school groups). Lastly, it is important for you as the clinician to develop all interventions that are culturally appropriate for each diverse family you will work with.

Conclusion

In summary, as behavior analysts we have a long way to go in terms of learning how to practice within a cultural lens that supports the clients we work with on a daily basis among the ASD community. There are much-needed training standards on diversity to be developed within our field for both graduate preparation programs and continuing education efforts to turn us from incompetent behavior analysts to those that become more culturally aware and sensitive to lead to cultural humility and eventually competency.

CASE STUDY 1

Picture this: you are a white, female behavior analyst who works in the home setting. You are assigned a new case and come to find out that the child you will be working with comes from a Muslim background. During your initial meeting with the family, you suspect some potential obstacles you may not be able to tackle. The child's father starts to question your credentials and experience as a behavior analyst. Through conversation, you learn that the parents are skeptical that you can carry out your work duties because you are a white female. Knowing this information, you feel uncomfortable that you will get parent buy-in with your programming for their child. You follow the ethics code (1.05c) and regrettably leave the case to someone who might be able to work effectively with this family.

CASE STUDY 2

Congratulations! You just passed the exam and finally can call yourself a BCBA®! You find a job within a school district and work for their ABA home program department. You role is to go into your assigned student's home, observe behaviors, run assessments, and interview parents about the goals they would like their child to accomplish under your supervision. Within the first few sessions, you notice your student engages in intense self-injurious behavior each time the therapist presents task demands. You decide the behavior is too intense to take baseline data and hold an emergency meeting with the parents to come up with an immediate intervention plan to reduce this dangerous behavior. The parents express they are not concerned about the self-injurious behavior (SIB), but instead would rather work on the student's motor and vocal stereotypy. Your training tells you to address the SIB since it is an extreme priority to keep your student safe. But the parents continue to insist the motor and vocal stereotypy is embarrassing to them, and their family – who recently visited from India – also made remarks that these repetitive behaviors make the child appear withdrawn from society. Upon learning this, you suspect a cultural boundary and want to respect the family's beliefs, but as a behavior analyst you must keep your priorities in line to address the SIB.

DISCUSSION QUESTIONS

For both case studies, apply these questions and answer them based upon the information provided.

1. As a behavior analyst, what would your next step be in handling each of these scenarios?
2. Which ethics codes could you potentially refer to when encountering these scenarios?
3. How might you resolve each of these situations while balancing the cultural needs of the clients and your professional/ethical obligations as a behavior analyst?

References

Autism Speaks Autism Treatment Network. (2014). *Demographic/diagnosis statistics.* Retrieved from http://asatn.org/node/223

Behavior Analyst Certification Board. (2019). *Professional and ethical compliance code for behavior analysts.* Retrieved from www.bacb.com/wp-content/uploads/BACB-Compliance-Code-english_190318.pdf

Bennett, A. (2012). *Parental involvement in early intervention programs for children with autism.* Unpublished master theses, St. Catherine University, St. Paul, MN.

Burkett, K., Morris, E., Manning-Courtney, P., Anthony, J., & Shambley-Ebron, D. (2015). African American families on autism diagnosis and treatment: The influence of culture. *Journal of Autism and Developmental Disorders, 45*(10), 3244–3254. https://doi.org/10.1007/s10803-015-2482-x.

Conners, B., Johnson, A., Duarte, J., Murriky, R., & Marks, K. (2019). Future directions of training and fieldwork of diversity issues in Applied Behavior Analysis. *Behavior Analysis in Practice*, *12*, 767–776. https://doi.org/10.1007/s40617-019-00349-2

Dyches, T. T., Wilder, L. K., Sudweeks, R. R., Obiakor, F. E., & Algozzine, B. (2004). Multicultural issues in autism. *Journal of Autism & Developmental Disorders*, *34*(2), 211–222.

Fong, E. H., Catagnus, R. M., Brodhead, M. T., Quigley, S., & Field, S. (2016). Developing the cultural awareness skills of behavior analysts. *Behavior Analysis Practice*, *9*(1), 84–94.

Hayes, S. C., & Plumb, J. C. (2007). Mindfulness from the bottom up: Providing an inductive framework for understanding mindfulness processes and their application to human suffering. *Psychological Inquiry*, *18*(4), 242–248. https://doi.org/10.1080/10478400701598314

Jibaja, M. L., Sebastian, R., Kingery, P., & Holcomb, J. D. (2000). The multicultural sensitivity of physician assistant students. *Journal of Allied Health*, *29*, 79–85.

Lillis, J., & Hayes, S. C. (2007). Applying acceptance, mindfulness, and values to the reduction of prejudice: A pilot study. *Behavior Modification*, *31*(4), 389–411.

Manghi, E. R. (2013). Multicultural challenges: Co-occurring Down syndrome and autism. In M. Froehlke, R. Zaborek, M. Foehlke, & R. Zaborek (Eds.), *When Down syndrome and autism intersect: A guide to DS-ASD for parents and professionals* (pp. 187–199). Bethesda, MD: Woodbine House.

Montgomery, W. (2001). Creating culturally responsive, inclusive classrooms. *Teaching Exceptional Children*, *33*(4), 4–9.

Randall-David, E. (1989). *Strategies for working with culturally diverse communities and clients*. Washington, DC: Association for the Care of Children's Health.

Skinner, B. F. (1971). *Beyond freedom and dignity*. New York: Alfred A. Knopf.

Skinner, B. F. (1974). *About behaviorism*. New York: Alfred A. Knopf.

Sugai, G., O'Keefe, B. V., & Fallon, L. M. (2012). A contextual consideration of culture and school wide positive behavior support. *Journal of Positive Behavior Interventions*, *14*(4). 197–208.

Tervalon, M., & Murray-Garcia, J. (1998). Cultural humility versus cultural competence; a critical distinction in defining physician training outcomes in multicultural education. *Journal of Health Care for the Poor and Underserved*, *9*(2), 117–125.

Tourinho, E. Z. (2006). Private stimuli, covert responses, and private events: Conceptual remarks. *The Behavior Analyst*, *29*(1), 13–31.

Vandenberghe, L. (2008). Culture-sensitive functional analytic psychotherapy. *The Behavior Analyst*, *31*(1), 67.

Zuckerman, K. E., Sinche, B., Mejia, A., Cobian, M., Becker, T., & Nicolaidis, C. (2014). Latino parents' perspectives on barriers to autism diagnosis. *Academic Pediatrics*, *14*(3), 301.

11

Creating a Culturally Competent Clinical Practice

Sara Gershfeld Litvak and Hanna Rue

Learning Objectives

- Describe the proposed standards for cultural competence in behavior analysis.
- Describe the influence of culture on ethical service delivery, professional development, and organizational considerations.
- State practices that behavior analysts in the position of organization leadership can engage in to increase cultural awareness and competence.

Today's behavioral organizations service more ethnically, socio-economically, and racially diverse individuals than ever before (Fong & Tanaka, 2013). Most applied behavior analysis (ABA) services are delivered in a tiered delivery model in which a behavior analyst provides clinical oversight to either an assistant behavior analyst or a behavior technician (Behavior Analyst Certification Board® [BACB®], 2014a, 2014b). This tiered model operates under the umbrella of a legal entity referred to as an ABA therapy organization. To better serve consumers from different cultures, the therapy provider must be aware of the patient experience and situations throughout the patient's lifecycle that can contribute to a more positive patient experience.

The patient lifecycle refers to the stages of a patient's therapeutic experience ranging from diagnosis to discharge. Although an ABA therapy organization often interacts with a patient through the lifecycle of their patient experience, few organizations understand the impact of each stage on patient satisfaction and outcome. In a behavioral practice, the patient lifecycle typically includes intake, billing, treatment planning, therapy delivery, caregiver training, coordination of care, and fading and discharge.

Who Are Our Patients?

Prior to understanding how to better serve our patients with cultural competence, we must understand who are represented as patients. It was once believed that autism spectrum disorder (ASD) occurred more frequently in upper-middle-class families (Bettelheim, 1967); however recent evidence indicates that the prevalence of individuals with ASD exists independent of race, ethnicity, country of origin, or economic status (Fombonne, 2007; Tincani, Travers, & Boutot, 2009). Although prevalence is the same, minorities are less likely to receive an early diagnosis of autism than Caucasian children (Mandell, Listerud, Levy, & Pinto-Martin, 2002; Mandell et al., 2009; Centers for Disease Control and Prevention, 2006). Minorities are also more likely to be misdiagnosed with another disorder such as attention-deficit/hyperactivity disorder (ADHD) during their initial visit (Mandell, Itlenbach, Levy, & Pinto-Martin, 2007). Patients with ASD belonging to minority populations often face a longer road toward diagnosis and access to services later in life. Independent of cultural background, each of these patients can and should receive culturally competent services.

The importance of the therapeutic relationship is one of the key factors of success when receiving therapy (Taylor, LeBlanc, & Nosik, 2018). The interaction with the clinical organization, not just the individual therapist, contributes to this therapeutic relationship. The National Center for Cultural Competence, Georgetown University, indicates a rationale for organizational cultural competence standards including improving the quality of services and outcomes to those served and eliminating long-standing disparities in the health status of people of diverse backgrounds (Goode, Jones, & Mason, 2002). The center states that providing services with a culturally competent lens is not just important for social justice, but also has implications on business sustainability. If an organization is questioning whether there is a need to enhance their cultural competence, the following provides benefits and goals of implementing standards for cultural competence.

First, organizations should respond to current and projected demographic changes in the United States to ensure long-term sustainability of their service model. As demographics change, organizations must adjust to the needs of the population around them. Not only will this help to eliminate long-standing disparities in the health status of people of diverse racial, ethnic, and cultural backgrounds, but it will help organizations gain a competitive edge in the marketplace. Second, many individuals with diverse background have a longer path to receiving medically necessary services. As such, expanding services to provide therapy with a culturally competent approach will ensure that these individuals are able to receive clinically sound services. Third, all health care organizations aim to impact the outcomes of their patients. Outcomes are greatly improved when an organization is able to meet the cultural and ethnic needs of the population they serve. Lastly, organizations should ensure they meet legislative, regulatory, and accreditation mandates regarding service equity (Health Research & Educational Trust, 2013). We will summarize some of the regulatory requirements related to providing culturally competent services. By addressing these needs, an organization will decrease the likelihood of liability and malpractice claims.

As noted previously, clients make contact with different staff members when receiving therapeutic services. At each point of contact, clients and their families should encounter well-informed staff members who are equipped to manage a variety of questions and situations. The purpose of this section is to provide details of how to implement culturally sensitive practices at each point of contact at the organizational level.

Intake

The intake process is designed to obtain basic information from the prospective patient or their family member. Key pieces of information discussed during intake include the type of services the patient is seeking, the presenting problem, identification of ongoing educational or mental health services, and how payment of services will be handled. Some organizations have an intake team dedicated to onboarding patients to receive services. Obtaining and transferring information accurately is vital to maintaining consistent care and preventing the patient from needlessly repeating information.

Initial contact with a prospective patient begins with a phone call or interaction with a website. Setting up access to multilingual options for the organization's telephone service and website assists in overcoming communication barriers at the outset. Imagine being in a country in which you are not fluent in the native language. Daily life can be a challenge. Now imagine attempting to obtain behavioral health care services for a loved one. All of these life stressors, combined with having to make phone calls to providers and browsing websites for reliable information, becomes stressful and daunting when language is a barrier.

Relationship building between the patient and the organization begins with the intake staff members. Intake staff members should be familiar with the surrounding community including racial and ethnic makeup, languages spoken, the various religions practiced, and information about the lesbian, gay, bisexual, and transgender (LGBT) populations. Learning how to manage inquiries from social workers, foster parents, and extended family members is also beneficial. Training may include information regarding the population makeup of the cities and counties in the area. This information can be obtained from city or county websites, the US Census Bureau website, or other local organizations serving diverse populations. Additionally, the US Census Bureau maintains information regarding languages spoken in homes at the state and county level. Consider maintaining an up-to-date list of community resources for linguistically diverse populations who may need assistance beyond what the ABA organization provides. If there are no clinicians who are competent to practice with a given population, clinical staff should be prepared to obtain consultation or refer to another organization.

Organizations receiving payment for services via Medicaid may be required to provide translation services to clients. The Office of Civil Rights of the Department of Health and Human Services developed federal regulations regarding translation services for individuals with limited English proficiency (LEP). These regulations are part of Section 1557, which is the civil rights provision of the Affordable Care Act (ACA) of 2010 (United States Department of Health and Human Services, 2010). Section 1557 provides protections for individuals with LEP by requiring organizations to take reasonable steps to provide a patient with access to translation services. Further, there are regulations requiring organizations that receive federal funds to post information regarding translation services in the top 15 languages identified in the state. Including this information in training regarding diverse populations is essential to ensure all staff members are adhering to federal regulations.

Training programs should result in a clinician obtaining a basic level of knowledge and putting that knowledge into action impacts patient outcomes. Self-assessment provides clinicians with an opportunity to reflect on beliefs and behaviors that may negatively impact their practice. The results of the self-assessment can guide clinicians in the development of self-monitoring strategies to support culturally sensitive clinical practice. For instance, if a self-assessment suggests that insensitive language is used with clients, a clinician may develop and practice new phrases to communicate with patients. These culturally sensitive phrases could be included in a self-monitoring checklist the clinician uses to achieve behavior change. Assessments published by the Substance Abuse and Mental Health Services Administration (2014) and the American Speech-Language-Hearing Association (ASHA, 2010) can be adapted for behavior analysts.

There are some data to support the notion of matching behavioral health care clinicians to clients in terms of cultural or linguistic similarities (e.g., Spanish speaking, Jewish, or American Indian) (Sue, 1998). That is not to say that clinicians are unable to provide effective behavior analytic services if they do not share the same culture. However, some families may request direct care staff or behavior analysts that share the same culture. Leaders at a clinical organization should be prepared to manage such requests and address family concerns. It may be that a better understanding of the family's needs and goals for therapy requires more time to develop a relationship with the direct care staff or behavior analyst.

Assessment

Assessment for ABA services can take many forms. Assessing behaviors that may lead to injury or property destruction typically include indirect methods (e.g., interview and checklists) and direct methods (e.g., observation and experimental functional analysis). Assessments for skill acquisition programs include criterion-based tools (e.g., the Verbal Behavior Milestones Assessment and Placement Program), norm-referenced measures (e.g., Vineland Adaptive Behavior Scales), and informally assessing for the presence/absence of skills. Understanding the impact of culture and language is necessary to complete and properly interpret assessment results.

For instance, consider clients from multilingual households. Assessment for skill acquisition programs may be a challenge as clients can demonstrate strengths when using one language, but not the other. For example, a young patient may be able to tact "shoe" in Hindi, but not in English. Lang et al. (2011) demonstrated that language (i.e., Spanish or English) used during discrete trial training impacted the percentage of correct responding and level of challenging behavior. Having multilingual staff and clinicians can overcome many barriers. If language is a barrier to treatment, clinicians may consider referring the family to an agency with multilingual clinical staff. According to the BACB® Professional and Ethical Compliance Code (2014b) guideline 2.01, behavior analysts are to only accept clients whose needs "are commensurate with the behavior analysts' education, training, experience, available resources, and organizational policies" (p. 6). There are situations in which multilingual clinical staff may not be available in the clients region of the country. If this is the case, guideline 2.01 states that a behavior analyst is to seek supervision or consultation from an appropriately trained clinician.

The initial assessment is the prime opportunity to have an open discussion regarding the family's values, preferences, customs, and expectations. Clinicians should use this opportunity to inform parents that an understanding of their family can better equip the clinician with information to design an effective treatment plan to meet their needs. Behavior analytic assessments typically include observation. Including notes of how family members interact with each other, names or nicknames used, and rituals around routines (e.g., eating or hygiene) can provide insight into the family's adherence to various cultural practices. For instance, consider possible differences between two families that emigrated from mainland China to the United States. One family may maintain many cultural traditions while the other family adopts more Western traditions. Limited information regarding traditions of the one family may severely impact the success of treatment for the patient. Further, it may be that multiple generations within one family adhere to cultural traditions differently. Expecting that all caregivers in a home with multiple generations can result in varying levels of implementation integrity, adjustments to a treatment plan may be necessary for different family members.

Assessment results, parental concerns, and clinical observation are used to inform the development of treatment goals. The BACB® Professional and Ethical Compliance Code (2014) is very clear in describing involvement of clients in treatment planning and obtaining consent for treatment. This information is outlined in guidelines 4.02, 4.03, and 4.04 (BACB®, 2014). Guideline 4.03 states that behavior analysts must individualize each behavior change program. This is where variables related to culture come into play. It may be that a Jewish family does not schedule treatment to occur on the Sabbath. Families from the Middle East, parts of India or Africa may forbid the use of the left hand at the dinner table as it is seen as unclean. Consider a situation in which direct care staff members are implementing self-feeding goals and prompting a child to use her left hand, but a grandmother in the home is blocking use of the left hand. It can be confusing for the staff members, the client, and the family.

Many ABA programs for young children with autism include goals that target social questions or questions about a patient's community. These questions can bring up sensitive topics if a family experienced loss, separation, or trauma. Regardless of a family's cultural background, it is important to review all information that will be targeted in such programs. Keep in mind that family members may face deportation, experience mental health issues related to adjusting to different social norms if emigrating from another country, or experience discord in the family as some members adhere to traditions differently.

Parent Training

There are numerous ABA studies highlighting the importance of parent training when treating a child with autism and other developmental disabilities (e.g., Hsieh, Wilder, & Abellon, 2011; Lafasakis & Sturmey, 2007; Najdowski et al., 2010; Reagon, & Higbee, 2009). The National Professional Development Center (NPDC) identified parent implemented interventions as an evidence-based practice (Wong et al., 2013). There are few studies in ABA that highlight patient or family culture as a variable to consider when designing or implementing behavior change programs. Fortunately, there is research available from related fields that may provide guidance in adapting ABA parent training and some examples provided in chapters in this book.

Buzhardt, Rusinko, Heitzman-Powell, Trevino-Maack, and McGrath (2016) described an innovative approach to providing training to Hispanic parents of children with autism. The authors adapted a parent-training model for Hispanic parents and outlined the adaptions that were made in five different areas (i.e., language, persons, content, methods, and context). The authors described one aspect of content modification that included use of the word *familismo* to encourage parents to teach strategies to other family members. The authors also provide suggestions regarding how to handle use of clinical terms in English that have no Spanish equivalent. Bernal, Jiménez-Chafey, and Domenech Rodríguez (2009) provide an in-depth discussion regarding cultural adaptations of evidence-based practices.

Behavior analysts designing parent-training programs are encouraged to consider the following variables:

1. The capacity of the parent to participate in a training program. Male and female family members may embrace different gender roles that are defined by their culture.
2. Disciplinary practices that may be influenced by cultural norms.
3. Educational and literacy deficits. Parents may not be able to access materials that are translated because of their inability to read.

Incorporating these considerations into an evidence-based training model provides a systematic way to approach parent training. Behavior skills training (BST) is often used in staff training programs but has been demonstrated as effective for parent training (Dogan et al., 2017; Harriage, Blair, & Miltenberger, 2016). BST includes providing instructions, modeling, rehearsal, and feedback to trainees (e.g., Ward-Horner & Sturmey, 2012). Each component of BST allows for an opportunity to individualize training to meet unique needs of parents and families. This includes use of language and gestures familiar to family members.

Fading and Discharge

Behavior analysts begin the discussion of fading and discharge at the start of the therapeutic relationship. During intake and assessment process, clinicians should review the contingencies regarding length of treatment and how discharge from treatment occurs. There are some funders of ABA services that require a discharge plan be outlined in each progress report submitted for reauthorization. The BACB® Ethical and Professional Compliance Code (2014) provides guidance regarding interruption (2.15) and discontinuation (4.11) of ABA services (BACB®, 2014).

Patients from diverse populations may find it challenging to identify community supports that are helpful after discontinuing ABA services. The clinician can assist the family in identifying community programs that are inclusive and supportive of diverse families. The community programs may provide a good opportunity for generalization training and social skills development for the patient. Working with the family on the timeline of the fading and discharge is critical for a smooth transition. Review key dates and provide supports such as calendars and checklists that can be recreated by the family after discharge from services. Finally, it is not unusual for patients to periodically require behavioral supports that can include consult to the family. Provide parents with information on how to access services in the future should the need arise.

Ethical and Professional Standards and Commitments to Diversity

Inherent in our work is that behavior analysts must function in accordance with the values, ethics and standards that govern our field. Cultural competence is as vital an asset for behavior analysts as scientific, technological, and clinical skills (Fong & Tanaka, 2013). Within the behavior analytic community, the following organizations have provided a framework for behavior analysts to consider regarding diversity and some provide resources and guidance on how to integrate these concepts into practice.

Association for Behavior Analysis International (ABAI)

Per their website, "ABAI seeks to be an organization comprised of people of different ages, races, nationalities, ethnic groups, sexual orientations, genders, classes, religions, abilities, and educational levels. ABAI opposes unfair discrimination." ABAI has also created a Culture and Diversity Special Interest Group (SIG). The goal of the SIG at ABAI is to "create a network of behavior analysts who speak a language or have a skill set relevant to a given population with people who need those services, as well as to connect behavior analysts with others who share common interests." (Culture and Diversity SIG, 2019). The SIG publishes and presents, mentors students, supports professional advancement, and improves service delivery. The SIG also advocates that diversity enhances our profession, benefits our community, and that culture is an important topic of research. Some efforts made by the SIG include creating awareness around the need to recruit more diverse, global professionals into our field; remove barriers to their education, success and advancement; and encourage diversity of thought, interdisciplinary expertise, and experience.

Behavior Analyst Certification Board® (BACB®)

The BACB® serves as the primary regulatory body for behavior analysts and provides several areas that behavior analysts should be attuned to related to cultural competence cited within the BACB's® Professional and Ethical Compliance Code (BACB®, 2014). A few of these areas are noted in Table 11.1.

Both code items refer to an individual behavior analyst's responsibility to ensure that they have received adequate training with the population they serve. When creating a culturally competent clinical practice, clinical leadership should ensure that their supervisory and clinical staff receive regular training regarding cultural differences and ensure that staff are matched appropriately based on competence.

Behavioral Health Center of Excellence® (BHCOE®)

BHCOE® serves as an accrediting body for behavioral organizations and provides guidance on several areas that organizations should be attuned to related to cultural competence cited within the BHCOE® Standards for Effective Applied Behavior Analysis Organizations (BHCOE®, 2019). A few of these areas are noted in Table 11.2.

All three standard items relate to an organization's responsibility to provide adequate training to staff to ensure clinical competence, including those areas related to cultural competence. The standards also indicate that an organization should make reasonable efforts to involve parents/guardians in treatment planning, which relates to an organization's responsibility to consider patient cultural preferences into their treatment program and planning. Lastly, all organizations accredited by BHCOE® are required to follow applicable federal, state, and local

TABLE 11.1 Select BACB® Professional and Ethical Compliance Code Items Related to Cultural Competence

BACB's® Professional and Ethical Compliance Code	
1.02 Boundaries of Competence	Behavior analysts should only provide services within the boundaries of their competence related to training, education and experience. Some considerations include working with new populations, including those populations that represent new cultural norms. It is recommended that individuals seek appropriate consultation from persons who are competent in those areas (BACB, 2019, p. 4).
1.05 (c) Professional and Scientific Relationships	Where differences of age, gender, race, culture, ethnicity, national origin, religion, sexual orientation, disability, language, or socioeconomic status significantly affect behavior analysts' work concerning particular individuals or groups, behavior analysts obtain the training, experience, consultation, and/ or supervision necessary to ensure the competence of their services, or they make appropriate referrals (BACB, 2019, p. 4).

TABLE 11.2 BHCOE® Standards for Effective Applied Behavior Analysis Organizations

1.05 Staff Hiring and Training	Participating organization provides training to ensure competency in clinical tasks (e.g., assessment processes, goal creation, intervention design, progress reporting, etc.) and administrative tasks (e.g., staff training, feedback delivery, BACB supervision standards, ethical billing practice, etc.).
3.04 Collaboration	Participating organization makes reasonable efforts to involve parents/guardians in training, participation and treatment planning.
4.09 Ethics and Consumer Protection	Participating organization obeys all applicable federal, state and local laws related to health, safety, and employment.

laws related to employment. For example, recently a federal judge recently ordered the Equal Employment Opportunity Commission (EEOC) to require affected employers to provide a revised version of the annual EEO-1 Report, which restores the gathering and reporting of certain compensation information (US Equal Employment Opportunity Commission, 2019). The implications of following these reporting requirements relates to compliance of organizations that employ 100 or more employees. The survey requires reporting employers to categorize company employment data by race/ethnicity, gender, and job category. Though laws are different regionally, organizations should be aware of changes that are occurring related to employment, as ignorance is not an adequate defense in the legal system.

Commitments to Diversity

It is recommended that all organizations have a statement related to the organization's commitment to diversity and inclusion. A diversity statement can range from one sentence to a few paragraphs. Diversity statements should be written at grade-level readability and avoid jargon or technical language. A diversity statement should also tie back to the organization's mission and be clear and specific. Table 11.3 provides examples of well-crafted diversity statements.

It is important to note that corporate diversity statements are promising, but an organization should ultimately be judged by their behaviors and systems to promote such diversity. A good way to check on whether diversity statements are translated into action relates to their ability to create an inclusive culture. Here are some suggestions for organizations to ensure diversity and cultural competency in their staff:

1. Ensure diverse hiring practices.
2. Match patient and therapeutic staff based on similar ethnic or cultural backgrounds.

3. Check for cultural competence of new staff during the interview/onboarding process.

4. Development and implement training related to cultural competence

5. Emphasize communication and relationship-building across multiple groups within your community.

6. Teach staff to engage in active listening.

7. Create sensitivity to language barriers or linguistic divisions.

8. Encourage sensitivity to issues like religion, customs, and etiquette.

9. Request feedback from your staff as they put training to use in their therapeutic environment to ensure validity of the training.

10. Implement additional coaching as needed.

TABLE 11.3 Sample Diversity Statement

Diversity Statement	Key Components
Google Headline: *Making progress on diversity, equity, and inclusion* Google's mission is to organize the world's information and make it universally accessible and useful. When we say we want to build for everyone, we mean everyone. To do that well, we need a workforce that's more representative of the users we serve. Google is committed to creating a diverse and inclusive workforce. Our employees thrive when we get this right. We aim to create a workplace that celebrates the diversity of our employees, customers, and users. We endeavor to build products that work for everyone by including perspectives from backgrounds that vary by race, ethnicity, social background, religion, gender, age, disability, sexual orientation, veteran status, and national origin. (Google Diversity, 2019).	• Relates to the organization's mission • Flesch-Kincaid Grade Level: 8.71
Salesforce Headline: We're greater when we're Equal Sub-headline: Together, we can reach Equality for all. Equality is a core value at Salesforce. We believe that businesses can be powerful platforms for social change and that our higher purpose is to drive Equality for all. Creating a culture of Equality isn't just the right thing to do, it's also the smart thing. Diverse companies are more innovative and better positioned to succeed in the Fourth Industrial Revolution. We strive to create workplaces that reflect the communities we serve and where everyone feels empowered to bring their full, authentic selves to work. There is more work to be done, but with the help of our entire Ohana – our employees, customers, partners, and community – we can achieve #EqualityForAll. (Salesforce Equality, 2019)	• Relates to organization's mission • Flesch-Kincaid Grade Level: 9.95

As a practitioner, it can be challenging to know whether an organization engages in practices that support diversity, inclusion, and cultural competence. Below are some questions that job-seekers can ask when looking for an organization that values diversity and inclusion:

1.   What efforts does your organization make to ensure a culturally sensitive workplace?
2.   Does your organization offer cultural competence training to employees?
3.   What are some of the difference cultures that your organization interacts with when providing therapeutic services?
4.   What do you do to ensure your staff are adequately prepared to work with different cultures?

Summary of Recommendations

Recommendations to ensure cultural competence focus on understanding the population served, ensuring a diverse workforce, and eliminating systemic barriers to patients receiving culturally competent care. In addition, organizations can ensure their staff members are culturally competent by enhancing training opportunities and self-identification of clinical competence. Leadership within ABA organizations may also consider activities such as journal clubs, a speaker series, or emails used to disseminate recent publications as mechanisms to share research regarding cultural diversity.

ABA organizations using the strategies discussed in this chapter can aid in our understanding of cultural sensitivity and competence in training and service delivery. There are numerous ways to measure the impact and outcomes of including cultural competence training for staff members. Social validity measures can capture trainee perception of specific elements related to cultural competence and guide the evolution of a training program. Social validity measures designed for parents can assess their perception of how clinicians and the organization respond to needs related to cultural and linguistic diversity. Direct observation provides insight into how intake and assessment methods change following training. Quality checklists applied to treatment plans and progress reports provide a means of measuring how training impacts how clinicians case conceptualization. Regional and national conferences and peer-reviewed publications provide a platform for sharing organizational endeavors to incorporate diversity training in ABA.

TABLE 11.4 Resources

Organization	Website
National Standards for Culturally and Linguistically Appropriate Services in Health and Health Care	https://thinkculturalhealth.hhs.gov/pdfs/EnhancedNationalCLASStandards.pdf
National Center for Cultural Competence, Georgetown University	https://nccc.georgetown.edu
US Census Bureau, Language Use	www.census.gov/topics/population/language-use/about.html
US Department of Health and Human Services, Office of Public Affairs	www.hhs.gov/ash/oah/resources-and-training/tpp-and-paf-resources/cultural-competence/index.html

CASE STUDY

Jumpstart for Kids is an organization providing behavior analytic services to children and adults with developmental disabilities. The founder and president of Jumpstart, Rachel, is a BCBA® with 10 years of experience in the field. Jumpstart is located just outside a city in the northeastern part of the United States. Rachel recently hired a newly minted BCBA®, Miriam, who is bilingual (English and Spanish) and interested in working with families from diverse populations. Rachel is thrilled at the opportunity to serve Spanish-speaking families. Miriam is assigned several new patients including one Spanish-speaking family, the Santos family. After several weeks, Rachel receives a call from Mrs. Santos requesting a change in BCBA®. Rachel requests a meeting with Mrs. Santos to better understand her concerns. It turns out that although Miriam is a great BCBA®, she is not fluent in the dialect of Spanish that the Santos family speaks. Miriam continuously prompts the wrong Spanish words during tacting programs, among other issues. Miriam is fluent in a Spanish dialect particular to Mexico and not the Dominican Republic. She did not take the time during the initial assessment to identify the family's country of origin or understand how the family communicates in both English and Spanish. Further, there was little information regarding the Santos family's language preferences gathered during the intake process.

Rachel decides this is a great opportunity to evaluate her organization's cultural sensitivity training. Rachel brings in a colleague with extensive experience as a consultant providing training to BCBA®s regarding culturally sensitive clinical practice. Training for clinicians begins with a review of the relevant BACB® Professional and Ethical Compliance Code including 1.02, Boundaries of Competence; 2.01 Accepting Clients; 3.01 Behavior-Analytic Assessment; and 4.02, Involving Clients in Planning and Consent, among other guidelines. The consultant has the clinicians review their self-assessment results and consider self-monitoring for any behaviors that may not align with culturally sensitive practice. In addition to working with clinicians, the consultant works with Rachel to support the intake, billing, and administrative staff in working with diverse populations. There is also a review of the Jumpstart's website and documents, which are revised to include more accessible language and are translated into the top three languages spoken in the region.

DISCUSSION QUESTIONS

1. Describe the barriers to accessing behavior analytic services that families from minority populations may face.

2. What can an ABA organization's leadership do on an organizational level to ensure diverse populations can access services?

3. Identify the organization's staff members in the case study who would likely benefit from training in cultural sensitivity.

4. How might a clinician ensure she is engaging in culturally sensitive behavioral assessment?

5. What are three BACB® Professional and Ethical Compliance Code guidelines that are relevant when considering service provision to diverse populations?

References

American Speech-Language-Hearing Association. (2010). *Cultural competence checklist: Personal reflection.* Retrieved from www.asha.org/uploadedFiles/Cultural-Competence-Checklist-Personal-Reflection.pdf.

Behavior Analyst Certification Board. (2014a). *Applied behavior analysis treatment of autism spectrum disorder: Practice guidelines for healthcare funders and mangers.* Littleton, CO: Author.

Behavior Analyst Certification Board. (2014b). *Professional and ethical compliance code for behavior analysts.* Littleton, CO: Author.

Behavioral Health Center of Excellence (2019). *BHCOE® standards for effective applied behavior analysis organizations.* Retrieved from: https://bhcoe.org/resources/code-of-effective-behavioral-organizations/

Bernal, G., Jiménez-Chafey, M. I., & Domenech Rodriguez, M. M. (2009). Cultural adaptations of treatments: A resource for considering culture in evidence-based practice. *Professional Psychology: Research and Practice, 40,* 361–368. https://doi.org/10.1037/a0016401

Bettelheim, B. (1967). *The empty fortress: Infantile autism and the birth of the self.* Oxford, UK: Free Press of Glencoe.

Buzhardt, J., Rusinko, L, Heitzman-Powell, L. Trevino-Maack, S., & McGrath, A. (2016). Exploratory evaluation and initial adaptation of a parent training program for Hispanic families of children with autism. *Family Process, 55,* 107–122. https://doi.org/10.1111/famp.12146

Centers for Disease Control and Prevention (CDC) (2006). *Mental health in the United States: parental report of diagnosed autism in children aged 4–17 years—United States, 2003–2004.* Retrieved from http://www.cdc.gov/

Culture and Diversity SIG. (2019, March 24). *Multicultural alliance of behavior analysts.* www.facebook.com/ Facebook Update Re: SIG. Retrieved from www.facebook.com/CultureandDiversitySIG/

Dogan, R. K., King, M. L., Fischetti, A. T., Lake, C. M., Mathews, T. L., & Warzak, W. J. (2017). Parent-implemented behavioral skills training of social skills. *Journal of Applied Behavior Analysis, 50,* 805–818.

Fombonne, E. (2007). Epidemiological surveys of pervasive developmental disorders. In *Autism and pervasive developmental disorders* (2nd ed., pp. 33–68). Cambridge: Cambridge University Press. https://doi.org/10.1017/CBO9780511544446.003

Fong, E. H., & Tanaka, S. (2013). Multicultural alliance of behavior analysis standards for cultural competence in behavior analysis. *International Journal of Behavioral Consultation and Therapy, 8,* 17–19.

Goode, T., Jones, W., & Mason, J. (2002). *A guide to planning and implementing cultural competence organization self-assessment.* Washington, DC: National Center for Cultural Competence, Georgetown University Child Development Center.

Google Diversity. (2019). Retrieved from https://diversity.google/

Harriage, B., Blair, K.S.C., & Miltenberger, R. (2016). An evaluation of a parent implemented in situ pedestrian safety skills intervention for individuals with autism. *Journal of Autism and Developmental Disorders, 46,* 2017–2027. https://doi.org/10.1007/s10803-016-2730-8

Health Research & Educational Trust. (2013, June). *Becoming a culturally competent health care organization.* Chicago, IL: Illinois. Health Research & Educational Trust. Retrieved from www.hpoe.org.

Hsieh, H. H., Wilder, D. A., & Abellon, O. E. (2011). The effects of training on caregiver implementation of incidental teaching. *Journal of Applied Behavior Analysis, 44*(1), 199–203. https://doi.org/10.1901/jaba.2011.44-199

Lafasakis, M., & Sturmey, P. (2007). Training parents implementation of discrete-trial teaching: Effects on generalization of parent teaching and child correct responding. *Journal of Applied Behavior Analysis, 40,* 685–689.

Lang, R., Rispoli, M., Sigafoos, J., Lancioni, G., Andrews, A., & Ortega, L. (2011). Effects of language of instruction on response accuracy and challenging behavior in a child with autism. *Journal of Behavioral Education, 20*(4), 252–259. http://doi.org/10.1007/s10864-011-9130-0

Mandell, D. S., Itlenbach, R. F., Levy, S. E., & Pinto-Martin, J. A. (2007). Disparities in diagnoses received prior to a diagnosis of autism spectrum disorder. *Journal of Autism and Developmental Disorders, 37*(9), 1795–1802. https://doi.org/10.1007/s10803-006-0314-8

Mandell, D. S., Listerud, J., Levy, S. E., & Pinto-Martin, J. A. (2002). Race differences in the age at diagnosis among Medicaid-eligible children with autism. *Journal of the American Academy of Child and Adolescent Psychiatry, 41*(12), 1447–1253. https://doi.org/10.1097/00004583-200212000-00016

Mandell, D. S., Wiggins, L. D., Carpenter, L. A., Daniels, J., DiGuiseppi, C., Durkin, M. S. . . . Kirby, R. S. (2009). Racial/ethnic disparities in the identification of children with autism spectrum disorders. *American Journal of Public Health, 99*(3), 493–498. https://doi.org/10.2105/AJPH.2007.131243

Najdowski, A. C., Wallace, M. D., Reagon, K., Penrod, B., Higbee, T. S., & Tarbox, J. (2010). Utilizing a home based parent training approach in the treatment of food selectivity. *Behavioral Interventions, 25*(2), 89–107. http://doi.org/10.1002/bin.298

Reagon, K. A., & Higbee, T. S. (2009). Parent-implemented script fading to promote play-based verbal initiations in children with autism. *Journal of Applied Behavior Analysis, 42*(3), 659–664. https://doi.org/10.1901/jaba.2009.42-659

Salesforce Equality. (2019). Retrieved from www.salesforce.com/company/equality/

Substance Abuse and Mental Health Services Administration. (2014). *Improving cultural competence.* Treatment Improvement Protocol (TIP) Series No. 59. HHS Publication No. (SMA) 14–4849. Rockville, MD: Substance Abuse and Mental Health Services Administration.

Sue, S. (1998). In search of cultural competence in psychotherapy and counseling. *American Psychologist, 53*(4), 440–448. http://doi.org/10.1037/0003-066X.53.4.440

Taylor, B. A., LeBlanc, L. A., & Nosik, M. R. (2018). Compassionate care in behavior analytic treatment: Can outcomes be enhanced by attending to relationships with caregivers? *Behavior Analysis in Practice.* https://doi.org/10.1007/s40617-018-00289-3

Tincani, M., Travers, J., & Boutot, A. (2009). Race, culture, and autism spectrum disorder: Understanding the role of diversity in successful educational interventions. *Research & Practice for Persons with Severe Disabilities, 34,* 81–90.

United States Department of Health and Human Services. (2010). *Patient Protection and Affordable Care Act, 42 U.S.C. § 18001 et seq.* Retrieved from www.hhs.gov/civil-rights/for-individuals/section-1557/index.html

United States Equal Employment Opportunity Commission (2019, October). *Fact sheet for EEO-1 Survey Filers.* Retrieved from www.eeoc.gov/employers/eeo1survey/fact_sheet_filers.cfm

Ward-Horner, J., & Sturmey, P. (2012). Component analysis of behavior skills training in functional analysis. *Behavioral Interventions, 27,* 75–92. https://doi.org/10.1002/bin.1339

Wong, C., Odom, S. L., Hume, K. Cox, A. W., Fettig, A., Kucharczyk, S. . . . Schultz, T. R. (2013). *Evidence-based practices for children, youth, and young adults with Autism Spectrum Disorder.* Chapel Hill, NC: The University of North Carolina, Frank Porter Graham Child Development Institute, Autism Evidence-Based Practice Review Group.

12

Cultural Accommodations in Caregiver Training

Juliana Aguilar and Casey J. Clay

Learning Objectives

- Understand the commonalities between behavior analytic caregiver trainings and manualized caregiver trainings in the field of psychology.
- Evaluate the history and effects of cultural accommodations on manualized caregiver trainings.
- Identify the current research in ABA on cultural accommodations to caregiver trainings.
- Understand professional ethical standards in regards to cultural accommodations and review best practices to stay in compliance with those standards.

Caregiver Training

The term "caregiver" can refer to biological or adopted parents, extended family members, or legal guardians of an individual who provide direct care for an individual ("Caregiver," n.d.). Caregivers are teachers for children across the lifetime. For children to receive applied behavior analysis (ABA) interventions in all contexts and environments, caregivers need to be trained in these procedures. The literature on training caregivers to implement behavior analytic procedures can be traced back to the 1960s (Engelin, Knutson, Laughy, & Garlington, 1968; Russo, 1964; Straughan, 1964; Wahler, Winkel, Peterson, & Morrison, 1965). In these early studies, modeling and reinforcement were used to train mothers on behavior analytic procedures. In 1979, Forehand et al. used instructions, modeling, rehearsal, and feedback to successfully train a mother on behavior analytic procedures. Training packages containing instructions, modeling, rehearsal, and feedback are now recognized as behavioral skills training (BST; Miltenberger, 2012). In the past two decades BST has been implemented with caregivers to train behavior analytic procedures such as reinforcement and redirection of problem behavior (Sawyer, Crosland, Miltenberger, & Rone, 2015), guided compliance or three-step prompting (Drifke,

Tiger, & Wierzba, 2017; Miles & Wilder, 2009), discrete trial instruction (Lafasakis & Sturmey, 2007; Ward-Horner & Sturmey, 2008), food selectivity interventions (Seiverling, Williams, Sturmey, & Hart, 2012), incidental teaching (Hsieh, Wilder, & Abellon, 2011), functional assessment and intervention planning (Shayne & Miltenberger, 2013), and functional analysis procedures (Ward-Horner & Sturmey, 2012).

Caregiver training is equally important to other related fields. The California Evidence-Based Clearinghouse for Child Welfare Parent Training Programs (2006) has listed the following caregiver training programs: Parent-Child Interaction Therapy (PCIT), The Incredible Years (IY), and Parent Management Training–Oregon Model (PMTO) with the highest scientific rating: "well-supported by research evidence" (defined by the strength of the evidence published in peer-reviewed journals). As part of these caregiver training programs (i.e., PMTO, PCIT, and IY), clinicians implement similar training components present in BST by providing caregivers with instructions (e.g., verbal rationale, didactic trainings, or written manuals); modeling (e.g., in-vivo role plays or video vignettes); rehearsals (role play with therapists or live practice with child); and corrective and positive feedback (e.g., bug-in-ear systems, direct observational feedback, or feedback on completed assignments) (Kaminski, Valle, Filine, & Boyle, 2008; Martinez & Eddy, 2005; Pearl, 2009; Postorino et al., 2017).

These caregiver training programs are based on behavior analytic theories developed by B. F. Skinner (Pearl, 2009). For example, in the 1950s multiple research groups in the United States generated a set of core principles for the current caregiver training programs (including PMTO, IY, and PCIT): (1) caregivers should serve as treatment agents, (2) caregivers learn to track and collect data on observable behavior, and (3) caregivers utilize positive reinforcement and mild negative sanctions as contingency management to discourage problem behavior (Dishion, Forgatch, Chamberlain, & Pelham, 2016). Kaminski and colleagues (2008) defined two aspects commonly found within caregiver training programs that are behavior analytic in nature. One variable in the parent training programs is disciplinary communication; this requires the parents to provide children with "clear and developmentally appropriate directions; setting limits and rules; stating behavioral expectations and consequences" (Kaminski et al., 2008, p. 575). They also defined discipline and behavior management as including "examining specific reinforcement and punishment techniques: e.g. planned ignoring, positive reinforcement, and time out" (Kaminski et al., 2008, p. 575). Pearl (2009) reported a similar finding, stating that while an explicit analysis of the maintaining variables of disruptive behavior is not discussed, they do focus on the behavior establishing and maintaining principles of reinforcement.

The research on caregiver training programs extends back decades. The literature demonstrates an increase in appropriate caregiver behavior as well as a clinically significant decrease in disruptive behaviors, especially compared with waitlist or no treatment control groups once caregiver trainings are implemented (Pearl, 2009). However, researchers failed to report specific participant demographics, such as ethnicity (Kaminski et al., 2008; Ortiz & Del Vecchio, 2013), which makes it difficult to assess the significance of these trainings with specific cultural groups. With limited information on specific results and limitations based on minority families, there could be cultural influences shaping the effectiveness of these interventions.

Cultural Effects on Caregiver Training

B. F. Skinner (1981) defined culture as a process of operant conditioning working together with natural selection. Culture evolves when an individual's specific behaviors contact reinforcement and are maintained and strengthened and those behaviors contribute to the success of the group (Skinner, 1981). It becomes that the success of the group, not the immediate contact of reinforcement for the individual, is responsible for the evolving culture (Skinner, 1981). Exploring the cultural contingencies affecting family units with whom behavior analysts interact is important to assist in identifying socially significant behaviors and treatments. When developing treatment protocols there is merit to defining cultural preferences, which could be referred to as conditioned reinforcers, as they are stimuli that have gained their value by being paired with primary reinforcers over the individual's lifetime (Fong, Catagnus, Brodhead, Quigley, & Field, 2016). Examination of cultural preferences through cultural accommodations is needed to produce evidence-based parent training interventions. Cultural accommodations can include access to language services such as an interpreter, translated materials, or bilingual staff, as well as a focus on determining culturally relevant content for training

Caregiver training interventions have been shown to be successful in training caregivers to implement antecedent and consequence management strategies. However, caregiver training interventions reflecting the goals and values of the majority culture could clash with the cultural contingencies that guide parenting values of ethnic minority parents (Forehand & Kotchick, 1996). It is important to remember that individuals belong to many different cultural groups and that different contingencies can maintain behaviors in a family. Each family unit contains individuals who are contacting contingencies in many environments. Caregivers build cultural contingencies within the home but may also contact contingencies tied to a dominant culture in a work and social environment. Children encounter the cultural contingencies maintained by their caregivers in their home environment but also contact the contingencies of the dominant culture in their educational and social settings. Some of the questions that should be evaluated are (1) How are problem behaviors defined across groups? (2) Is the intervention/parenting skill being trained acceptable to the parenting style of the parent? (3) Do children respond in the same way to parent behaviors (reinforcement, time out, etc.) across groups? Due to the concerns expressed above, a large line of research has evolved evaluating the potential effects of cultural accommodations on manualized caregiver training programs such as the PCIT, PMTO, and IY.

Accommodations in Manualized Therapies

There have been three major frameworks for developing and implementing cultural accommodations when examining the manualized trainings of PCIT, IY, and PMTO. The first two frameworks for exploring cultural accommodations involves the selection of the content and type of cultural accommodation; the third addresses the process in which those accommodations are developed and implemented (Baumann et al., 2015). The Ecological Validity Model

(EVM) by Bernal, Bonilla, and Bellido (1995) and the Cultural Sensitivity Framework (CSF) developed by Resnicow, Soler, Braithwaite, Ahluwalia, and Butler (2000) deal with content selection of cultural accommodations. The third framework, the Cultural Adaptation Process Model (CAPM) was developed by Domenech-Rodriguez and Wieling and colleagues (2004; Domenech-Rodriguez and colleagues, 2012) and describes the process by which to complete cultural accommodations. It starts with including all players of interest to discuss the literature and the needs of the community. The process continues with implementing, measuring, and reviewing the initial adaptations and ends with a tailored intervention (see Table 12.1).

Multiple reviews have been conducted on the effects of culturally accommodated caregiver training in psychotherapies (Baumann et al., 2015; Van Mourik et al., 2017). One review compared caregiver programs with deep sensitivity accommodations, surface sensitivity accommodations, and programs with no accommodations (Van Mourik et al., 2017). Their primary dependent variable was changes in parenting behavior, with a secondary dependent

TABLE 12.1 Major Frameworks for Developing and Implementing Cultural Accommodations

Model	Description	Studies	Relevant findings
EVM; Bernal et al. (1995)	Considers eight dimensions when creating a culturally sensitive treatment: (1) language, (2) persons, (3) metaphors, (4) content, (5) concepts, (6) goals, (7) methods, and (8) context	Domenech-Rodriguez, Bauman, and Schwartz (2011); Domenech-Rodriguez and Wieling (2004); Matos, Bauermeister, and Bernal (2009); Matos, Torres, Santiago, Jurado, and Rodriguez (2006)	Effective PMTO and PCIT caregiver trainings have been adapted using the eight domains considered by the EVM.
Cultural Sensitivity Framework (CSF); Resnicow et al. (2000)	Levels of CS: (1) "Surface accommodations." At this level, accommodations may include matching materials and messages utilized during treatment to a groups/individual's language, geographical location, or physical appearance. (2) "Deep accommodations". These types of accommodations can include elements of common behavioral practices within that group's culture.	Martinez and Eddy (2005); Matos et al. (2006); Matos et al. (2009); Van Mourik, Crone, de Wolff, and Reis (2017)	Review compared caregiver programs with deep sensitivity accommodations, surface sensitivity accommodations, and programs with no accommodations. Overall, researchers found a small, but significant, difference between intervention and comparison groups.

Model	Description	Studies	Relevant findings
Cultural Adaptation Process Model (CAPM); Domenech-Rodriguez and Bernal (2012); Domenech-Rodriguez and Wieling (2004)	Three phases: (1) setting the stage, (2) initial adaptations, and (3) adaptation iterations	Parra-Cardona, Bybee, Sullivan, Domenech-Rodriguez, Dates, Tams, and Bernal (2017); Cardona et al. (2012); Domenech-Rodríguez et al. (2011); Matos et al. (2006); Matos et al., 2009; McCabe and Yeh (2009); McCabe, Yeh, Garland, Lau, and Chavez (2005); McCabe, Yeh, Lau, and Argote (2012)	The CAPM may not be directly cited in the accommodation process; however, similar features can be seen across the caregiver training literature: (1) expert review of the current literature; (2) inclusion of a community advisory board or the use of focus groups; (3) request input from cultural and context expert; (4) direct observation and data collection of initial accommodations; and (5) continued assessment and accommodation of the intervention.

variable exploring the changes in parental perceptions and child psychosocial behavior. Overall researchers found a small but significant difference between intervention and comparison groups. Also, there was a small difference between groups favoring the intervention group when examining child behavior outcomes. Interestingly, the greatest effect noted was for deep-level accommodations. Researchers noted that few of the studies reported guidelines on how choices were made regarding accommodations, and which stakeholders were involved in the accommodation process (Van Mourik et al., 2017). These findings led to the importance of the CAPM, which suggests a process for developing and implementing cultural accommodations.

Some studies of adapted caregiver training did not specify their process in developing or implementing cultural accommodations, nor did they specifically describe what their accommodations were, which made identifying frameworks difficult. However, the overwhelming results show that evidenced-based caregiver training programs such as the PMTO, PCIT, and IY can be successfully accommodated for caregivers of many backgrounds. When compared to a no-intervention control group, the gains were significant using a culturally adapted caregiver training program (Gross et al., 2009; Martinez & Eddy, 2005; Matos et al., 2006, 2009). However, when comparing manualized caregiver trainings (i.e., PCIT) to a culturally accommodated version of that training (i.e., GANA), there were no significant differences noted on any measure of parent or child behavior (McCabe et al., 2012; McCabe & Yeh, 2009).

While there is some potential evidence that cultural accommodations may not be a fundamental element in effective caregiver training with psychotherapies, there is still significant research that needs to be completed before any conclusions can be drawn. Lau (2006) discovered that trying to manualize strategies for culturally framed caregiver training was overly prescriptive and denied the provider the ability to be flexible in addressing heterogeneity within cultures. Examining how cultural accommodations impact a more individualized process of caregiver training could provide alternative results. Behavior analytic caregiver training techniques, such as BST (i.e. instructions, modeling, rehearsal, and feedback) can be the individualized treatment where cultural accommodations may be more effective.

Cultural Accommodations to Caregiver Training in ABA

Referencing the cultural accommodations to caregiver training literature in psychotherapies can give us a foundation on how to examine our own evidence-based practices and provide appropriate adaptations to our clients. Some aspects of caregiver training are specific to ABA and must be considered when reviewing the literature from related fields. It is important to note that ABA treatments should be individualized (Behavior Analyst Certification Board® [BACB®], 2016). As discussed previously, adapted caregiver trainings were found to be effective when the adaptations were attempted on an individual family basis instead of as an overall manualized treatment (Lau, 2006; McCabe et al., 2005). However, limited research has been conducted on cultural accommodations through ABA methodology. The basic mechanics of the caregiver training have a foundation in the BST model of instructions, modeling, rehearsal, and feedback. Therefore, parallels can be drawn and studies have been conducting involving these components.

A pilot study conducted by Buzhardt, Rusinko, Heitzman-Powell, Trevino-Maack, and McGrath (2016) evaluated cultural accommodations implemented with an online-based caregiver-training program known as the Online and Applied System for Intervention Skills (OASIS). The OASIS was originally found to be effective at training caregivers in ABA techniques with children with ASD living in remote areas (Heitzman-Powell, Buzhardt, Rusinko, & Miller, 2013). The web-based training consists of instruction paired with live coaching and feedback completed through web-based videoconferencing. The web-based modules allow for assessment of the caregiver's knowledge of ABA procedures and techniques, while the videoconferencing allows for rehearsal and immediate feedback for the caregiver and their child. The study evaluated if there were differences in knowledge and skill acquisition between a Hispanic, Spanish-speaking participant and other English-speaking participants completing the online-based training. The only accommodation offered by researchers was the addition of an interpreter for all training sessions. Researchers found that while the Spanish-speaking participant was able to reach mastery criterion in the knowledge assessments, it required several attempts and there were limitations in her skill acquisition (i.e., the participant was not able to meet mastery criterion during the live coaching sessions). The Spanish-speaking participant was in training for 36 weeks in comparison to 15–25 weeks averaged by the English-speaking participants (Buzhardt et al., 2016).

To revise and accommodate the program for Hispanic families, a focus group that consisted of Hispanic caregivers, Hispanic educators, and family service providers were asked to provide suggestions on the types of cultural accommodations that may further benefit Hispanic participants (Buzhardt et al., 2016). While not yet evaluated, the research team will implement the following changes to the OASIS-H (Hispanic) Parent Training Program: (1) translate all trainee materials and coach scripts into Spanish, (2) use a bilingual coach rather than an interpreter during coaching sessions, (3) encourage parents to promote the strategies among their extended family, and (4) include extended family into the training.

This preliminary evaluation of the OASIS with a Hispanic family provided the field with two important findings (Buzhardt et al., 2016). The first being that a Hispanic caregiver was able to benefit from the original core concepts of the intervention with the simple addition of an interpreter. The second finding is that while there was improvement in knowledge scores (after multiple attempts), larger gains were made by the non-Hispanic participants in a shorter amount of time. ABA researchers have also explored the need and effectiveness of cultural accommodations on a more individualized treatment style.

Garcia, Bloom, Campos, and Bell (2018) developed and evaluated the Culturally-Adapted Response Evaluation Survey (CARES) to assist in the development and implementation of cultural accommodations. The survey is a structured interview tool that assists practitioners in obtaining culturally relevant information about participants and their families specifically for the implementation of functional communication training (FCT; for discussion see Tiger, Hanley, & Bruzek, 2008). FCT is a "differential reinforcement procedure in which an individual is taught an alternative response (i.e., functional communication response [FCR]) that results in the same class of reinforcement identified as the maintaining problem behavior" (Tiger et al., 2008, p. 16).

The CARES is administered in two parts. The first part of the survey addresses what type of FCR the caregiver finds most appropriate. The second part of the survey assesses caregiver's acceptability of the FCR. Prior to implementation, the survey was evaluated by experts (behavior analysis faculty and doctoral students with at least one year or more of Board Certified Behavior Analyst® (BCBA®) certification and at least one year or more of implementing functional communication training). Once refined by experts, CARES was implemented with three children with a diagnosis of autism whose caregivers identified as Latino (Garcia et al., 2018). Caregivers were seeking assistance with the management of challenging behavior, and researchers planned to implement FCT as a part of treatment. Two FCRs were selected for evaluation: one was a standard functional communication response (S-FCR) and the second was a culturally adapted functional communication response (C-FCR), which was selected using the CARES. Both the standard and culturally adapted FCT led to a significant reduction in challenging behavior and an effective increase in the FCR. However, post-FCT caregivers were presented with choice sessions in which they selected the FCR they preferred to use during treatment. When provided with the option, caregivers selected the C-FCR. While the cultural accommodation did not result in a significant difference across the effectiveness of the intervention, there was an effect noted in the social validity (parent selection) of the intervention.

Accommodations to a caregiver training program at a university-based autism clinic have also been examined (Aguilar, 2018). In this study, three parent-child dyads were trained in the implementation of behavior analytic techniques such as differential reinforcement, FCT, BST, and guided compliance, through the components of BST. All three parents had requested an interpreter be present during all medical treatment in the university health care system, and they reported their primary language as Spanish. Interpreter services were provided through an interpreter-based videoconferencing system where an interpreter was contacted via a third-party contractor and was connected with the clinician and the caregivers in the clinic setting via a video call. All parties were able to communicate via audio and had real-time visual feeds of each other. During the training each parent was initially provided written instructions that were reviewed in English and translated via the video-based interpreter system. The parents were then asked to implement the behavior analytic technique; first, with a confederate who was instructed to make errors and demonstrate challenging behavior, and second, with their child in the clinic setting. Once a stable baseline of performance was reached, clinicians implemented BST in English via the video-based interpreter system to train the behavior analytic skills selected for each participant. Five sessions of BST in English were programmed for each caregiver in this phase. If they were unable to reach mastery criterion within the five session video-based training period, then BST was provided in Spanish by a bilingual clinician with translated materials. This phase was implemented until the participants demonstrated mastery of the skill. Researchers found caregivers were able to reach mastery criterion for most of the skills with the use of an interpreter, however for all three caregivers during at least one behavior analytic skill (varied across dyads), BST in Spanish was necessary to reach mastery criterion.

Researchers also gathered data on preference for the different training arrangements. One participant reported a high level of proficiency in English and Spanish, while two of the participants reported a high level of proficiency only in Spanish. Two of the three participants reported preference for BST in Spanish, while one participant showed no preference for English or Spanish BST. The level of language proficiency matched the preferred training method. This study also demonstrates that for most behavior analytic skills trained, having an interpreter present (surface accommodation) may be sufficient in training a behavior analytic technique. However, there may be a preference for receiving that treatment in their dominant language, thus affecting the social validity of the treatment.

While not specifically developed for behavior analysis or evaluated in the field, the Culturally Informed Functional Assessment (CIFA) interview is an open-ended assessment and treatment interview that could be beneficial for providers working with caregivers (Tanaka-Matsumi, Seiden, & Lam, 1996). The CIFA was originally developed for use to inform cognitive behavioral treatment as a means to assist providers in defining challenging behavior accurately and demonstrate respect for the client's culture. The CIFA is an instrument to assist clinicians in comparing and contrasting the values and points of view of the client, family, culture, and the clinician's own biases to arrive at solutions that are acceptable to all parties.

It guides providers and caregivers through culturally accepted norms for the role of the target behavior, culturally relevant definition of target behaviors, expectations regarding intervention, and culturally sanctioned change agents (Tanaka-Matsumi et al., 1996). Researchers use the CIFA to evaluate the cultural match or mismatch between client and provider and to determine the need for an interpreter or cultural consultant. The CIFA requires family/cultural informants to assess cultural meanings of problems and to what extent such behaviors are deviant in terms of excesses and deficits.

The second portion of the interview addresses the assessment of challenging behavior. It focuses on causal explanations and examining behaviors considering cultural norms. This portion of the interview assists the clinician in familiarizing themselves with the cultural variables that will provide them with a normative baseline followed by the completion of a functional assessment (Tanaka-Matsumi et al., 1996). Once a hypothesis is reached, the clinician compares the results with the client's explanation of the problem. Clinician and client synthesize their views on the (1) definitions of terminology, (2) causation, and (3) the decision about whether to apply a specific label to the problem.

The final phase of the interview is the treatment plan. The interview guides the creation of culturally acceptable treatment goals, target behaviors, change agents, and techniques. The CIFA allows interventionists to explore the acceptability and consequences of data collection with the client and family. The structure of treatment duration, course, and expected outcome is discussed. The clinician and client/family must come to a mutual agreement upon the course of action. If this is accomplished, then an ethical and acceptable treatment is in place and the interview is complete. As mentioned previously, while this has not been evaluated in the field of behavior analysis, it is a useful framework for addressing the issues of culture in an individualized treatment setting.

Cultural Accommodations and Professional Ethics

The BACB® has laid out a code that dictates professional and ethical behavior. While this code does not directly address issues of cultural accommodations, there are some important features of culture addressed in the code. In code 1.02, Boundaries of Competence, the BACB® states:

(a) All behavior analysts provide services, teach, and conduct research only within the boundaries of their competence, defined as being commensurate with their education, training, and supervised experience.

(b) Behavior analysts provide services, teach, or conduct research in new areas (e.g., populations, techniques, behaviors) only after first undertaking appropriate study, training, supervision, and/or consultation from persons who are competent in those areas.

(BACB®, 2016, p. 4)

Beaulieu, Addington, and Almeida (2018) surveyed BCBAs on the amount of training they received on working with people from diverse backgrounds. They additionally assessed whether those BCBAs thought the training was relevant, how competent they personally felt on the topic, and their utilization of accommodations for different populations (Beaulieu et al., 2018).

Beaulieu and colleagues (2018) reported low levels of exposure and training to cultural content, which may create situations where behavior analysts are acting outside their scope of competence. This could lead to poor results in the assessment and intervention of individuals and have negative effects on the practitioner (Brodhead, Quigley, & Wilczynski, 2018). According to the Multicultural Alliance of Behavior Analysis, now called the Culture and Diversity Special Interest Group, cultural competency can be included within this ethical standard (Fong & Tanaka, 2013).

Fong and Tanaka (2013) listed the following as imperative to the demonstration of cultural competency: (1) self-awareness of BCBAs'[®] own personal, cultural values, beliefs and potential biases, (2) cross-cultural application – the use of appropriate culturally sensitive methodological approaches, skills, and techniques, (3) awareness of personal and professional limitations, (4) provide and advocate for the dissemination of behavior analytic information in the client's dominant language, and (5) make the appropriate referrals when needed. Code 1.05: Professional and Scientific Relationships refers to cultural competency in subsections (d) and (e), which address the dangers of lacking awareness of your personal biases and conflicts. These sections state that behavior analysts will not engage in discrimination or harassment of any groups based on age, gender, race, culture, ethnicity, national origin, religion, sexual orientation, disability, language, socioeconomic status, or any basis proscribed by law. In section (f), the BACB[®] states the following: "Behavior analysts recognize that their personal problems and conflicts may interfere with their effectiveness. Behavior analysts refrain from providing services when their personal circumstances may compromise delivering services to the best of their abilities" (BACB[®], 2016, p. 5). The initial step in complying with this code is to have awareness of your individual biases.

In an equally important section of code 1.05: Professional and Scientific Relationships, section (b) states: "when behavior analysts provide behavior-analytic services, they use language that is fully understandable to the recipient of those services while remaining conceptually systematic with the profession of behavior analysis" (BACB[®], 2016, p. 5). Fong, Ficklin, and Lee (2017) cite the National Standards on Culturally and Linguistically Appropriate Services (CLAS) standards for providing culturally and linguistically appropriate treatment. Among these standards is the need to offer and provide language assistance services, including bilingual staff and interpreter services at no cost to the client. This expectation is for both verbal and written communication. As part of the proposed cultural competence standards for behavior analysis, Fong and colleagues (2017) provided the recommendation of "Language Diversity," which states: "Behavior Analysts shall seek to provide or advocate for the provision of information, referrals, and services in the language appropriate to the client, which may include the use of interpreters" (p. 4). All of the research described in this article included an accommodation regarding language services (i.e. interpreter services, translation services, or bilingual staff).

There has been a string of legislation over the past 50 years that has focused on the inclusion of language access in health care settings (Chen, Youdelman, & Brooks, 2007). Title VI of the Civil Rights Act of 1964 states that no person can be excluded from participation in, be denied the benefits of, or be subjected to discrimination under any program or activity receiving federal financial assistance (Title 42, 2019). Under this legislation, language access is included under "national origin" and "federal financial assistance" including funding such as Medicaid, SCHIP, and Medicare payment, National Institute of Health grants, and Centers for Disease Control and Prevention monies (Chen et al., 2007). While it is federally mandated to provide language access services, it is not mandated that Medicaid fund this service (Medicaid, n.d.). To bridge the gap between services and funding, states have implemented language-based legislation (Chen et al., 2007). The inclusionary requirements of state legislation vary based on condition, language, and institution (Chen et al., 2007). It is behavior analysts' responsibility to be familiar with their federal and state mandates regarding language access services for their organizations. It is also their duty to advocate for language assistance services for clients with limited English proficiency and their families to stay in compliance with their professional and ethical standards.

Outside of cultural competence and language-access services, cultural accommodations are necessary for the inclusion of behavior analysts' clients and their families in treatment goal setting, planning, and implementation. Codes 4.02: Involving Clients in Planning and Consent, 4.03: Individualized Behavior-Change Programs, and 4.07: Environmental Conditions that Interfere with Implementation all focus on the idea of individualization, including families in the treatment development program, and to examine potential barriers to the success of that treatment (BACB®, 2016). One barrier is lacking cultural competency, which can prevent behavior analysts from recognizing their own biases and limiting awareness of potential cultural conflicts. Methods to prevent behavior analysts' personal biases are discussed in this chapter and can assist in the development of appropriate cultural accommodations.

Best Practice Recommendations

Previous findings demonstrated the potential for limitations in skill demonstration and extended training lengths if caregivers are not receiving sufficient cultural accommodations (Buzhardt et al., 2016). Other recent research reports potential limitations in caregivers' acceptance of standard models of caregiver training without cultural accommodations (Aguilar2018; Garcia et al., 2018). Therefore, it seems researchers and practitioners need to increase social validity.

Social validity was defined by Wolf (1978) as social significance and acceptability of interventions with different communities and populations. He described three aspects of social validity: (1) social significance of treatment goals, (2) acceptability of treatment procedures, and (3) assessing the significance of the effects of treatment (Wolf, 1978). There are many ways to utilize the principals of ABA in accordance with our professional and ethical codes to increase our effectiveness in both treatment outcomes and social validity. Adding cultural accommodations may be an additional avenue that behavior analysts can explore to increase the level of social validity in behavior analytic treatments.

Cultural competency in its simplest form is recognizing one's cultural identity (Fong, Catagnus, Brodhead, Quigley, & Field, 2016). Recognizing one's cultural identity equates to recognizing distinguishable stimulus and response classes regarding one's "values, preferences, characteristics, and circumstances and how those differ from others" (Fong et al., 2017, p. 3). Recognition of one's cultural identity can assist in avoidance of unintentional biased perceptions or disregard for other's cultural beliefs (Fong et al., 2017). It is important to avoid biases and place emphasis on client's cultural beliefs to increase the social validity of our treatments, but also because it is required in our professional and ethical codes.

Fong et al. (2016, 2017) describe methods to obtain cultural competence. To increase cultural awareness Fong and colleagues recommended self-assessments to evaluate your current level of cultural competency. They recommended creating professional networks in which cultural and diversity issues can be discussed and feedback can be received are another useful tool in growing cultural competence (Fong et al., 2016). Attending and participating in cultural trainings as part of educational and professional development could serve to develop cultural competence (Fong et al., 2016, 2017). Developing cultural competency can assist in meeting ethical standard 1.02 by developing that personal awareness of biases and building the skills to address and evaluate social validity with new populations.

Language accommodations are the most commonly used form of cultural accommodations and are often mandated by law. In the previously mentioned survey provided to BCBAs®, most respondents reported rarely or never interpreted materials for clients whose second language was English, but often used an interpreter for treatment (Beaulieu et al., 2018). In caregiver training previously described in this chapter, language accommodations involved considering the caregivers' literacy level (Matos et al., 2006; McCabe et al., 2005) and accommodations for the caregivers' dominant language, including the use of bilingual staff/ practitioners (Aguilar, 2018; Brotman et al., 2011; Buzhardt et al., 2016; Cardona et al., 2012; Domenech-Rodriguez & Wieling, 2004, Domenech-Rodriguez et al., 2011, 2012; Garcia et al., 2018; Gross et al., 2003, 2009; Martinez & Eddy, 2005; Matos et al., 2006, 2009; McCabe et al., 2005; McCabe et al., 2012; McCabe & Yeh, 2009). Lacking these basic accommodations is not only a danger to the quality of treatment being provided but also to the legality of the services being provided. Therefore, behavior analysts must include these language accommodations.

While not evaluated in the field of ABA, the cultural accommodations frameworks of the EVM, CSF, and CAPM could be explored and evaluated in single-subject design literature. Some features of these frameworks have been successfully utilized in the ABA literature. Buzhardt and colleagues (2016) implemented focus groups and community advisory boards in order to develop their cultural accommodations. Garcia and colleagues (2018) utilized a culturally aimed survey to develop a culturally sensitive functional communication response.

Culturally aimed surveys, such as the CIFA and the CARES, allow you to include the family in the development of the treatment goals and treatment plan and to receive information from those most competent in the cultural contingencies maintaining their behavior. Finally, data collection and the evaluation of progress throughout the intervention and communication with caregivers and clients throughout the process is necessary to continuously evaluate the need for cultural accommodations.

Discussion and Future Directions

The research in the field of ABA on cultural accommodations in the area of caregiver training is sparse. However, we have a vast amount of literature to reference in evidence-based psychotherapies such as PCIT, PMTO, and IY. The similarities between the implementation of these manualized caregiver trainings and the common training packages implemented in ABA provide for a point of reference between these two fields. While neither field has found significant effect differences between standard interventions and those interventions with cultural accommodations, ABA researchers have noted differences when assessing social validity. Additional research is required to make any definitive conclusions about the importance of cultural accommodations to caregiver training.

Future researchers can examine some of the frameworks (e.g., EVM, CSF, and CAPM) used to culturally accommodate manualized caregiver trainings in individualized behavior analytic investigations. Pieces of these frameworks are already being utilized in ABA using interpreters, bilingual staff, and the translation of materials. However, we can continue to explore the differences between surface and deep accommodations (i.e. translating materials versus including specific cultural content). Also, in ABA we have the potential to utilize the EVM and CAPM since our clients are our cultural experts. Through repeated measures we are pilot testing and repeatedly tailoring our interventions as treatment progresses.

In conclusion, behavior analysts need to begin considering where, when, and how to make cultural accommodations to treatments to adhere to the BACB® professional and ethical standards, the Multicultural Alliance of BCBAs® Cultural Competency Standards, and federal and state legislation. To ensure that behavior analysts are providing the most effective and socially valid treatment available to our clients, behavior analysts must explore their own biases through cultural competency training and look to our clients and their families for guidance, as they are the cultural experts of their learning histories. It is imperative that behavior analysts involve their clients in the development of interventions under a culturally sensitive framework. Most importantly, behavior analysts must track behavior through data, analyze interventions based on that information, and convey this information in a way that clients from different backgrounds would be able to understand, process, and become involved in the treatment process.

CASE STUDY

As a behavior analyst you began a caregiver training intervention with a family of a preschool child with a diagnosis of autism. You know the family has had to communicate with your clinic through an extended family member to schedule the initial appointment and fill out all new patient paperwork.

Prior to this appointment you have received very little contact with cultural awareness training. It was not part of your master's program and you have not contacted any continuing education opportunities on the topic.

DISCUSSION QUESTIONS

1. What are some steps you can take before meeting with the family to increase your competence (code 1.02) in working with a family from a different background?

2. Should the family rely on an extended family member to provide all language access services for your care?

3. When conducting the initial consultation with the family, what are some tools you can use to facilitate a culturally competent interview?

4. What is an evidence-based package that can be used to train caregivers and families to implement behavior analytic techniques?

References

Aguilar, J. (2018). *The effects of culturally-based accommodations on behavioral skills training.* Master's thesis. Retrieved from ProQuest Dissertations & Theses Global database. (UMI No. 13850732).

Baumann, A. A., Powell, B. J., Kohl, P. L., Tabak, R. G., Penalba, V., Proctor, E. K. . . . Cabassa, L. J. (2015). Cultural adaptation and implementation of evidence-based parent-training: A systematic review and critique of guiding evidence. *Children and Youth Services Review, 53,* 113–120. https://doi.org/10.1016/j.childyouth.2015.03.025

Beaulieu, L., Addington, J., & Almeida, D. (2018). Behavior analysts' training and practices regarding cultural diversity: The case for culturally competent care. *Behavior Analysis in Practice, 12*(3), 557–575. https://doi.org/10.1007/s40617-018-00313-6

Behavior Analyst Certification Board. (2016). *Professional and ethical compliance code for behavior analysts.* Retrieved from www.bacb.com/wp-content/uploads/BACB-Compliance-Code-english_190318.pdf.

Bernal, G., Bonilla, J., & Bellido, C. (1995). Ecological validity and cultural sensitivity for outcome research: Issues for the cultural adaptation and development of psychosocial treatments with Hispanics. *Journal of Abnormal Child Psychology, 23*(1), 67–82. http://doi.org/10.1007/bf01447045

Brodhead, M. T., Quigley, S. P., & Wilczynski, S. M. (2018). A call for discussion about scope of competence in Behavior Analysis. *Behavior Analysis in Practice, 11*(4), 424–435. https://doi.org/10.1007/s40617-018-00303-8

Brotman, L. M., Calzada, E., Huang, K.-Y., Kingston, S., Dawson-McClure, S., Kamboukos, D., . . . Petkova, E. (2011). Promoting effective parenting practices and preventing child behavior problems in school among ethnically diverse families from underserved, urban communities. *Child Development, 82*(1), 258–276. https://doi.org/10.1111/j.1467-8624.2010.01554.x

Buzhardt, J., Rusinko, L., Heitzman-Powell, L., Trevino-Maack, S., & McGrath, A. (2016). Exploratory evaluation and initial adaptation of a parent training program for Hispanic families of children with autism. *Family Process, 55*(1), 107–122. https://doi.org/10.1111/famp.12146

California Evidence-Based Clearinghouse for Child Welfare. (2006). *Parent training programs that address behavior problems in children and adolescents.* Retrieved October 27, 2019, from www.cebc4cw.org/topic/parent-training-programs-behavior-problems/

Cardona, J.R.P., Domenech-Rodriguez, M., Forgatch, M., Sullivan, C., Bybee, D. . . . Bernal, G. (2012). Culturally adapting an evidence-based parenting intervention for Latino immigrants: The need to integrate fidelity and cultural relevance. *Family Process, 51*(1), 56–72. https://doi.org/10.1111/j.1545-5300.2012.01386.x

Caregiver. (n.d.). *Merriam Webster Online.* Retrieved October 27, 2019, from www.merriam-webster.com/dictionary/caregiver?utm_campaign=sd&utm_medium=serp&utm_source=jsonld#other-words

Chen, A. H., Youdelman, M. K., & Brooks, J. (2007). The legal framework for language access in healthcare settings: Title VI and beyond. *Journal of General Internal Medicine, 22*(Suppl 2), 362–367. https://doi.org/10.1007/s11606-007-0366-2

Dishion, T., Forgatch, M., Chamberlain, P., & Pelham III, W. E. (2016). The Oregon Model of behavior family therapy: From intervention design to promoting large-scale system change. *Behavior Therapy, 47*(6), 812–837. https://doi.org/10.1016/j.beth.2016.02.002

Domenech-Rodríguez, M. M., Baumann, A. A., & Schwartz, A. L. (2011). Cultural adaptation of an evidence based intervention: From theory to practice in a Latino/a community context. *American Journal of Community Psychology, 47*(1–2), 170–186. https://doi.org/10.1007/s10464-010-9371-4

Domenech-Rodriguez, M. M., Bernal, G., & Guillermo, B. (2012). Frameworks, models, and guidelines for cultural adaptation. In *Cultural adaptations: Tools for evidence-based practice with diverse populations* (pp. 23–44). Washington, DC: American Psychological Association.

Domenech-Rodríguez, M. M., & Wieling, E. (2004). Developing culturally appropriate evidence based treatments for interventions with ethnic minority populations. In M. Rastogi & E. Wieling (Eds.), *Voices of color: First person accounts of ethnic minority therapists* (pp. 313–333). Thousand Oaks, CA: Sage Publications.

Drifke, M. A., Tiger, J. H., & Wierzba, B. C. (2017). Using behavioral skills training to teach parents to implement three-step prompting: A component analysis and generalization assessment. *Learning and Motivation, 57*, 1–14. https://doi.org/10.1016/j.lmot.2016.12.001

Engelin, R., Knutson, J., Laughy, L., & Garlington, W. (1968). Behaviour modification techniques applied to a family unit: A case study. *Journal of Child Psychology and Psychiatry, 9*(3–4), 245–252. https://doi.org/10.1111/j.1469-7610.1968.tb02226.x

Fong, E. H., Catagnus, R. M., Brodhead, M. T., Quigley, S., & Field, S. (2016). Developing the cultural awareness skills of behavior analysis. *Behavior Analysis Practice, 9*(1), 84–94. https://doi.org/10.1007/s40617-016-0111-6

Fong, E. H., Ficklin, S., & Lee, Y. H. (2017). Increasing cultural understanding and diversity in applied behavior analysis. *Behavior Analysis: Research and Practice, 17*(2), 103–113. https://doi.org/10.1037/bar0000076.

Fong, E. H., & Tanaka, S. (2013). Multicultural alliance of behavior analysis standards for cultural competence in behavior analysis. *International Journal of Behavior Consultation and Therapy, 8*(2), 17–19. http://doi/org/10.1037/h0100970

Forehand, R., & Kotchick, B. A. (1996). Cultural diversity: A wake-up call for parent training. *Behavior Therapy, 27*(2), 187–206. https://doi.org/10.1016/S0005-7894(96)80014-1

Forehand, R., Sturgis, E. T., McMahon, R. J., Aguar, D., Green, K., Wells, K. C., & Breiner, J. (1979). Parent behavioral training to modify child noncompliance: Treatment generalization across time and from home to school. *Behavior Modification, 3*(1), 3–25. https://doi.org/10.1177/014544557931001

Garcia, A. R., Bloom, S.E., Campos, C., & Bell, M. C. (2018, May). *A cultural adaptation of functional communication training.* Paper presented at the meeting of Association for Behavior Analysis International 43rd Conference, San Diego, CA.

Gross, D., Fogg, L., Webster-Stratton, C., Garvey, C., Julion, W., & Grady, J. (2003). Parent training of toddlers in day care in low-income urban communities. *Journal of Consulting and Clinical Psychology, 71*(2), 261–278.

Gross, D., Garvey, C., Julion, W., Fogg, L., Tucker, S., & Mokros, H. (2009). Efficacy of the Chicago Parent Program with Low-Income African American and Latino Parents of Young Children. *Prevention Science, 10*(1), 54–65.

Heitzman-Powell L. S., Buzhardt, J., Rusinko, L. C., Miller, & T. M. (2013). Formative evaluation of an ABA outreach training program for parents of children with autism in remote areas. *Focus on Autism and Other Developmental Disabilities, 29*(1), 23–38. https://doi.org/10.1177/1088357613504992

Hsieh, H.-H., Wilder, D. A., & Abellon, O. E. (2011). The effects of training on caregiver implementation of incidental teaching. *Journal of Applied Behavior Analysis, 44*(1), 199–203. https://doi.org/10.1901/jaba.2011.44-199

Kaminski, J. W., Valle, L. A., Filene, J. H., & Boyle, C. L. (2008). A meta-analytic review of components associated with parent training program effectiveness. *Journal of Abnormal Child Psychology, 36*(4), 567–589. https://doi.org/10.1007/s10802-007-9201-9

Lafasakis, M., & Sturmey, P. (2007). Training parent implementation of discrete-trial teaching: Effects on generalization of parent teaching and child correct responding. *Journal of Applied Behavior Analysis, 40*(4), 685–689. https://doi.org/10.1901/jaba.2007.685-689

Lau, A. S. (2006). Making the case for selective and directed cultural adaptations of evidence-based treatments: Examples from parent training. *Clinical Psychology: Science and Practice, 13*(4), 295–310. https://doi.org/10.1111/j.1468-2850.2006.00042.x

Martinez Jr., C. R., & Eddy, J. M. (2005). Effects of culturally adapted parent management training on Latino youth behavioral health outcomes. *Journal of Consulting and Clinical Psychology, 73*(5), 841–851. https://doi.org/10.1037/0022-006X.73.5.841

Matos, M., Bauermeister, J. J., & Bernal, G. (2009). Parent-child interaction therapy for Puerto Rican preschool children with ADHD and behavior problems: A pilot efficacy study. *Family Process, 48*(2), 232–252. https://doi.org/10.1111/j.1545-5300.2009.01279.x

Matos, M., Torres, R., Santiago, R., Jurado, M., & Rodriguez, I. (2006). Adaptation of parent-child interaction therapy for Puerto Rican families: A preliminary study. *Family Process, 45*(2), 205–222. https://doi.org/10.1111/j.1545-5300.2006.00091.x

McCabe, K. M., & Yeh, M. (2009). Parent-child interaction therapy for Mexican Americans: A randomized clinical trial. *Journal of Clinical Child and Adolescent Psychology: The Official Journal for the Society of Clinical Child and Adolescent Psychology, American Psychological Association, Division 53, 38*(5), 753–759. https://doi.org/10.1080/15374410903103544

McCabe, K. M., Yeh, M., Garland, A. F., Lau, A. S., & Chavez, G. (2005). The GANA program: A tailoring approach to adapting parent child interaction therapy for Mexican Americans. *Education and Treatment of Children, 28*(2), 111–129.

McCabe, K. M., Yeh, M., Lau, A., & Argote, C. B. (2012). Parent-child interaction therapy for Mexican Americans: Results of a pilot randomized clinical trial at follow-up. *Behavior Therapy, 43*(3), 606–618. https://doi.org/10.1016/j.beth.2011.11.001

Medicaid (n.d.). *Translation and interpretation services.* Retrieved from https://www.medicaid.gov/medicaid/financial-management/medicaid-administrative-claiming/translation-and-interpretation-services/index.html

Miles, N. I., & Wilder, D. A. (2009). The effects of behavioral skills training on caregiver implementation of guided compliance. *Journal of Applied Behavior Analysis, 42*(2), 405–410. https://doi.org/10.1901/jaba.2009.42-405

Miltenberger, R. G. (2012). *Behavior modification: Principles and procedures* (5th ed.). Belmont, CA: Wadsworth, Cengage Learning.

Ortiz, C., & Del Vecchio, T. (2013). Cultural diversity: Do we need a new wake-up call for parent training? *Behavior Therapy, 44*(3), 443–458. https://doi.org/10.1016/j.beth.2013.03.009

Parra-Cardona, J. R., Bybee, D., Sullivan, C. M., Rodriguez, M. M. D., Dates, B., Tams, L., & Bernal, G. (2017). Examining the impact of differential cultural adaptation with Latina/o immigrants exposed to adapted parent training interventions. *Journal of Consulting and Clinical Psychology, 85*(1), 58–71. https://doi.org/10.1037/ccp0000160

Pearl, E. S. (2009). Parent management training for reducing oppositional and aggressive behavior in preschoolers. *Aggression and Violent Behavior, 14*(5), 295–305. https://doi.org/10.1016/j.avb.2009.03.007

Postorino, V., Sharp, W. G., McCracken, C. E., Bearss, K., Burrell, T. L., Evans, A. N., & Scahill, L. (2017). A systematic review and meta-analysis of parent training for disruptive behavior in children with Autism Spectrum Disorder. *Clinical Child and Family Psychology Review, 20*(4), 391–402. https://doi.org/10.1007/s10567-017-0237-2

Resnicow, K., Soler, R., Braithwaite, R. L., Ahluwalia, J. S., & Butler, J. (2000). Cultural sensitivity in substance use prevention: Bridging the gap between research and practice in community-based substance abuse prevention. *Journal of Community Psychology, 28*(3), 271–290. https://doi.org/10.1002/(SICI)1520-6629(200005)28:3<271::AID-JCOP4>3.0.CO;2-I

Russo, S. (1964). Adaptations in behavioral therapy with children. *Behavior Research and Therapy, 2*(1), 43–47. https://doi.org/10.1016/0005-7967(64)90054-3

Sawyer, M. R., Crosland, K. A., Miltenberger, R. G., & Rone, A. B. (2015). Using behavioral skills training to promote the generalization of parenting skills to problematic routines. *Child & Family Behavior Therapy, 37*(4), 261–284. https://doi.org/10.1080/07317107.2015.1071971

Seiverling, L., Williams, K., Sturmey, P., & Hart, S. (2012). Effects of behavioral skills training on parental treatment of children's food selectivity. *Journal of Applied Behavior Analysis, 45*(1), 197–203. https://doi.org/10.1901/jaba.2012.45-197

Shayne, R., & Miltenberger, R. G. (2013). Evaluation of behavioral skills training for teaching functional assessment and treatment selection skills to parents. *Behavioral Interventions, 28*(1), 4–21. https://doi.org/10.1002/bin.1350

Skinner, B. F. (1981). Selection by consequences. *Science*, *213*(4507), 501–504.

Straughan, J. H. (1964). Treatment with child and mother in playroom. *Behaviour Research and Therapy*, *2*(1), 37–41. https://doi.org/10.1016/0005-7967(64)90053-1

Tanaka-Matsumi, J., Seiden, D. Y., & Lam, K. N. (1996). The culturally informed functional assessment (CIFA) interview: A strategy for cross cultural behavioral practice. *Cognitive and Behavioral Practice*, *3*(2), 215–233. https://doi.org/10.1016/S1077-7229(96)80015-0.

Tiger, J. H., Hanley, G. P., & Bruzek, J. (2008). Functional communication training: A review and practical guide. *Behavior Analysis and Practice*, *1*(1), 16–23. https://doi.org/10.1007/BF03391716

Title 42 – *The public health and welfare*. Retrieved from www.govinfo.gov/content/pkg/USCODE-2010-title42/pdf/USCODE-2010-title42-chap21-subchapV.pdf

Van Mourik, K., Crone, M. R., de Wolff, M. S., & Reis, R. (2017). Parent training programs for ethnic minorities: A meta-analysis of adaptations and effect. *Prevention Science*, *18*(1), 95–105. https://doi.org/10.1007/s11121-016-0733-5

Wahler, R. G., Winkel, G. H., Peterson, R. F., & Morrison, D. C. (1965). Mothers as behavior therapists for their own children. *Behaviour Research and Therapy*, *3*(2), 113–124. https://doi.org/10.1016/0005-7967(65)90015-X

Ward-Horner, J., & Sturmey, P. (2008). The effects of general-case training and behavioral skills training on the generalization of parents' use of discrete-trial teaching, child correct responses, and child maladaptive behavior. *Behavioral Interventions*, *23*(4), 271–284. https://doi.org/10.1002/bin.268

Ward-Horner, J., & Sturmey, P. (2012). Component analysis of behavior skills training in functional analysis. *Behavioral Interventions*, *27*(2), 75–92. https://doi.org/10.1002/bin.1339

Wolf, M. M. (1978). Social validity: The case for subjective measurement or how applied behavior analysis is finding its heart. *Journal of Applied Behavior Analysis*, *11*(2), 203–214. https://doi.org/10.1901/jaba.1978.11-203

13

Accounting for Cultural Differences to Make Parent Training More Socially Significant

Adriana Rodriguez and April Michele Williams

Learning Objectives

- Readers will name positive effects of parent training.
- Readers will identify ways to increase parents' engagement in therapy.
- Readers will identify ways to become more culturally aware.
- Readers will list ethical consideration when working with Latin American families.

Introduction

Many researchers have found positive effects of parent training regarding the details of behavior analytic procedures being implemented with their children (Koegel, Bimbela, & Schreibman, 1996; McConachie & Diggle, 2007; Sanders & Glynn, 1981). In some types of interventions, such as for the acquisition of social and communication skills, behavior analysts should collaborate with parents because they spend the most time with their children and therefore can affect more meaningful change (Meadan, Ostrosky, Zaghlawan, & Yu, 2009). The importance of parent training is not limited to social and communication behavior change programs, however. For example, Marcus, Swanson, and Vollmer (2001) evaluated the relation between parents' behavior and changes in the behavior of four children diagnosed with developmental disabilities. Results indicated that, when parent training was provided as part of behavior analytic interventions implemented for the reduction of problem behaviors, the child's behavior improved as a function of the parent's performance improving. A benefit that is secondary to the increased improvement in the child's behavior, but certainly no less important, is the reduction of stress reported by parents who have received training on their child's behavior analytic programs (Koegel et al., 1996).

Despite the research demonstrating the benefits of parent training when working with children who have developmental disabilities and are receiving ABA therapy, the success of parent-conducted behavioral procedures depends greatly on the ability of the parents or caregivers to integrate those interventions into the context in which problem behavior occurs (Moes & Frea, 2002). In addition, the engagement of parents in treatment depends on the context of therapy and the therapist's ability to communicate with the parents effectively. It has been suggested that engagement in therapy might be higher if the therapist is able to understand the client's history, culture, values, and sociopolitical orientation (Bernal & Flores-Ortiz, 1982). Therefore, making sure the programs selected by the therapist align with the parents' values and culture could potentially be of great benefit for the success of interventions. Because of the necessity of cultural alignment, in this chapter we focus on parent training that is designed specifically to be conducted with Latin American families. More directly, we focus on adapting behavior analytic interventions for these families when they are from a different background than the behavior analyst. Next, a case study will be described along with the ethical considerations when providing services to parents from Latin American countries. Finally, more general recommendations as to how to become a culturally aware behavior analyst will be provided.

Throughout this chapter, we use the term "Latinx" to refer to people born in any Latin American country, including Brazil. More specifically, we use the term "Hispanic" to refer people from countries within Latin America with Spanish as their native language.

Description of Intersection of Diversity Issues and Clinical Subject Area

Practitioners of ABA implement behavior analytic interventions to solve problems of social significance (Baer, Wolf, & Risley, 1968). Socially significant behaviors targeted for change include anything that would facilitate the individual's independence and adaptation to their environment (e.g., communicating wants and needs effectively to parents, teachers, and friends). Behavior analysts accomplish this by manipulating environmental variables to ameliorate existing skills deficits (e.g., using words to communicate with others) and, in conjunction, reduce the likelihood of behaviors that may otherwise interfere with those new skills (e.g., tantrums as a mode of communication). By understanding the importance of culture, behavior analysts can ensure the specific goals selected for those behavior change interventions (such as the language that is taught) are aligned with their clients' cultural values and are considered socially significant by parents, teachers, and anyone else in the child's environment.

Cultural differences have been cited by previous researchers regarding how family and professional relationships are viewed, how business is conducted, and how culture affects and shapes our behavior overall (Wood & Eagly, 2002). Over 35 years ago, Skinner (1981) raised the importance of developing a knowledge of people's cultural values, preferences, characteristics, and circumstances for understanding their behavior. This is beneficial not only for clients but for society as well, because socially important goals for diverse populations can only be achieved when the behavior analyst is aware of the importance of cultural influences on behavior (Fong, Catagnus, Brodhead, Quigley, & Field, 2016).

As the discipline of ABA continues to mature, behavior analysts are beginning to emulate more long-standing professions, such as psychology (American Psychological Association, 2017) and social work (National Association of Social Workers, 2003), in stressing the importance of identifying cultural differences between professionals and the families they serve. For example, Moes and Frea (2002) evaluated specific variables pertaining to family context (e.g., the family's values, culture, and social interaction). Specifically, they incorporated family context into individualizing functional communication training (FCT; Carr & Durand, 1985) treatment packages. Three families of children with autism participated in the study in a multiple-baseline design across participants. First, participants were studied under a baseline condition in which each child was observed over the course of two separate household routines previously selected by the parents. No feedback was provided to the parents during this initial phase.

Following the baseline condition, the behavior analyst and the parents discussed teaching appropriate means of communication as an alternative to their child's maladaptive behavior. Next, parent training began with the parents first selecting their child's target communication response and then being taught to implement the FCT treatment package based on one of the routines identified during the initial interview. After that training session, the FCT phase was initiated. During this phase, one to two training sessions were conducted each week with each family. During the FCT treatment package, parents were asked to provide relevant information about the family's context (i.e., how they organized and constructed daily routines). Based on the parents' responses, modifications were made to the existing FCT protocols to ensure contextualization of the FCT treatment package. Results indicated that FCT can be adapted to incorporate the individual needs of families. Results also indicated that adaptation to an existing FCT protocol does not compromise the efficacy of standardized behavioral intervention. In a social validity assessment, the researchers asked the parents who participated in this study to rate the sustainability of the intervention packages (i.e., standard FCT and contextualized FCT). Parents reported they preferred the contextualized FCT more than they preferred the standard FCT. In other words, the parents stated they were more likely to use the FCT protocol that was in line with their daily routine than an arbitrary one (Moes & Frea, 2002).

Clinical Applications

There are three factors that make it more likely that all behavior analysts in America will eventually serve individuals from another part of the world. The first is the projected growth for the profession of ABA, in which the number of advertised positions for Board Certified Behavior Analysts® increased by 127% from 2017 to 2018 (Burning Glass Technologies, 2019). The second is an expected continuing influx in immigrants (particularly from Latin American countries) to the United States (Colby & Ortman, 2014). Finally, when you add in the rapidly increasing rates of autism spectrum disorders (Centers for Disease Control and Prevention, 2019), the area in which over 60% of behavior analysts work (Association for Professional Behavior Analysts, 2014), all three factors combined makes it more likely that most behavior analysts in America will eventually serve individuals from another part of the world. Cultural awareness, therefore, becomes even more important than in the past and is something that we have to make sure we address. In this section, we will discuss research that has been conducted with Hispanic families in the field of ABA to provide examples of how cultural awareness can be incorporated when providing services to Hispanic families.

Buzhardt, Rusinko, Heitzman-Powell, Trevino-Maack, and McGrath (2016) evaluated and adapted the Online and Applied System for Intervention Skills (OASIS), an evidence-based training program for parents of children with autism. They sought to determine if adaptations to this program were necessary when training Hispanic parents. Four families (one Hispanic, the others non-Hispanic) participated in this study. An interpreter was used during assessments and coaching sessions for the Hispanic family (one of the adaptions of the program). Results showed that, based on pre- to post-test knowledge assessment, the Hispanic mother had a greater knowledge gain than the non-Hispanic parents. However, the Hispanic mother scored lower compared to the non-Hispanic parents when measuring skill mastery gains, and the training for the Hispanic parents took longer than training for the non-Hispanic parents. Overall, this research demonstrated that an adaptation of a parent training protocol for Hispanic parents can be beneficial when teaching parents ABA interventions.

Rodriguez (2018) also assessed the effects of incorporating variables related to families' culture into a behavior analytic intervention (specifically FCT). In addition, Rodriguez evaluated parents' preference for interventions by incorporating a choice phase. Three mother–child dyads were included in this study. The children were 5 years old and had been attending an early intervention clinic for at least one year prior. Two of the mothers were from Puerto Rico and one was from Mexico. All mothers' English comprehension was very limited. Prior to the beginning of the experiment, a pairwise functional analysis was conducted to verify the children's maintaining variables for problem behaviors. Afterward, a task analysis of the appropriate FCT protocol was given to each mother, both in English and Spanish, based on their child's identified maintaining consequence. A nonconcurrent multiple-baseline across participants with an embedded alternating-treatments design was used in the experiment to evaluate parent training effectiveness and child's behavior. The experiment was divided into four phases. First, baseline measurements were taken. Second, the FCT protocol was taught to the mothers using behavioral skills training with a confederate (i.e., an adult who acted as the child). Third, in situ training was implemented with each child. Finally, a choice phase was implemented to identify the mothers' language preferences (i.e., English or Spanish) to be used to deliver the protocol. Results indicated that, once the mothers were trained on the implementation of protocols, they were able to correctly implement FCT regardless of the language used. This study also showed that the implementation of FCT reduced each child's problem behaviors.

Kuhn et al. (2019) also culturally adapted an evidence-based intervention and then applied it to a group transition program for Hispanic families of youth with ASD. For the first goal of the research, adapting an evidence-based intervention, Kuhn et al. (2019) analyzed a nine-step process to identify possible cultural adaptations to the intervention. The steps consisted of:

1. Identifying the need and interest of the families involved in the experiment.
2. Creating a community partnership to learn about the characteristic of families being served.
3. Conducting a literature review to identify beliefs and values that are common to Hispanic families and how these values affect behavior.
4. Creating or translating and adapting the curriculum of the intervention being used for this research.
5. Obtaining feedback from community partners on the new culturally adapted intervention.
6. Making changes based on the feedback provided by the community partners.
7. Implementing the culturally adapted program with the Transitioning Together (TT) program, designed to increase parents' knowledge, skills, and readiness for supporting their child when transitioning to adulthood (DaWalt, Greenberg, & Mailick, 2018).
8. Collecting feedback from the participants at the end of the training.
9. Making changes based on the feedback provided by the participants and the experience of the developer of the program.

The results indicated that the Hispanic families who participated in this research were very satisfied when provided with a culturally adapted intervention that was designed to help them with the transition of their children to adulthood.

Ethical and Professional Standards

As behavior analysts, we are required to abide by the Behavior Analyst Certification Board's® Professional and Ethical Compliance Code (BACB®, 2017). By becoming culturally aware professionals who implement interventions in a culturally competent manner, we ensure that our clients are not only getting the best services possible but that we remain in compliance with our ethics code. For example, one of the strategies used to incorporate adaptations to programs implemented with families with different backgrounds is to involve them in the planning of the intervention. As described previously, researchers have asked members of the community and families receiving services about their preferences and cultures, thus involving the clients in the planning of the programs they will be receiving (code 4.02). Another relevant code is 4.03, which states that behavior analysts should provide individualized behavior-change programs. In other words, programs provided to the families we serve should be customized to address their specific needs. These individualized programs, therefore, should include specific adaptations based on the family's culture, beliefs, and values.

Providing culturally competent services is not only beneficial for the families and the populations we serve, but also for the field overall in terms of disseminating behavior analysis (code 6.02; BACB®, 2017). The more families we can serve, the more we are able to disseminate and teach people about behavior analysis. In addition, the more we learn about different cultures and the more we adapt our evidence-based interventions to the specific needs of the different cultures, the better we will become at disseminating ABA worldwide.

Best Practice Recommendations

In this section of the chapter, we will be making recommendations as to how to become a culturally competent behavior analyst. Some of these recommendations have been mentioned in the behavior analysis literature and others have been part of the first author's experiences. It is our hope that these recommendations serve as a guide when providing culturally appropriate ABA services.

Identify the Definition of Culture

One of the most important actions taken by applied behavior analysts is to clearly and objectively define behaviors. This is helpful because it allows them to experimentally evaluate the efficacy of specific interventions and for others to replicate and extend the research, furthering the development of the field. In other words, identifying a concise, objective, and clear definition is necessary before analyzing a specific behavior. For the same reason, identifying a precise definition for culture is important when trying to include it within the field of behavior analysis. For example, Skinner (1953) defined culture as variables that are arranged by other people that affect an individual. Fong et al. (2016) defined culture as contingencies controlled by humans that affect the behavior and the environment of a person or a group of people. In other words, culture is a set of rules put in place by a group of people so that members of this group will behave in line with the set rules. These rules, then, are what set these individuals apart from other groups of individuals.

Acknowledge the Importance of Culture

Acknowledging the importance of culture is key for behavior analysts because they then will be able to identify what is the norm for their clients and thus what therapeutic goals are appropriate when providing behavior analytic services. This is not only important for identifying culturally aware goals but also to identify contingencies currently in place. It is also helpful for determining possible reinforcers to increase appropriate behaviors. There are some steps that can be taken for behavior analysts to learn to understand various cultures. One example is for the behavior analyst to ask the client questions about their specific culture. They can also ask about the differences and similarities between the new culture and the client's culture. Behavior analysts should also be aware of the impact of making a judgment based on one's own opinion; we should do our own research and study our client's or client's parents' culture.

Develop Cultural Awareness of Oneself

Once we understand culture and its importance, the next step is to develop cultural aware-ness of oneself. According to Fong et al. (2016), before developing cultural awareness of their clients, behavior analysts should attempt to identify the key components of their own culture. For example, does the culture of the analyst focus on teaching children equal responsibilities around the house, or does it focus on girls doing housework while boys learn how to provide for their families? This is important because when the analyst doesn't have a clear understand-ing of the differences between their own culture and their clients' cultures, there may be a resulting mismatch in recommendations.

Fong et al. (2016) provided recommendations as to how to develop cultural awareness of self. They suggested analysts discuss their client interactions with other professionals in the field (through writing journal articles, conducting mentorship meetings, participating in self-reflective exercises, etc.). They also suggested behavior analysts test hypotheses rather than imposing their own personal norms. Fong et al. also suggested behavior analysts carefully examine their own private events while observing the client's interactions and to focus on the information provided by the client and the families. Lastly, they suggested the use of self-assessment tools. Two such tools are the Diversity Self-Assessment Tool (Montgomery, 2001), which helps professionals identify their understanding of diversity, and How Do You Relate to Various Group of People in Society (Randall-David, 1989), which can help professionals identify how they might react to different groups of people.

Develop Cultural Awareness of Others

After the behavior analyst has identified the key components of his or her culture, then he or she can focus on identifying the differences between their own culture and their client's cul-ture (Fong et al., 2016). This can be accomplished by learning about cultural identity, or how much the client's family identifies with their own culture. Fong et al. (2016) recommended learning about a client's cultural identity by asking members of the same culture (without identifying the client's family themselves). This is helpful because it allows the behavior analyst to identify specific questions to ask prior to conducting the initial assessment with the families. Another way to develop cultural awareness is to identify the family's level of acculturation (i.e., their assimilation to their new culture, or how much of the new culture has been adopted by the client's family).

Provide Culturally Aware Assessments

After a behavior analyst has a clear understanding of his or her own culture as well as the cli-ent's family's culture, only then can he or she can provide assessments that are culturally aware. That involves changing assessments to focus on the specific client's needs (as identified after taking into account the cultural variables) in addition to the purpose for which the assess-ment was created. One recommendation is to use assessments that are translated or written in the families' primary language. Another suggestion is to incorporate feedback collected from members of the community to the existing assessments (Kuhn et al., 2019). In addition, behavior analysts should incorporate feedback from the families they serve to the existing assessment. One thing to keep in mind, though, is that more research is needed in this area, so when choosing to change aspects of the existing assessments, the behavior analyst needs to be aware of the implications of such changes and how they might affect the assessment's validity.

Provide Culturally Aware Interventions

Implementing culturally aware assessments makes it easier for the analyst to be able to provide culturally aware interventions. Identifying what is important for the client and what is the norm in his or her culture is one of the first steps to providing culturally aware interventions. As mentioned previously in this chapter, this is of great importance to increase the social validity of interventions among families with diverse cultural backgrounds (e.g., incorporating a specific family's routine, values, culture, and language; Buzhardt et al., 2016; Kuhn et al., 2019; Moes & Frea, 2002; Rodriguez, 2018).

Discussion/Conclusion

One of the aims of this chapter is to emphasize the importance of providing culturally competent services for Hispanic families. This chapter provided ways to culturally adapt evidence-based interventions as well as suggestions on becoming a more culturally competent behavior analyst. We hope that this chapter serves as a guide for behavior analysts interested in learning about adapting behavior analytic interventions when working with families from Latin America and other cultures. Furthermore, we hope this chapter serves to inspire others to continue to add to the research in this area. A limitation for behavior analysts seeking to become more culturally aware is that every culture is different and within every culture there are subcultures. Thus, learning about a specific culture might be never-ending. However, knowing the steps for identifying a client's cultural identity and becoming culturally aware will help behavior analysts provide services that are more customized to clients and their families. University programs in ABA should move to include cultural awareness classes as part of their curriculum (Fong et al., 2016). In addition, clinics and job sites should also promote the learning and maintenance of cultural awareness.

CASE STUDY

Carlos was a 2-year-old boy diagnosed with pervasive developmental disorder, not otherwise specified (PDD-NOS). His family had moved to the United States from a Latin American country. His mother was hoping to find services that could assist him with learning skills that could eventually help him become more independent. The mother had heard about ABA therapy and was convinced

(continued)

(continued)

that this was going to help them. When Carlos started receiving services, he was not able to communicate his wants and needs. Due to this skill deficit, he engaged in problem behaviors until his mother or another adult was able to identify what he needed.

After an assessment was conducted and the maintaining consequences were identified, skill acquisition programs were put in place. Skills such as appropriately manding for attention, food, and toys were among the programs implemented. After a year of intensive ABA services, Carlos was able to appropriately communicate his needs. Although some skill deficits still existed and problem behaviors continued to occur, progress was apparent. He was a sweet boy who always gave a kiss and a hug to everyone in the room when he arrived at the clinic in the morning; he also gave hugs and kisses when he was leaving at the end of his sessions. The clinic staff was very happy with his progress and the changes that they were able to see after only a year of ABA.

Once, when Carlos's ABA therapists were meeting to talk about Carlos's progress and programs, their supervisor brought to the therapist's attention his demonstrations of affection. She mentioned that Carlos's way of greeting and saying goodbye was "cute" then, as he was only 3 years old, but that they needed to think of the future and how giving kisses and hugs to strangers when he first entered or left a room was not appropriate. She then suggested that they begin thinking about potentially not reinforcing this behavior any longer. As one of the therapists was reflecting on their conversation, she thought about her own culture. For herself, originally from a Latin American country where giving hugs and kisses is considered the appropriate way of greeting and saying goodbye, this was the norm. The next day, the therapist spoke with the supervisor about her thoughts and explained the social norms of a Latin American country. They then spoke to the mother about this behavior and what she considered appropriate, incorporating code 4.02 (involving client in the planning of interventions; BACB®, 2017). As a result, they were both able to grow from this experience and realize that cultural considerations need to be a part of the services they provided.

In summary, sometimes we as behavior analysts focus so much on the results of a non-culturally aware assessment or on what should be the norm that we forget to analyze and take the client's culture into consideration. Thankfully, in recent years, more and more behavior analysts are recognizing the need to be more culturally aware and provide services that are culturally sensitive. Taking culture into consideration will make us better, more well-rounded behavior analysts who are able to adapt evidence-based interventions to any culture. It will also keep us in line with our own Professional and Ethical Compliance Code (BACB®, 2017). Code 1.02a states that behavior analysts are only to provide services within the boundaries of their competence. By contrast, code 1.02b states that a behavior analyst can provide services outside of their area of competence if the behavior analyst has undertaken appropriate training and supervision from a person competent in that area. In other words, in order to provide competent services to Hispanic families or families from a different cultural background than the analyst, the behavior analyst assigned to work with families should be aware of the cultural differences between the family and the analyst and, if different, should seek to remediate any deficits in understanding.

DISCUSSION QUESTIONS

1.   Discuss the importance of becoming a culturally aware behavior analyst.
2.   Describe the importance of adapting behavior analytic interventions for Hispanic families.
3.   List ways in which evidence-based interventions can be adapted for Hispanic families.
4.   When working with Latin-American families, identify some recommendations to ensure behavior analysts are providing culturally aware services.
5.   How can behavior analysts learn and maintain cultural awareness?

References

American Psychological Association. (2017). *Multicultural guidelines: An ecological approach to context, identity, and intersectionality.* Retrieved from www.apa.org/about/policy/multicultural-guidelines.pdf

Association for Professional Behavior Analysts. (2015, June). *2014 U. S. professional employment survey: A preliminary report.* Retrieved from www.apbahome.net/global_engine/download. aspx?fileid=04E4737B-0C81–494D-82A2–4C35F78ECD70&ext=pdf

Baer, D. M., Wolf, M. M., & Risley, T. R. (1968). Some current dimensions of applied behavior analysis. *Journal of Applied Behavior Analysis, 1*(1), 91–97. https://doi.org/10.1901/jaba.1968.1-91

Behavior Analyst Certification Board. (2017). *BACB® professional and ethical compliance code for behavior analysts.* Retrieved from www.bacb.com/wp-content/uploads/BACB-Compliance-Code-english_190318.pdf

Bernal, G., & Flores-Ortiz, Y. (1982). Latino families in therapy: Engagement and evaluation. *Journal of Marital and Family Therapy, 8*(3), 357–365. https://doi.org/10.1111/j.1752-0606.1982.tb01458.x

Burning Glass Technologies. (2019). *US employment demand for behavior analysts: 2010–2018.* Retrieved from www.bacb.com/wp-content/uploads/US- Employment-Demand-for-Behavior-Analysts_2019.pdf

Buzhardt, J., Rusinko, L., Heitzman-Powell, L., Trevino-Maack, S., & McGrath, A. (2016). Exploratory evaluation and initial adaptation of a parent training program for Hispanic families of children with autism. *Family Process, 55*(1), 107–122. https://doi.org/10.1111/famp.12146

Carr, E. G., & Durand, V. M. (1985). Reducing behavior problems through functional communication training. *Journal of Applied Behavior Analysis, 18*(2), 111–126. https://doi.org/10.1901/jaba.1985.18-111

Centers for Disease Control and Prevention. (2019). *Data & statistics on autism spectrum disorder.* Retrieved from www.cdc.gov/ncbddd/autism/data.html

Colby, S. L., & Ortman, J. M. (2014). *Projections of the size and composition of the U.S. population: 2014 to 2060.* Washington, DC: US Census Bureau.

DaWalt, L. S., Greenberg, J. S., & Mailick, M. R. (2018). Transitioning together: A multi-family group psychoeducation program for adolescents with ASD and their parents. *Journal of Autism and Developmental Disorders, 48*(1), 251–263. https://doi.org/10.1007/s10803-017-3307-x

Fong, E. H., Catagnus, R. M., Brodhead, M. T., Quigley, T., & Field, S. (2016). Developing the cultural awareness skills of behavior analysts. *Behavior Analysis in Practice*, *9*(1), 84–94. https://doi.org/10.1007/s40617-016-0111-6.

Koegel, R. L., Bimbela, A., & Schreibman, L. (1996). Collateral effects of parent training on family interactions. *Journal of Autism and Developmental Disorders*, *26*(3), 347–359.

Kuhn, J. L., Vanegas, S. B., Saldago, R., Borjas, S. K., Magana, S., DaWalt, L. S. (2019). The cultural adaptation of a transition program for Latino families of youth with autism spectrum disorder. *Family Process*. https://doi.org/10.1111/famp.12439

Marcus, B. A., Swanson, V., & Vollmer, T. R. (2001). Effects of parent training on parent and child behavior using procedures based on functional analyses. *Behavioral Interventions*, *16*(2), 87–104. https://doi.org/10.1002/bin.87

McConachie, H., & Diggle, T. (2007). Parent implemented early intervention for young children with autism spectrum disorder: A systematic review. *Journal of Evaluation in Clinical Practice*, *13*(1), 120–129. https://doi.org/10.1111/j.1365–2753.2006.00674.x

Meadan, H., Ostrosky, M., Zaghlawan, H., & Yu, S. (2009). Promoting the social and communicative behavior of young children with autism spectrum disorders. *Topics in Early Childhood Special Education*, *29*(2), 90–104. https://doi.org/10.1177/0271121409337950.

Moes, D., & Frea, W. (2002). Contextualized behavioral support in early intervention for children with autism and their families. *Journal of Autism and Developmental Disorder*, *35*(6), 519–533. https://doi.org/10.1023/A:1021298729297.

Montgomery, W. (2001). Creating culturally responsive, inclusive classrooms. *Teaching Exceptional Children*, *33*(4), 4–9.

National Association of Social Workers. (2003). *NASW standards for cultural competence in social work practice*. Washington, DC: National Association of Social Workers.

Randall-David, E. (1989). *Strategies for working with culturally diverse communities and clients* (pp. 7–9). Washington, DC: Association for the Care of Children's Health.

Rodriguez, A. (2018). *A comparison of traditional and culturally sensitive parent training of functional communication training*. Unpublished master's thesis, Rollins College, Winter Park, FL. Retrieved from https://scholarship.rollins.edu/mabacs_thesis/7

Sanders, M. R., & Glynn, T. (1981). Training parents in behavioral self-management: An analysis of generalization and management. *Journal of Applied Behavior Analysis*, *14*(3), 223–237. http://doi.org/10.1901/jaba.1981.14-223

Skinner, B. F. (1953). *Science and human behavior*. New York: Collier-Macmillan.

Skinner, B. F. (1981). Selection by consequences. *Science*, *213*(4507), 501–504. https://doi.org/10.1126/science.7244649

Wood, W., & Eagly, A. H. (2002). A cross-cultural analysis of the behavior of women and men: Implications for the origins of sex differences. *Psychological Bulletin*, *128*(5), 699–727. https://doi.org/10.1037//0033-2909.128.5.699

14

How to Integrate Multiculturalism and Diversity Sensitivity Into the Training and Ethical Skill Set of Behavior Analysts

Mary Jane Weiss, Ksenia Gatzunis, and Wafa Aljohani

Learning Objectives

- Readers will identify some of the current issues in the field of behavior analysis in regard to cultural competence.

- Readers will describe the importance of understanding cultural sensitivity and diversity, and particularly the impact on clinical service delivery.

- Readers will identify existing behavior analytic literature describing cultural sensitivity issues, as well as the need for additional behavior analytic literature that discusses cultural sensitivity issues in clinical practices.

- Readers will be able to identify concrete practices to improve their own competence in regard to cultural sensitivity in clinical settings.

- Readers will be able to identify future directions to guide research in the field of behavior analysis on cultural sensitivity and diversity issues.

Introduction

Culture has been defined as "the extent to which a group of individuals engage in overt and verbal behavior reflecting shared behavioral learning histories, serving to differentiate the groups from other groups, and predicting how individuals within the group act in specific setting conditions" (Sugai, O'Keeffe, & Fallon, 2012). In other words, culture denotes a set of behaviors that are both shared (by members of the group) and distinct (from other groups) (Skinner, 1953). It is often associated with additional variables such as beliefs, values, and traditions.

A failure to understand and adapt to cultural variables might reduce the effectiveness of applied behavior analysis (ABA) providers. Since both professionals in the field and the clients they serve come from diverse backgrounds, the need for fostering cultural competency and building cultural awareness within clinical settings has been increasingly identified as essential and relevant (Fong, Ficklin, & Lee, 2017). This is especially relevant, as the US Census Bureau predicts that by 2044, more than half of the individuals in the United States will "belong to a minority group (any group other than non-Hispanic White alone)" (Colby & Ortman, 2015, p. 1). Within the field of behavior analysis, there has been explicit support for additional focus on diversity and culture. For example, the Association for Behavior Analysis International's (ABAI) Diversity Policy states that the organization

> encourages diversity and inclusiveness in the field of behavior analysis broadly, and within the organization specifically. Diversity refers to differences in race, ethnicity, sexual orientation, gender identity, age, country of origin, religious or spiritual beliefs, ability, and social and economic class.
>
> (Association for Behavior Analysis International, 2019)

Despite this increased attention, many areas remain in need of definition and improvement, such as sharing more guidelines for practitioners and organizations and developing empirically validated interventions to teach relevant skills to practitioners (Brodhead & Higbee, 2012). This chapter will provide an overview of existing resources both within and outside of the field, including practice recommendations for practitioners, and will discuss current limitations and ideas for future directions.

Current Relevance to Clinical Settings

As our field continues to expand, so will the diversity of practitioners and clients within clinical settings. To gain more insight on the status quo, a number of recent surveys have been conducted with either practitioners or stakeholders. Despite the known limitations of survey data, both of the following studies should be considered in regard to the importance of considering culture within clinical applications.

Taylor, LeBlanc, and Nosik (2018) obtained data pertaining to parent perspective regarding the services that they have received from their behavior analyst. While the majority of the study focused on other aspects of service delivery, one question asked about cultural respect and sensitivity. Using a Likert scale, respondents answered with the degree to which they felt that the behavior analyst working with their child showed respect for their family's cultural values and beliefs. Only 67% of respondents indicated that they were in agreement that their behavior analyst demonstrated respect for their cultural values and beliefs. This result indicates that there is a need to address this issue further, particularly from a consumer perspective.

Interestingly, Beaulieu and colleagues (2018) conducted a survey largely focused on questions regarding culture and diversity. They surveyed 703 Board Certified Behavior Analysts® (BCBAs®) and Board Certified Behavior Analyst – Doctoral™ (BCBA-Ds™) across 40 questions using a Likert scale. The survey asked questions regarding the respondents' demographics, their opinions on the value of obtaining training on working with diverse populations, their own perceived levels of skill and comfort in working with diverse clients, and the amount of relevant training they have received through coursework, practicum, continuing education, and training provided by their employers. The survey yielded some noteworthy results. For instance, 86% of behavior analysts perceived themselves as being "moderately skilled" or "extremely skilled" in regard to working with diverse populations, demonstrating a difference in perception in comparison to the consumer data obtained from Taylor and colleagues (2018). Additionally, 57% of the respondents stated that *greater than half of the clients on their caseload came from diverse backgrounds* and at least 84% of the respondents identified themselves as white. Therefore, there is a high number of practitioner-client relationships in which the two do not have shared backgrounds, resulting in a need for practitioners to obtain more information regarding the cultures of many of their clients, rather than relying on assumptions of shared values, beliefs, and norms.

Ethical and Professional Standards

Behavior analysts have a variety of resources available for guidance in ethical decision-making including the Behavior Analyst Certification Board's® (BACB®) Professional and Ethical Compliance Code, published articles, and books. The following section will focus on BACB's® Professional and Ethical Compliance Code (Behavior Analyst Certification Board®, 2019), as well as several interpretations of its application to clinical practice.

BACB's® Professional and Ethical Compliance Code outlines the ethical responsibilities of behavior analysts across a wide variety of professional contexts (Behavior Analyst Certification Board®, 2019). Currently, a limited number of codes specifically guide behavior analysts in situations involving cultural relevance within practice. Code 1.05 is one of particular relevance to the current discussion. Code 1.05 states that whenever there are differences between the behavior analyst and their clients across a variety of factors, behavior analysts "obtain the training, experience, consultation, and/or supervision necessary to ensure the competence of their services, or they make appropriate referrals" (Behavior Analyst Certification Board®, 2019, p. 5). In addition, practitioners do not discriminate against others, and "do not knowingly engage in behavior that is harassing or demeaning to persons with whom they interact in their work" based on "age, gender, race, culture, ethnicity, national origin, religion, sexual orientation, disability, language, or socioeconomic status, in accordance with law" (Behavior Analyst Certification Board®, 2019, p. 5). This code is similar to the analogous portions of the ethics guidelines of other professional organizations such as the American Psychological Association

(APA, 2017) and the American Speech-Language-Hearing Association (ASHA, 2016). Due to the increased need for knowledge and competency in this area, additional codes should be developed to capture a wider variety of ethical concerns related to diversity and culture.

A unique perspective on the BACB's® Professional and Ethical Compliance Code has recently been offered by Beirne and Sadavoy (2019). In the book *Understanding Ethics in Applied Behavior Analysis*, the primary authors offer not only their interpretations of the BACB's® Professional and Ethical Compliance Code, but also many applied examples based on their personal experiences working in North America, Africa, Europe, Asia, and South America. The book also includes a wide variety of guest contributors, including an autistic self-advocate, BCBAs®, psychologists, and educators. Through these diverse perspectives, practitioners can gain an understanding of the gray areas that exist, especially when working within different cultures. Gaps in understanding can be identified, which could influence skill identification and training.

It is important for us all to define and to critically analyze cultural competence. Rosenberg and Schwartz (2019) highlight the importance of considering cultural variables when answering the question of what makes a behavior analyst ethical. Is it simply compliance to the BACB's® Professional and Ethical Compliance Code? What if the Code conflicts with cultural norms and values, or if two or more parts of the Code conflict with one another in a given situation? The authors describe ways in which these potential issues can impact service delivery and demonstrate how ethical decision-making is oftentimes not black and white. Rosenberg and Schwartz (2019) emphasize that "culture always matters," and that "it is impossible to propose a set of rules that fits every cultural situation" (p. 476). Therefore, compliance to the BACB's® Professional and Ethical Compliance Code without consideration for the culture variations of our consumers can result in a variety of consequences ranging from offending our clients to a family's decision to terminate ABA services. With our field's continued expansion to other areas of the world, the need to take a culturally relevant approach to ethics becomes paramount. Brodhead (2019) expands the conversation in his published response to the article. He argues that the BACB's® Professional and Ethical Compliance Code "unintentionally underplays the importance of culture" and, in conjunction with Rosenberg and Schwartz, calls for behavior analysts to join the discussion with an ongoing critical analysis of the Code (Brodhead, 2019, p. 1).

In taking Brodhead's advice, let's take a look at a commonly discussed section of the Code, 1.06(d), which prohibits behavior analysts from accepting gifts from clients due to concerns regarding multiple relationships (BACB®, 2019). Witts, Brodhead, Adlington, and Barron (2018) question the cultural relevance of this code. In a survey, they found that the majority of behavior analysts surveyed responded "yes" to the statement "For the clients I work with, it is offensive to refuse a gift offer" (Witts et al., 2018, p. 5) Additionally, some behavior analysts agreed with the BACB's® argument regarding dual relationships, while some others stated that it is "inappropriate/awkward" to refuse a gift or that refusing gifts will be harmful to the practitioner-consumer relationship (Witts et al., 2018, p. 5). On the other hand, Bailey and Burch (2016) argue that since behavior analysts are not "guests" of the families with whom they work, they must not accept gifts, as doing so may result in a dual relationship or produce a slippery slope (p. 73). A risks and benefits analysis seems warranted, and some consideration of cultural fallout might help identify unintended negative consequences. More nuanced discussion around this issue might help the field to refine this analysis and might lead to clinical guidelines for navigating such challenges.

Additional ABA Resources

In addition to the BACB's® Professional and Ethical Compliance Code and the resources discussed in the previous section, the following behavior analytic resources add to the dialogue. Fong, Catagnus, Brodhead, Quigley, and Field (2016) provide recommendations for behavior analysts to improve their cultural awareness skills. The authors suggest ways to develop cultural awareness of self and clients and describe specific recommendations for practitioners, including the following:

- *Be mindful of the language used during assessment and treatment* (e.g., avoid jargon, consider which type of communication is easiest for the client, provide an interpreter or translation services if needed).

- *Understand the cultural identity of the client and the community* (e.g., ask relevant questions during the intake process, obtain additional information about the culture and language from other resources, use culturally appropriate terminology, understand how norms and values may affect the acceptability of treatment).

- *Use existing resources and materials* (see Fong and colleagues (2016) for a list of recommended resources to supplement the resources discussed in the present chapter).

- *Following assessment, make appropriate decisions* (e.g., accept the client or refer them to a clinician who may be more culturally knowledgeable, seek additional information and training).

Fong and colleagues (2016) also list recommendations for organizations and for professional development programs (e.g., graduate schools). These recommendations include appointing a person within the organization that is in charge of addressing the development and improvement of cultural competence, including cultural awareness training as a part of the supervision process, and including these discussion and trainings within BACB® coursework.

Miller, Re Cruz, and Ala'i-Rosales (2019) further discuss the relevance of culture and diversity to the field. The authors describe current limitations seen in practice and offer recommendations for both practitioners and organizations. Miller and colleagues recommend allocating resources and time to discussing culture within the workplace, seeking to share new experiences and forming relationships with individuals from other cultural backgrounds, utilizing available resources and learning from other professions, and reflecting and evaluating progress toward our goals. Within ABA, the discussion has begun, and the problem has been identified.

The challenge is to move the discussion from a review of the issue into an implementation phase.

Resources Available From Related Professions

It is imperative that services are delivered in a culturally relevant manner. Offensive or disrespectful interactions, intentional or otherwise, may interfere with the outcomes of intervention and may reduce the family's investment in treatment beyond the current context. Several resources exist that might help behavior analysts operationally define target behaviors for treatment provision. As the discussion of this topic is currently in its infancy within our field, it is beneficial to also reference the resources available within other human service fields, such as psychology and speech and language pathology.

Self-Assessments for Practitioners

ASHA's (2010a) *Cultural Competence Checklist: Personal Reflection* asks practitioners to personally reflect on the extent to which their behavior reflects cultural sensitivity. Items range from general cultural respect (e.g., "I treat all clients with respect for their culture") to an assessment of prohibited actions (e.g., "I do not participate in insensitive comments and behaviors") (ASHA, 2010a). In addition, the assessment examines the influence of dialect, disability, and family structure, and challenges the interventionist to examine the extent to which their own prejudices might influence treatment, interaction, or communication. Furthermore, the practitioner is reminded that culture can influence a wide range of issues including sleep, feeding, and self-help skills. Finally, the checklist alerts the practitioner to areas of communication and interaction that might be influenced by culture including eye contact, turn taking, and the use of humor. Such a checklist helps to remind the practitioner that culture is omnipresent and bidirectional. Norms, customs, and expectations are held by both the service provider and the client. Bridging those gaps is imperative to ensure sensitive and respectful service delivery. It is recommended that an analogous self-assessment be developed for behavior analytic practitioners. Additionally, the development of a more objective, measurable tool that could be used by supervisors and trainers would be largely beneficial.

The National Association of School Psychologists has the Self-Assessment Checklist for Personnel Providing Services and Supports to Children and their Families (Goode, 2009), which extends this response class in interesting ways. Practitioners are asked to examine the physical environment and materials that are used. For example, do the magazines and reading materials reflect the culture of those commonly served? Do the videos used in training reflect the community served? Are the foods offered representative of the culture of the clients? This resource also focuses specifically on the use of familiar language and dialectical phrases, as well as the availability of translators, to ease the experience for clients. Finally, it focuses on the behavior of the provider in preparing to meet with and serve a new family. This sets the expectation that an effort will be made to become informed about and to be responsive to cultural preferences, characteristics, norms, and values. Examples from the checklist include items relating to male and female roles, the definition of the family, the role of elders, and the desire or lack of desire for acculturation (Goode, 2009). Following the completion of checklist, the practitioner should become aware of changes to be made within their own service delivery, as well within their organizations and programs.

ASHA's (2010c) Cultural Competence Checklist: Service Delivery outlines some common and important contexts for the demonstration of cultural sensitivity. Items include behaviors such as learning about the culture, providing translated items and interpreters, respecting alternative ways of providing information (such as storytelling), and incorporating supplemental communication strategies to facilitate comprehension (such as visual aids and modeling). The items all underscore ways to welcome families and make them feel more comfortable in the service provision context by ensuring that information will be shared in comprehensible ways. Many elements of this checklist are quite concrete, are easily measured, and are fully consistent with the philosophical underpinnings of the science of ABA.

Self-Assessment for Organizations

In addition to examining how individual practitioners can be helped to develop cultural competence, it is also helpful to look at how organizations can foster cultural sensitivity in service provision. Indeed, organizations set the tone for the individuals within them and can provide guiding policies and procedures and a climate that supports diversity, tolerance, and respect. Policies, procedures, and systems can all support cultural sensitivity at an organizational level. In addition, such policies provide a statement to individual clinicians about the importance of culturally relevant service delivery.

ASHA offers a self-assessment for organizations that is instructive in how one can create organizational scaffolding for cultural competence. ASHA's (2010b) Cultural Competence Checklist: Policies and Procedures examines aspects of organizational leadership in this context. Items include attention to the inclusion of cultural competence in the mission statement, the availability of translators, the existence of diversity in the workforce, the inclusion of diverse personnel in leadership roles, the extension of benefits for non-traditional family arrangements, and the recognition of a broad variety of holidays. It is important for organizations to align with members of the communities they serve, to ensure that they are meeting the needs of these constituents in accurate and appropriate ways. Organizations can partner with local leaders in the areas or communities they are working in to ensure that this expertise is provided at an organizational level.

Relevance to ABA

Social validity and the individualization of assessment, goals, and treatment are the heart of ABA (Wolf, 1978). Therefore, practitioners cannot discount the relevance of cultural norms, beliefs, and values within the assessment and treatment process. The aforementioned tools from other professions can serve as a valuable starting point to increase the cultural sensitivity of our services.

While the BACB®, APA, and ASHA all prohibit discrimination against others, attention to what they *should* do to ensure the delivery of culturally respectful clinical practices is not yet widely articulated in the field of behavior analysis. It may be the case that the field's value on operationally defined, observable, and measurable behaviors is an impediment in the development of these tools. In fact, the tools developed in other professions rely heavily on subjective impressions of the extent to which such behaviors are exhibited. Many of the targets are attitudinal or values based. Some may even seem mentalistic. However, a few elements of behavior analysis should strengthen our commitment to embracing these goals and to developing a conceptually systematic approach to achieving them. Additionally, research must be conducted to assess the effectiveness of training procedures that specifically target the recommended skills to provide empirical support and validity to the practice recommendations and assessment tools.

Hence, it is entirely conceptually systematic to seek to refine the definitions and procedures associated with culturally competent ABA service provision. The challenge may be to refine the ways in which such behaviors operationally defined and are judged as presently exhibited. It seems that behavior analysts are well suited to developing a more objective and observable definition of culturally competent service provision. It also seems that components of culturally sensitive workplace environments could be identified.

Practice Recommendations

Based on the resources described within this chapters, the following is a list of considerations for ensuring that clients feel supported and respected, and that their cultural differences are included within assessment and intervention planning:

1. Clinicians should use resources that are currently available, including the assessments, articles, and books discussed throughout this chapter (Fong et al., 2016).

2. Clinicians should regularly seek feedback from the individuals with whom they work, as survey data have shown that parent and practitioner perspectives may differ regarding service delivery (Beaulieu et al., 2018; Taylor et al., 2018).

3. Clinicians must consider the role of cultural beliefs and norms in everyday activities such as parenting styles and activities of daily living such as feeding, toileting, self-care, and sleeping. Roles of different family and community members should also be considered. This information should begin to be gathered as early as the intake process (American Speech-Language-Hearing Association, 2010a; Fong et al., 2016). This must be considered throughout assessment, treatment development, and service delivery.

4. Clinicians must consider how cultural and linguistic diversity impact behavior analytic services (e.g., making sure to implement culturally appropriate language acquisition programs; Brodhead, Durán, & Bloom, 2014).

5. Clinicians and organizations should make every effort to ensure that translators are present for meetings and discussions with families for whom the primary language of the area is not the natively spoken language.

6. Clinicians should seek out additional training, professional development, and supervision opportunities related to culture and diversity whenever possible. This is particularly important for behavior analysts, as the majority report limited to no formal training in this area (Beaulieu et al., 2018)

7. Clinicians and organizations should make every effort to have the environment be hospitable for individuals from all cultures, including using training materials that reflect the diverse clientele served.

8. Steps should be taken to ensure that practitioners do not inadvertently offend clients.

Additional Extensions

Behavior analysts must not only consider the cultural differences between practitioner and client but also take into consideration how differences in cultural beliefs, norms, and values may impact the relationship between employers and employees, professors and students, and supervisors and supervisees. Fong and colleagues (2017) provide practical recommendations for academic, training, and work settings to increase the understanding and diversity within our field. It is imperative that those in leadership and administrative roles within their organizations work to create systems that foster respectful and comfortable environments for all individuals regardless of their cultural backgrounds or identities.

A number of steps can be taken to increase sensitivity toward a diverse workforce (e.g., Atkinson, Casas, & Neville, 1994; Fong et al., 2017). Strategies include:

- Recognizing the unique abilities for professionals who are fluent in multiple languages.
- Making appropriate accommodations when needed for those who are not native speakers in the main vocal language spoken in the workplace.
- Allocating time to learn about the different backgrounds and cultures of each employee.
- Assigning minority professionals to provide mentorship to younger minority professionals to build a sense of belonging and satisfaction celebrating holidays across cultures for employees, such as Eid al-Fitr and Eid al-Adha for Muslims and Diwali for Hindus.
- Planning a variety of culturally sensitive team building activities (while keeping in mind others' cultural, religious, or other restrictions).
- Staying updated with current events, including showing support and empathy to the professionals and coworkers who identify with any cultures or groups of people who may have been affected by both national and global events (e.g., shootings in places of worship, war, natural disasters).

Behavior analysts should continue to discuss this important topic and expand the ways in which all practitioners feel accepted and support regardless of their identities or backgrounds. Workplaces can do a great deal to advance these goals by increasing their sensitivity to these issues and expanding their reach in these ways.

Discussion

Behavior analysis is a relatively new profession, and many elements of professionalism are still being articulated. Other human service professions have examined these issues and outlined strategies for cultural competence to a greater extent than behavior analysis. This is not surprising, but it should not discourage us. We can benefit from the work of those professionals who have considered these competencies. They can serve as foundations for our own resources.

At the heart of behavior analysis, individualized assessment and intervention guide our work. As a field, we have always looked at change on an individual level. In research designs, we seek indicators of change at the level of the individual, and we doubt the significance of studies that demonstrate group differences only. These values, and this compass, need to also lay the foundation for addressing cultural competence. The effectiveness and efficiency of our interventions will be enhanced by improvements in cultural sensitivity. Furthermore, the extent to which clients feel supported, understood, and empowered will likely improve as a result of improvements in cultural competence among ABA practitioners.

DISCUSSION QUESTIONS

1. Why are cultural beliefs, norms, and values important to consider within the context of behavior analytic service delivery?

2. Discuss the current reported discrepancy between consumer and practitioner opinion regarding levels of cultural competence of behavior analysts.

3. Provide a brief critical analysis of the BACB's® Professional and Ethical Compliance Code in terms of its consideration for cultural differences, including a list of three to five proposed recommendations for future revisions of the Code.

4. Describe several available ABA resources for practitioners to use as a guide to improve cultural competence. Consider the limitations that could be addressed within the development of future ABA resources.

5. Discuss the advantages and limitations of behavior analysts utilizing the resources that are currently available within other professions. Consider what steps behavior analysts can take to increase the objectivity and measurability of these resources.

6. List and describe ways in which practitioners can improve their approaches to service delivery to increase their cultural sensitivity.

7. List and describe ways in which organizations can help foster a work environment that promotes increased cultural sensitivity.

CASE STUDY

Read through the follow scenarios and consider whether cultural sensitivity was demonstrated and whether ethical issues were properly managed. Reflect on alternative routes that could have been taken, as well as prevention strategies that should have been considered.

Do You Understand Me?

You are at an IEP meeting with an Arabic-speaking family. At the last minute, the interpreter cancels. The family speaks very limited English, and you and the rest of the professionals at the meeting do not speak any Arabic. The head of the IEP meeting decides that because this interpreter has cancelled multiple times and there is a deadline approaching, the meeting should be held as planned and should not be once again rescheduled for another time. The meeting proceeds, and although you try to explain your portion in parent-friendly language, it does not appear that the parents fully understand the information you are trying to share in their non-native language. You feel pressure to continue from the rest of the team, and no one else seems to be concerned about this issue. You continue with the meeting as planned.

In this scenario, it may be argued that code 1.05c was not adhered to. This situation may be less clear, as it was a team decision to continue the meeting; however, the behavior analyst did not stay true to providing competent services, as they did not relay information to the parents in a way that was understandable to them. This also violates code 1.05b, which requires the use of "language that is fully understandable to the recipient of those services" (BACB®, 2019, p. 5). The behavior analyst should have recommended that the meeting not continue until an interpreter was made available, whether through a service available through the phone (e.g., Interpreters Unlimited) or a different in-person interpreter on a future date.

You Remind Me of Someone

You are a Korean behavior analyst who was just assigned to a new Caucasian family. When you meet the parents for the first time, they tell you that they are concerned that their son will not react well to you because you look like an Asian preschool teacher that their son strongly dislikes. When you go into work the next day, your supervisor tells you that the family has requested to have you transitioned off of their case. You feel that you are being discriminated against, but your supervisor rationalizes the decision by stating that he cannot send you back into their home against the parents' wishes. Instead, the case will be reassigned to a white coworker. What are some considerations in this case?

A discussion with the team could include the very difficult topic of discrimination based on race or ethnicity. While it may seem like reassignment is condoning racism, it is must also be considered that the employer has an obligation to protect the employee from an uncomfortable work environment. An honest discussion of all of the angles of this circumstance could be very useful for all

(continued)

(continued)

members of the team and could widen the discussion of an often ignored dimension of experience in the workplace.

Mealtime

A family has recently relocated from another country and is just now receiving services. The behavior analyst conducts an intake assessment and lists as a presenting problem that their son does not know how to properly use a fork and spoon even though he is approaching young adulthood. When the family meets with the team, the behavior analyst states that the child needs to learn how to properly use all types of utensils, and that this should be one of the top priority goals. The family is confused, as they do not see this as a problem – their son can properly eat all family meals with his hands, the norm within their community. The behavior analyst is frustrated that the child does not have what she considers to be age-appropriate feeding skills, and that the family is not changing their minds about this goal.

This example is an excellent illustration of cultural insensitivity. It stems from a failure to consider the impact of culture during the assessment and goal-setting process. The clinician has inadvertently imposed a personal cultural norm on this family, failing to consider that different perspectives exist. More training and consideration for cultural norms could have prevented this from occurring.

References

American Psychological Association. (2017). *Ethical principles of psychologists and code of conduct.* Retrieved from www.apa.org/ethics/code/

American Speech-Language-Hearing Association. (2010a). *Cultural competence checklist: Personal reflection.* Retrieved from www.asha.org/practice/multicultural/self/

American Speech-Language-Hearing Association. (2010b). *Cultural competence checklist: Policies and procedures.* Retrieved from www.asha.org/practice/multicultural/self/

American Speech-Language-Hearing Association. (2010c). *Cultural competence checklist: Service delivery.* Retrieved from www.asha.org/practice/multicultural/self/

American Speech-Language-Hearing Association. (2016). *Code of ethics.* Retrieved from www.asha.org/policy

Association for Behavior Analysis International. (2019). *Policies and positions.* Retrieved from www.abainternational.org/about-us/policies-and-positions.aspx

Atkinson, D. R., Casas, A., & Neville, H. A. (1994). Ethnic minority psychologists: Whom they mentor and benefits they derive from the process. *Journal of Multicultural Counseling and Development, 22*(1), 37–48. https://doi.org/10.1002/j.2161-1912.1994.tb00241.x

Bailey, J. S., & Burch, M. R. (2016). *Ethics for behavior analysts* (3rd ed.). New York: Routledge.

Beaulieu, L., Addington, J., & Almeida, D. (2018). Behavior analysts' training and practices regarding cultural diversity: The case for culturally competent care. *Behavior Analysis in Practice, 12*(3), 557–575. https://doi.org/10.1007/s40617-018-00313-6

Behavior Analyst Certification Board. (2019). *Professional and ethical compliance code for behavior analysts.* Retrieved from www.bacb.com/ethics/ethics-code/

Beirne, A., & Sadavoy, J. A. (2019). *Understanding ethics in applied behavior analysis.* New York: Routledge.

Brodhead, M. T. (2019). Culture always matters: Some thoughts on Rosenberg and Schwartz. *Behavior Analysis in Practice, 12*, 826–830. https://doi.org/10.1007/s40617-019-00351-8

Brodhead, M. T., Durán, L., & Bloom, S. E. (2014). Cultural and linguistic diversity in recent verbal behavior research on individuals with disabilities: A review and implications for research and practice. *The Analysis of Verbal Behavior, 30*(1), 75–86. https://doi.org/10.1007/s40616-014-0009-8

Brodhead, M. T., & Higbee, T. S. (2012). Teaching and maintaining ethical behavior in a professional organization. *Behavior Analysis in Practice, 5*(2), 86–92. https://doi.org/10.1007/BF03391827

Colby, S. L., & Ortman, J. M. (2015). *Projections of the size and composition of the U.S. population: 2014 to 2060.* Retrieved from https://census.gov/content/dam/Census/library/publications/2015/demo/p25-1143.pdf

Conners, B., Johnson, A., Duarte, J., Murriky, R., & Marks, K. (2019). Future directions of training and fieldwork in diversity issues in applied behavior analysis. *Behavior Analysis in Practice, 12*, 767–776. https://doi.org/10.1007/s40617-019-00349-2

Fong, E. H., Catagnus, R. M., Brodhead, M. T., Quigley, S., & Field, S. (2016). Developing the cultural awareness skills of behavior analysts. *Behavior Analysis in Practice, 9*(1), 84–94. https://doi.org/10.1007/s40617-016-0111-6

Fong, E. H., Ficklin, S., & Lee, H. Y. (2017). Increasing cultural understanding and diversity in applied behavior analysis. *Behavior Analysis: Research and Practice, 17*(2), 103–113. https://doi.org/10.1037/bar0000076

Fong, E. H., & Tanaka, S. (2013). Multicultural alliance of behavior analysis standards for cultural competence in behavior analysis. *International Journal of Behavioral Consultation and Therapy, 8*(2), 17–19. https://doi.org/10.1037/h0100970

Goode, T. D. (2009). *Self-assessment checklist for personnel providing behavioral health services and supports to children, youth and their families.* Retrieved from https://nccc.georgetown.edu/resources/type.php

Miller, K. L., Re Cruz, A., & Ala'i-Rosales, S. (2019). Inherent tensions and possibilities: Behavior analysis and cultural responsiveness. *Behavior and Social Issues, 28*, 16–36. https://doi.org/10.1007/s42822-019-00010-1

Rosenberg, N. E., & Schwartz, I. S. (2019). Guidance or compliance: What makes an ethical behavior analyst? *Behavior Analysis in Practice, 12*(2), 473–482. https://doi.org/10.1007/s40617-018-00287-5

Skinner, B. F. (1953). *Science and human behavior.* New York: The Macmillan Company.

Sugai, G., O'Keeffe, B. V., & Fallon, L. M. (2012). A contextual consideration of culture and schoolwide positive behavior support. *Journal of Positive Behavior Interventions, 14*(4). 197–208. https://doi.org/10.1177/1098300711426334.

Taylor, B. A., LeBlanc, L. A., & Nosik, M. R. (2018). Compassionate care in behavior analytic treatment: Can outcomes be enhanced by attending to relationships with caregivers? *Behavior Analysis in Practice, 12*(3), 654–666. https://doi.org/10.1007/s40617-018-00289-3

Witts, B. N., Brodhead, M. T., Adlington, L. C., & Barron, D. K. (2018). Behavior analysts accept gifts during practice: So now what? *Behavior Analysis: Research and Practice* [Advance online publication]. http://doi.org/10.1037/bar0000117

Wolf, M. M. (1978). Social validity: The case for subjective measurement or how applied behavior analysis is finding its heart. *Journal of Applied Behavior Analysis, 11*(2), 203–214. https://doi.org/10.1901/jaba.1978.11-203

15

Examining Cross-Cultural Supervision in Applied Behavior Analysis

Elizabeth Hughes Fong

The requirements for the supervision of individuals who wish to become Board Certified Assistant Behavior Analysts® (BCaBA^{i}) or Board Certified Behavior Analysts® (BCBA^{i} or BCBA-D™) by the Behavior Analysis Certification Board (BACB^{i}) are well documented. Those seeking certification must be well versed in behavior analytic interventions and have received supervision by a BCBA®. Due to the sparsity of BCBAs®, some individuals seeking certification may use a supervisor from a different geographic location or from a different culture. This may assist the individual in getting their supervision requirements met, but the supervisor may not be well versed in the difference in cultures between the client, supervisee, and supervisor. Examples of differences in culture might be geographic location, religion, sexual orientation, age, or race – for instance, acceptance of applied behavior analysis (ABA) within the culture, availability of behavior analytic terms in the other language, differences in customs, traditions, values, or beliefs (Shupp & Mattingly, 2017). While the BACB® covers the nature of supervision, what is not clear is how to supervise those individuals who are from a different culture than the supervisor. Similarly, it is not well documented in behavior analytic literature how culture might impact the supervision relationship. Furthermore, there are currently no multicultural competencies within the discipline of ABA. Closely related fields have done a superior job of addressing such topics and assessing their impact on the supervisory experience, such as psychology's Multicultural Guidelines (American Psychological Association, 2017), nursing (Douglas et al., 2014), and social work (National Association of Social Workers, 2015).

The BACB® and Supervision

The BACB® lays out specific topics that an ethical supervisor should follow and cover when supervising staff in the BACB's® Professional and Ethical Compliance Code for Behavior Analysts (2018), specifically codes 5.01–5.07.

Within these standards there is a plethora of opportunities for a behavior analyst to be a culturally sensitive supervisor. For example, in code 5.01 Supervisory Competence, a behavior analyst could attend workshops, lectures, read scholarly articles, or attend other continuing education events to help them become more competent when working with diverse populations (BACB®, 2018). Similar to what a behavior analyst could do in order to become a more competent supervisor, a behavior analyst who is a supervisor could also encourage or provide opportunities for supervisees to attend workshops, lectures, read scholarly articles, or attend other continuing education events to help them become more competent when working with diverse populations. In doing so, this would demonstrate adherence to code 5.03 Supervisory Delegation (BACB®, 2018).

While there may not be a specific requirement for culturally sensitivity training for licensure or certification, it is possible for the supervisor to create defined goals around culturally sensitive service delivery under code 5.04 Designing Effective Supervision and Training (BACB®, 2018). Culturally sensitive service delivery may allow for a more socially valid intervention since the selection of goals, reinforcers, punishers, and other interventions will be more geared toward the individual's culture. Addressing this may start at the university level or at the training program that the supervisee attends – for example, having culture be taught under the Behavior-Change Procedures; Selecting and Implementing Interventions course content requirement, or teaching supervisees how to select and implement culturally sensitive interventions under the Behavior-Change Procedures; Selecting and Implementing Interventions course content requirement would be two options to train supervisees in how to be more culturally sensitive practitioners. In addition, teaching behavior analysts how to be culturally sensitive supervisors falls under the Personnel Supervision and Management course content requirement. Examples of goals around culturally sensitive service delivery might be checking to see if the clinician asked about the client's culture – are there are customs, holidays or other culturally norms that I should be aware of which might impact service delivery? Asking about social validity – are these goals and interventions acceptable to you? (caregiver, client, etc.).

To adhere to code 5.05 Communication of Supervision Conditions, should the supervising behavior analyst choose to include cultural trainings or competencies in supervision, the supervisor should ensure that these are behaviorally written, with clear, specific, observable behaviors to assess (BACB®, 2018). For example, in applying code 5.05, if the training is about assessing social validity, the supervisee could be assessed via checklist if they asked caregiver and/or client are the procedures appropriate and socially acceptable. These expectations should also be communicated to the supervisee as part of supervision sessions and periodically reviewed with the supervisee.

Due to the fact that supervisees may be coming from a different culture, which may use a different language, supervisors should be sensitive to the language and terms used by a supervisee's culture when providing feedback to a supervisee to remain in compliance with code 5.06 Providing Feedback to Supervisees (BACB®, 2018). A supervisor might consider providing both written and verbal feedback so that the supervisee has the opportunity to review what was discussed. If the supervisee speaks a different language than the supervisor, the use of an interpreter might be considered. If there is no formal interpreter, the supervisor should consider if they should take the individual as a supervisee or if an informal interpreter can be used. However, the ethics of either of these should be carefully assessed. Similar to a culturally sensitive intervention one might create for clients, the supervisor should also make sure that they are creating meaningful reinforcement systems that are sensitive to the supervisee's culture and values. This can be done by asking the supervisee the best way to deliver feedback and reinforce behaviors.

Code 5.07 Evaluating the Effects of Supervision highlights the importance of evaluation in the supervision process (BACB®, 2018). Since there is no standardized checklist for evaluating culturally sensitive practices in behavior analysis, a supervising behavior analyst might create a task analysis of what culturally sensitive supervision and practice might look like. This may be useful not only to assess the behavior of the supervisee but also as a self-reflection of the supervisor. This might include a discussion on values, worldview, and background of the supervisee and how they impact supervision and practice, and in addition, issues (stereotypes, values, biases, etc.) that might pose a barrier and problems in supervision and practice.

In recent years, behavior analysts have started to become more aware of the need for culturally sensitive practitioners. Specifically, there appears to be an increase in informal discussions, conference presentations, posters, and trainings on topics around culture. However, this also raises concerns as more supervisees are becoming more culturally aware; previously trained supervisors may not have had this training. Supervisees may want their supervisor to be well versed in how to handle cultural issues, and when these needs are not addressed they become frustrated or upset (Douglas et al., 2014). Basic ways in which a culturally sensitive supervisor could address culture and diversity might be when discussing the BACB® 5th edition Task List (2017) or Professional and Ethical Compliance Code (2018). BACB® 5th Edition Task List (2017) items that might lend themselves well for teaching during supervision include:

E-2 Behavior analysts' responsibility to clients.

E-5 Behavior analysts as supervisors.

F-3 Identify and prioritize socially significant behavior-change goals.

H-3 Recommend intervention goals and strategies based on such factors as client preferences, supporting environments, risks, constraints, and social validity.

H-9 Collaborate with others who support and/or provide services to clients.

I-8 Evaluate the effects of supervision (e.g., on client outcomes, on supervisee repertoires).

(BACB, 2017, p 3)

Under code E-2 Behavior Analysts' Responsibility to Clients (BACB®, 2017), the supervisor and supervisee could examine what are their responsibilities are as cross-cultural clinicians.
What considerations, accommodations, and tasks should be done to ensure effective treatment.

The supervisor should examine their behavior under code E-5 Behavior Analysts as Supervisors (BACB®, 2017) and also make the same considerations as they did under E-2, in terms of
what considerations, accommodations, and tasks should be done to ensure effective supervision.

Since not every culture values the same things, the supervisor should assist the supervisee with code F-3 Identify and Prioritize Socially Significant Behavior-Change Goals
(BACB®, 2017). Here a combination of the behavior analyst's expertise should be balanced
with what is also appropriate for the culture. Some exploration into social validity should
be discussed.

Similar to code F-3, code H-3 Recommend Intervention Goals and Strategies Based on Such
Factors as Client Preferences, should examine the role of culture when planning intervention
goals (BACB®, 2017). While a good behavior analyst should take client preference into account
and individualize each plan for their specific client, perhaps more specific questions should be
asked geared toward incorporating a client's culture into treatment. For example, is the family
more past, present, or future focused? A client that is coming from a culture that is not future
focused might have difficulty with the future-focused concept of the Premack principle.

Under H-9 Collaborate With Others Who Support and/or Provide Services to Clients
(BACB®, 2017), the supervisor could expand the idea of who is traditionally consulted and
when collaboration should occur. For example, religious leaders, advocates, or other cultural
experience might be able to be cultural brokers and provide important information. In addition,
it might assist with rapport building and getting the buy-in from the client for intervention.

Finally, under code I-8 Evaluate the Effects of Supervision (e.g., on client outcomes, on
supervisee repertoires) (BACB®, 2017), the supervisor and supervisee should discuss how the
supervisory relationship is impacting the supervisee's skill acquisition, specifically in identifying biases, self-awareness, and working cross-culturally.

The BACB's® Professional and Ethical Compliance Code for Behavior Analysts (2018)
items that may provide opportunities for discussion during supervision include codes 1.02b–
1.03, 1.05b–f, 2.01, 3.04, 4.03, and 5.03a–b.

Further explanation of how a supervisor might incorporate the compliance code and diversity into supervision can be found below.

For codes 1.02b and 5.03, the Assessment of Culturally Sensitive Practice in Behavior
Analysis Algorithm (see Figure 15.1) may be one solution to objectively determine how to
proceed when working with clients of varying background. The supervisor should take care

that the supervisee is providing culturally sensitive services. If they do not have the skills (see Figure 15.1), the supervising behavior analyst should either provide the necessary training (opportunities), co-consult, or remove the behavior analyst from the case if serious ethical concerns exist.

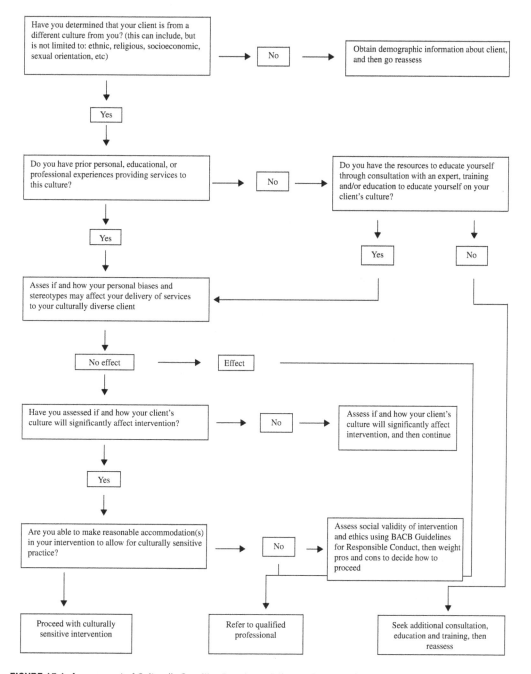

FIGURE 15.1 Assessment of Culturally Sensitive Practice in Behavior Analysis Algorithm

Under code 1.03, supervisors should attend and encourage their supervisees to attend professional development opportunities specifically around serving diverse clients. This may be inside or outside behavior analysis, as our discipline does not have as comprehensive theories on the subject as other fields such as psychology. However, behavior analysts and their supervisees should then discuss the application to behavior analysis, as it is important to maintain fidelity to our interventions.

Code 1.05 clearly makes ties to working with diverse clients and addressing issues around discrimination. A supervisor can expand upon these points by specifically discussing bias, microaggressions, and promote self-awareness and reflection by the supervisee. For example, thinking about how one felt when working with a client from a different background – what went well, was anything different, how did you feel? Microaggression in particular might be an important topic since these are more common now than overt racism, sexism, and so forth (Sue et al., 2007). Examples of microaggression in clinical practice might include calling someone "oriental" instead of Asian, or saying that a minority person speaks really good English for being from a particular minority group, asking a minority where they were born, telling a minority supervisee that they can succeed if they work just as hard as everyone else, telling a supervisee that race doesn't matter, that they see everyone as the same (Sue et al., 2007).

In code 3.04 Explaining Assessment Results, behavior analysts explain assessment results using language and graphic displays of data that are reasonably understandable to the client (BACB®, 2018). The supervisor should also have the supervisee practice explaining assessment results to the supervisor, in terms that might be understood by the diverse client. In some cases, when an interpreter is being used, care should be taken that the interpreter is familiar with the behavior analytic jargon being used in order to promote accurate translation. The BACBâ (2019a) has a list of translated documents that may be a useful resource.

Furthermore, code 4.03 Individualized Behavior-Change Programs. (a) Behavior analysts must tailor behavior-change programs to the unique behaviors, environmental variables, assessment results, and goals of each client (BACB®, 2017, p 12) incorporates the importance of social validity as a useful topic to discuss with supervisees when examining the application of this code. A good behavior analytic program will be individualized for each client's behaviors, but care should be taken to also specifically incorporate the client's culture – for example, when appropriate, ensuring culturally specific reinforcers are used and the development of socially valid goals and behaviors. For example, if remaining seated during the whole duration of a meal is important, a behavior analyst then might include this as a goal. Or of the client has certain ethnic foods that they like, those might be used as reinforcers. While some behaviors may be appropriate for a culture (e.g., aggression), they may not be appropriate in another. Therefore, discrimination training or assistance with prioritizing behaviors should be discussed. For example, a family may want to work on educational goals, as education is highly valued in the culture, but the client is displaying other destructive behavior. This could present a conflict that would need to be handled. One solution would be to discuss how we prioritize behaviors and suggest working on education later on, or concurrently if possible.

While the items do not fully encompass how to address culture and diversity in supervision, these skills can assist supervisors by providing a starting point for conversation.

Strengths of Cross-Cultural Supervision

Skinner (1953) defines culture as a collection of behavior or practices that includes variables "arranged by other people" (p. 419). Given that the varying cultures in America continue to grow, it is important for behavior analysts to consider how they can be effective supervisors for diverse populations. In general, cultural responsivity refers to the ability to learn from and relate respectfully to people from your own and other cultures (Seponski & Jordan, 2017). Includes a culturally sensitive worldview, a competent knowledge base, acting accord as a culturally sensitive individual, and the sharing of power with stakeholders. Cultural responsiveness in supervision refers to the supervisor's acknowledgment of the existence culture in the supervisory relationship and active exploration of the impact of culture on the relationship (Douglas et al., 2014). Culturally responsive supervisors acknowledge the fact that supervisees can be experts, with firsthand experience, on their culture and call upon that knowledge. They may also use cultural advisors, and work to distinguish differences between cross-cultural relationships (Seponski & Jordan, 2017). There is also the acknowledgement that a therapist's culture can impact the therapeutic relationship. For example, a supervisee whose culture values deference to people in authority might have a hard time challenging or speaking up to their supervisor. While inclusion of multicultural issues is especially important for the growth and development of minority supervisees, there are also benefits for non-minorities. These benefits include an increase in personal awareness of cultural issues, better consideration of culture in case conceptualization, increase levels of multicultural sensitivity, and an overall improved supervisory experience (Seponski & Jordan, 2017).

Including culturally responsive supervision can have a positive impact on the quality of supervision. For example, if the supervisor does not address cultural issues, the supervisee's interpersonal and professional growth may be hindered. For example, supervisees may feel offended, upset, distressed, uncomfortable, scared, and unable to meet clients' needs if their cultural needs are not addressed. Ideally, cross-cultural supervision should encourage the development and growth of the supervisees. Furthermore, it should address or alleviate any potential ethnic and cultural barriers within supervision and practice. Strengths of cross-cultural supervision include (1) getting to know another culture, (2) increased knowledge about your own culture, (3) learning more about yourself, (4) being self-aware and unafraid to address cultural differences, (5) supervisees may feel more comfortable, (6) having an improved supervision experience for both the supervisor and supervisee, (7) helping the supervisee develop a cultural identity, (8) realizing commonalities to bridge differences, (9) a mutual appreciation and understanding, and (10) enhanced professional and sensitized supervision practices (Wisker & Claesson, 2013).

For Supervisors

As discussed by Shupp and Mattingly (2017), supervisors who are self-aware of their own biases, have a solid cultural identity, are understanding of the complexities of culture, and can facilitate discussions around the topic of culture allow for supervisees to feel more supported, are able to establish trust with the supervisee, and are able to assist in the development and growth of the supervisee. One model proposed by Ancis and Ladany (2001) includes six dimensions of multicultural competencies. This begins with the supervisor obtaining additional knowledge or training on their own values, biases, and personal limitations, with the focus on their personal development. The supervisor should encourage the same self-reflection from their supervisee and help them explore their own identity (race, religion, gender, sexual orientation).

In the conceptualization stage, the supervisor should discuss topics such as how stereotyping may impact one's work with a client, including case conceptualizations, treatment goals, and interventions (Ancis & Ladany, 2001). It should be noted that there are some behavior analytic interventions that are more in line with American values. For example, the Premack principle is focused on the future, therefore cultures that may value the past might not adapt to this type of intervention as easily. These should also be discussed during supervision and make accommodations, providing the fidelity of the intervention can remain intact.

Another way to view stereotyping and the impact it might have on one's work is by exploring self-awareness. As discussed by Barnes-Holmes, Barnes-Holmes, Roche, and Smeets (2001) self-awareness can be defined as verbal discrimination of our own behavior. By developing self-awareness, we may prevent our biases from impeding how we serve culturally diverse clients. Similarly, Skinner (1974) emphasized the relationship between self-awareness and control over our own behavior, Skinner proposed that talking about our behavior is how we achieve self-awareness. We can help to be more aware of our biases, by being "mindful", fully attending and being alert in the moment, as well as alert us to those covert and overt behaviors that can cause bias. One way of doing this is by paying attention to clients and being active and alert, which can help to build rapport. For example, being aware of similarities and differences, and asking questions about observations when applicable.

In the skills dimension of multicultural supervision, supervisees should examine the use of nontraditional or alternative interventions; these might include indigenous interventions or ones better suited to the socioeconomic situation or religion of the client. It should be emphasized that the fidelity of the behavior analytic intervention should not be compromised, and clinicians will want to be careful when working with non-evidence-based interventions that some families might support. The supervisee should be able to demonstrate flexibility in intervention implementation while keeping the essential parts in place – for example, knowing what reinforcers are appropriate, what holidays are celebrated, what terms or language the client might use, or who to include in meetings. If a client wants to use a non-evidence-based practice, and assuming the alternative intervention does not cause any ethical concerns, the behavior analyst should share their concerns but also respect the culture of the client. One solution might be to use data to demonstrate the effectiveness (or non-effectiveness of the nontraditional or alternative intervention). In supervision, the behavior analyst might also have the supervisee explore non–behavior analytic theories such as racial identity, gender identity, sexual orientation, or ethnic identity theories if these will help the supervisee obtain additional skills.

Finally, in the outcome/evaluation stage proposed by Ancis and Landy (2001), the supervisor evaluates the supervisee's multicultural competencies. Competencies in this context do not necessary mean that the supervisee is competent, but rather that they demonstrate a set of skills. This final stage might prove challenging to the field of ABA since we do not have a single unified approach to assessing or conceptualizing this topic. Instead, supervisors should consider creating their own objective way to assess for multicultural competencies. If the supervisee is unable to demonstrate competency, the supervisor should provide more support in those areas where the supervisee is falling short.

Challenges of Obtaining Cross-Cultural Supervision in Behavior Analysis

The role of a supervisor is an important one. Specifically, the supervisor assists the supervisee in translating what they learned in their coursework into practice. While not behavior analytic, Sue, Arredondo and McDavis's (1992) seminal article outlined three multicultural competencies that a supervisor should address: (1) self-awareness, (2) knowledge, and (3) skills. While currently, in behavior analysis, there are no standard skills or ways to assess skills related to diversity, Fong, Catagnus, Broadhead, and Quigley (2016) described how behavior analysts can become more self-aware. The first step would be in understanding our own cultural systems. A self-aware behavior analyst might also reflect, discuss, or communicate through other mediums about one's diverse client interactions. Finally, a self-aware behavior analyst might engage in mindfulness and scientific mindedness and reflect on one's client interactions or private events. While it is not mandatory for topics around culture to be addressed, doing so may enhance the supervisory relationship.

Aside from the practical concerns over of a lack of standards or competencies for cross-cultural supervision, other challenges include differences in values, interactional styles, acculturation level, education, and socioeconomic status (Inman, 2008). This can result in miscommunications, hostility, or mistrust. For example, the supervisor might take the supervisee's lack of eye contact as a negative quality, when in fact the supervisee's culture believes that a lack of eye contact shows respect. Similarly, a supervisee might be taught never to question authority, so the supervisee will not speak up or ask questions during supervision (Inman, 2008). The supervisor might think the supervisee knows the material. In addition, there might be a lack of acknowledgement of power differences at cultural and professional levels. This might result in a lack of self-disclosure, safety, trust, or guarded communication. For example, a supervisee might be reluctant to raise topics related to race, culture, or any other part of culture to their supervisor. There might also be an unwillingness to request help, due to biases or fear of validating pre-existing -isms (Inman, 2008). For example, a female supervisee might not want to ask for a day off to watch her child because she is afraid she will confirm a perceived supervisor's opinion that mothers should not be working.

Suárez-Orozco et al. (2013) put forth a paper discussing best practices for working with immigrant populations. While this may seem restricted to only mental health professionals and immigrant clients, it can also be useful when working with minority supervisees with some expansion. For example, the concept of clinician bias may be reframed to supervisor bias. Here the tendency to apply a majority culture's module of illness to a supervisee or client is a key issue. By not taking into account how a supervisee might conceptualize a concern based on their cultural experience might negatively impact the supervisor/supervisee relationship, causing the minority supervisee to feel further marginalized. A better idea might be some education on how both groups conceptualize the issue. The supervisor should self-reflect on their own biases and expectations and when appropriate consult with others who are from a similar background as the supervisee. Similarly, if the supervisee is working with a minority client, they should also be careful not to force their model of treatment on the client without listening to the client's perspective. Similar to the above example with the supervisor/supervisee, the rapport may be negatively impacted between the supervisee and client. It might be advisable that the supervisor question if the supervisee has actively addressed the role of culture with the family.

The guidelines for working with immigrant-origin clients also discuss the importance of the clinicians' self-assessment (Suárez-Orozco et al., 2013). Here, supervisors and supervisees could be self-aware and examine how their socialization impacts their evaluation of the client's minority status. Lillis and Hayes (2007) discussed that given our cultural systems and the human tendency to evaluate judgments and thoughts, judgments are normal but practitioners should remain committed to acting positively based on our values. Supervisors should be aware that their attitudes and beliefs may negatively influence their perceptions of and interactions with individuals who are different from themselves (Suárez-Orozco et al., 2013). Similarly, they should encourage exploration and address this idea in their supervision sessions.

In terms of capacity, the supervisor should assess their capacity to provide supervision that will meet the needs of their supervisee across cultures (Suárez-Orozco et al., 2013). While these guidelines were not specifically written for behavior analysis, they can be translated into the idea that cultural competence involves three areas: (1) a behavior analyst's cultural knowledge, (2) the behavior analyst's attitudes and beliefs toward clients who may be from diverse backgrounds and self-understanding, and (3) the behavior analyst's ability and application of culturally appropriate interventions (Suárez-Orozco et al., 2013). When necessary, the behavior analyst should also know when to seek the assistance of others who are more familiar with the supervisee's culture or the culture of the family. This might include the use of interpretive services, religious pillars of the community, or other advocates.

One of the challenges in providing cross-cultural supervision is not being fully aware of what constitutes one's culture. Hall (1976) coined the term "cultural iceberg" as an analogy of culture. In this model, there are some portions of a culture that are visible (think above the water), but there is an even greater portion below the surface that we cannot see or are not aware of. More specifically, the external or conscious part of culture is what we can readily observe, which includes behaviors and some beliefs – this is the tip of the iceberg. Below the surface is the internal or subconscious part of culture, which includes some beliefs and the values and thought patterns that underlie behavior. The unconscious or internal components of a culture are often more difficult to change and are implicitly learned and subjective. In contrast, the conscious or external components of a culture are explicitly learned, more easily changed, and obtained through objective knowledge.

It is important to understand these differences, especially since the internal culture is harder to learn. Specifically, Hall (1976) believed that the only way to learn the internal culture of others is to actively participate in their culture. When first learning about a new culture, the most apparent differences might be the overt or observable behaviors. Does the individual shake hands or bow? What is their eye contact like? However, the more time that is spent within the culture, the culture's underlying beliefs, values, and thought patterns that govern the behavior can be discovered. If we apply this concept to supervision, a good first step is to observe the differences between cultures, but if the supervisor stops there, they are not doing a comprehensive job at understanding the cultural differences and similarities. The exploration should be intentional and comprehensive, allowing the supervisor and supervisee to explore how their experiences, expectations, and application of behavior analysis might differ between cultures. The supervisor should go beyond what is on the surface, or the tip of the iceberg, to uncover a deeper understanding.

There is also a logistical challenge in obtaining cross-cultural supervision. According to the BACB[i] website (2019b), there are 322,008 BCBAs. In a 2016 Job Task Analysis survey, 67.65% of BCBAs® self-reported that they work in autism, with the second largest area working in education (BACB®, 2019b). In addition, there may be multiple BCBAs® in some geographic locations, or none at all. Countries such as Armenia, Brunei Darussalam, Bulgaria, Estonia, Guam, and the Virgin Islands (US) do not have any BCBA-Ds™ or BCBAs[i] (BACB®, 2019b). In the United States, which has the largest number of certificants, every state has at least four BCBAs®, however, this does not ensure the availability of a BCBA® to provide supervision. Those seeking supervision by a BCBA® have an extra challenge if they are looking specifically for a certificant who speaks a certain language or has experience working with a specific population since that information is unavailable through the BACB® website. In those cases, the individual would have to contact certificants via a listserv or other tool to find a match.

Conclusion

Ultimately, all supervision could be considered multicultural because no two people have an identical experience (Falicov, 1995). Supervisors should take the necessary steps to ensure that they are prepared to provide a comprehensive supervision experience, whether this means attending professional development or creating standards, task analyses, or checklists. Even when supervisors and supervisees are from the same culture, there still can be challenges. There could be assumptions applied to the supervisor or supervisee based on a shared group identity that does not consider an individual's unique history (Shupp & Mattingly, 2017). By creating opportunities for professional development around the topic of culture and diversity, supervisors can be better prepared to address such topics in supervision.

References

American Psychological Association. (2017). *Multicultural guidelines: An ecological approach to context, identity, and intersectionality.* Retrieved from www.apa.org/about/policy/multicultural-guidelines.pdf

Ancis, J. R., & Ladany, N. (2001). A multicultural framework for counselor supervision. In L. Bradley & N. Ladany (Eds.), *Counselor supervision: Principles, process, and practice* (3rd ed., pp. 63–90). New York, NY: Brunner-Routledge.

Barnes-Holmes, Y., Barnes-Holmes, D., Roche, B., & Smeets, P. M. (2001). The development of self and perspective-taking: A relational frame analysis. *Behavioral Development Bulletin, 10*(1), 42–45. http://doi.org/10.1037/h0100482

Behavior Analyst Certification Board. (2017). *BCBA/BCaBA task list* (5th ed.) Retrieved from www.bacb.com/wp-content/uploads/2017/09/170113-BCBA-BCaBA-task-list-5th-ed-.pdf

Behavior Analyst Certification Board. (2018). *Professional and ethical compliance code for behavior analysts.* Retrieved from www.bacb.com/wp-content/uploads/BACB-Compliance-Code-english_190318.pdf

Behavior Analyst Certification Board. (2019a). *Translated documents.* Retrieved from www.bacb.com/translated-documents/

Behavior Analyst Certification Board. (2019b). *Mass email service.* Retrieved from www.bacb.com/services/o.php?page=100763

Douglas, M. K., Rosenkoetter, M., Pacquiao, D. F., Callister, L. C., Hattar-Pollara, M., Lauderdale, J., Milstead, J., Nardi, D., & Purnell, L. (2014). Guidelines for implementing culturally competent nursing care. *Journal of Transcultural Nursing, 25*(2), 109–121.

Falicov, C. J. (1995). Training to think culturally: A multidimensional comparative framework. *Family Process, 34*(4), 373–388.

Fong, E. H., Catagnus, R. M., Brodhead, M. T., Quigley, S., & Field, S. (2016). Developing the cultural awareness skills of behavior analysts. *Behavior Analysis in Practice, 9*(1), 84–94.

Hall, E. T. (1976). *Beyond culture.* New York: Doubleday.

Inman, A. G. (2008). *Race and culture in supervision: Challenges and opportunities.* Presented at the 116th American Psychological Association Conference, Boston, MA.

Lillis, J., & Hayes S. C. (2007). Applying acceptance, mindfulness, and values to the reduction of prejudice: A pilot study. *Behavior Modification, 31*(4), 389–411. doi: 10.1177/0145445506298413

National Association of Social Workers. (2015). *Standards and indicators for cultural competence in social work practice.* https://www.socialworkers.org/LinkClick.aspx?fileticket=PonPTDEBrn4%3D&portalid=0

Seponski, D. M., & Jordan, L. S. (2017). Cross-cultural supervision in an international setting: Foreign supervisors and native supervisees. *Journal of Family Therapy, 40*(2), 247–264. http://doi.org/10.1111/1467-6427.12157

Shupp, M. R., & Mattingly, R. S. (2017). A qualitative examination of cross-cultural supervision: Toward a revised model. *International Journal for Cross-Disciplinary Subjects in Education, 8*(1), 2954–2963.

Skinner, B. F. (1953). *Science and human behavior.* New York: Free Press.

Skinner, B. F. (1974). *About behaviorism.* Oxford, UK: Alfred A. Knopf.

Suárez-Orozco, C., Birman, D., Casas, J. M., Nakamura, N., Tummala-Nara, P., & Zárate, M. (2013). *Working with immigrant-origin clients: An update for mental health professionals.* Washington, DC: American Psychological Association.

Sue, D. W., Arredondo, P., & McDavis, R. J. (1992). Multicultural competencies/standards: A pressing need. *Journal of Counseling & Development, 70,* 477–486.

Sue, D. W., Capodilupo, C. M., Torino, G. C., Bucceri, J. M., Holder, A., Nadal, K. L., & Esquilin, M. (2007). Racial microaggressions in everyday life: Implications for clinical practice. *American Psychologist, 62*(4), 271.

Wisker, G., & Claesson, S. (2013). The impact of cross-disciplinary culture on student-supervisor perceptions. *International Journal of Doctoral Studies, 8,* 21–37.

16

Multiculturalism and Diversity Issues in Applied Behavior Analysis

Where Do We Go From Here?

Brian M. Conners

Demographic Data

The first area of improvement in our field is that we need to realistically know the demographics of the population of behavior analysts working in the field. As highlighted in previous chapters, the BACB® (2019) only releases certain data about certificants (e.g., number of certificants and areas worked), and some research has highlighted the number of females and males in the field (e.g., Nosik, Luke, & Carr, 2019). However, this is not enough information to understand the diversity of the field. Knowing the demographics of our field is important to better understand how diverse we are or if there truly is a lack of diversity or representation of groups within the profession. This can then allow professional organizations (e.g., BACB®, the Association for Behavior Analysis International (ABAI), and the Association of Professional Behavior Analysts (APBA)) to develop task forces to address the recruitment, retention, and training of diverse professionals into the field of ABA.

Ethical and Professional Standards in ABA

As highlighted throughout the chapters, the current BACB® (2019) *Professional and Ethical Compliance Code for Behavior Analysts* and the BACB® (2012, 2017) 4th and 5th Edition Task Lists make minimal mention about working with diverse populations, having the skill set needed to work with diverse populations, and being a culturally competent behavior analyst. Throughout the book, authors identified certain professional and ethical standards that may apply, but had to make the standards fit the topics within the current available standards. This is another area that can be focused on for improvement in the field by developing ethical and professional standards that embrace language around diversity and providing clarity of training and practice guidelines for working with diverse populations.

Graduate Training, Fieldwork, and Supervision

As noted in the chapters on working with diverse populations along with the supervision chapter, there is not much in terms of requirements for multiculturalism and diversity training in the field of ABA as part of graduate preparation. Therefore, since the BACB® creates the standards for training and ABAI does the approval of verified course sequences and accreditation of master's and doctoral ABA programs, there is a unique opportunity there to impact the profession by including training standards for future generations of ABA professionals entering the field.

Professional Development

Another area that is a future consideration for our field is examining our continuing education requirement as behavior analysts to include credit requirements for multiculturalism and diversity courses similar to the current professional development training standards for ethics and supervision. This would help to provide training to those individuals who are currently certified and working in the field who may never have had exposure to diversity training as part of their graduate preparation in ABA.

Research With Diverse Populations

The final major area that was observed throughout the chapters is that there has been minimal research done with diverse and international populations in ABA research literature. Professional organizations and ABA journals should be encouraging academics to produce scholarly research on applications of ABA principles with diverse and international populations and how behavioral treatments may need to be adapted in a culturally sensitive way to provide comprehensive ABA services to diverse groups.

Summary

In summation, as mentioned in the introductory chapter of this book, our hope is that publishing this book paves way for a larger discussion on multiculturalism and diversity issues among behavior analysts and our professional organizations. Furthermore, this book should have provided you as a reader with a stronger foundation and knowledge base of working with diverse populations. Again, no one book can cover every aspect of diversity or make you culturally competent, but this book was designed to begin a dialogue about this important topic and contribute to the shaping of the field of ABA.

References

Behavior Analyst Certification Board. (2012). *4th edition task list.* Retrieved from www.bacb.com/wp-content/uploads/2017/09/160101-BCBA-BCaBA-task-list-fourth-edition-english.pdf

Behavior Analyst Certification Board. (2017). *5th edition task list.* Retrieved from www.bacb.com/wp-content/uploads/2017/09/170113-BCBA-BCaBA-task-list-5th-ed-.pdf

Behavior Analyst Certification Board. (2019). *Professional and ethical compliance codes for behavior analysts.* Retrieved from www.bacb.com/wp-content/uploads/BACB-Compliance-Code-english_190318.pdf

Nosik, M. R., Luke, M. M., & Carr, J. E. (2019). Representation of women in behavior analysis: An empirical analysis. *Behavior Analysis: Research and Practice, 19*(2), 213–221. http://doi.org/10.1037/bar0000118

Test Bank for *Multiculturalism and Diversity in Applied Behavior Analysis*

Bridging Theory and Application

By Brian Conners and Shawn T. Capell

Chapter 2 Exam Questions

1. Indicate the correct aspects of culture included in the ADDRESSING model.

    a. Indigenous Heritage

    b. Gender Identify/Expression

    c. Age/Generation

    d. All of the above

2. You are a behavior analyst who was raised in a family who ascribes to the Catholic religion. You have had little interactions with families who ascribe to the Muslim religion within your professional career; however, you have been asked by your employer to take a case with a family who practices the Muslim faith. You do not feel comfortable with the family's practices within the home. How can you effectively address your concerns while still providing the learner with quality services?

    a. Identify what specific practices make you uncomfortable and speak with the parents about changing these practices while you are in the home.

    b. Identify what specific practices make you uncomfortable, identify peer-reviewed research regarding the specific practices, identify additional educational events specific to the practices you feel uncomfortable with, and speak with other professionals to identify possible solutions to your concerns.

c. Identify what specific practices make you uncomfortable and seek out other professionals in the field to speak with and identify possible solutions.

d. Speak with your supervisor and discontinue services due to you not feeling comfortable within the home.

3. It is important for a behavior analyst to be self-aware of their own personal, cultural values and beliefs for all of the following reasons except:

a. Knowledge of their own personal, cultural values and beliefs will better assist the behavior analyst in providing culturally competent services.

b. Knowledgeable of a behavior analyst's own personal, cultural values and beliefs can assist them in increasing cultural awareness.

c. When a behavior analyst is aware of their own personal, cultural values and beliefs, they can make more money by accepting more clients.

d. Knowledge of their own personal, cultural values and beliefs can better assist a behavior analyst in accepting clients with which they can be most effective.

4. The ADDRESSING framework includes which of the following nine components?

a. Age/Diagnosed Disability/Assumed Disability/Region/Ethnic Expression/Socioeconomic Status/Sexual Expression/Indigenous Heritage/National Identity/Gender Expression

b. Age/Congenital Disability/Acquired Disability/Religion/Ethnic Identity/Socioeconomic Status/Sexual Identity/Indigenous Heritage/National Origin/Gender

c. Appearance/Expressed Disability/Acquired Disability/Religion/Ethnic Expression/Socioeconomic Status/Sexual Identity/Indigenous Origin/National Origin/Gender

d. None of the above

5. Being a member of the dominant group within a domain can create which of the following blind spots specific to clinical practice?

a. Not fully understanding cultural contingencies and their possible effects on behavior

b. Behavioral missteps

c. Both A and B

d. None of the above

6. Indigenous Heritage refers to _____ while National Origin refers to _____.

a. original inhabitants of an area/people who were born in the country they live in

b. where a culture comes from/where a culture currently lives

c. people who were born in the country they live/original inhabitants of an area

d. where a culture was born/where cultures are accepted

7. You are a Caucasian behavior analyst who has been asked to provide services to an African American family. You have had little experience with African American families in the past, and from those experiences you view very few as being positive. Which domain of the ADDRESSING model should you use to evaluate your self-awareness?

    a. Age/Generation

    b. Religion/Spirituality

    c. Socioeconomic Status

    d. Ethnic and Racial Identity

8. You are a behavior analyst who has been working with an adult learner for many years. You have established a great professional relationship with the learner and their family. During your last session, your learner expressed his interest to start dating; however, he expressed his interest in someone of the same sex. You do not feel comfortable with this as it is not within your belief system. All are acceptable next steps for you except:

    a. Do not say anything and hope the learner forgets the conversation.

    b. Conduct a self-assessment regarding your personal belief system related to the topic of sexual identity.

    c. Speak with a supervisor/seasoned behavior analyst to identify how you can best provide services while respecting the client's wishes.

    d. Identify an alternative behavior analyst to continue providing services in the case until culturally competent services are available.

9. You are assigned to work with an adult who identifies as transgender, and you are unfamiliar with the client's gender identity. You should:

    a. Validate the client's gender identity.

    b. Seek out information specific to transgender individuals.

    c. Ask the client which pronouns they prefer and include this information in programming.

    d. All are respectful culturally sensitive steps.

10. A behavior analyst's awareness of deficits related to gender should lead to:

    a. Posting on a personal social media platform to gain advice.

    b. Taking no action.

    c. Seeking out more information from creditable sources.

    d. Asking the client questions that can be considered offensive.

Chapter 2 Answer Key

1. A
2. B
3. C
4. B
5. C
6. A
7. D
8. A
9. D
10. C

Chapter 3 Exam Questions

1. Which of the following examples best represents culturally sensitive practices in the field of applied behavior analysis?

   a. Obtaining programming ideas from the parents specific to the client's culture, but not implementing these goals during intervention sessions.

   b. Ensuring all written forms of communication are provided in the native language of the client.

   c. Providing clients with translators to increase understanding during parent training sessions, meetings, and all other required vocal communications.

   d. Ensuring programs are specific to the client's cultural practices regardless of the personal feelings of the behavior analyst.

2. All of the following examples illustrate the potential negative effects of a lack of culturally sensitive practice related to the client except:

   a. The potential breakdown of the client-clinician relationship.

   b. The potential increase in difficulties when implementing programming.

   c. An increased feeling of guilt from the behavior analyst.

   d. Lack of parent buy-in and community support.

3. Regarding the current BACB's® Professional and Ethical Compliance Code for Behavior Analysts (2019), limitations include that:

   a. The code does not effectively address all the needs required.

   b. The code is absent a moral philosophical framework.

   c. Unintentional racism may be promoted.

   d. All of the above

4. Once published, the *Multicultural Alliance of Behavior Analysts Standards for Cultural Competency in Behavior Analysis* was adopted by _____.

   a. The Association for Professional Behavior Analysts

   b. Applied Behavior Analysis International

   c. The Culture and Diversity SIG

   d. The BACB®

5. Which example best exemplifies a behavior analyst advocating for appropriate and culturally sensitive services?

   a. Requesting additional hours for a client due to a parent request.

   b. Ensuring all documentation is translated to the learner's native language and providing a translator during meetings to ensure effective communication.

c. Speaking with the parents to ensure the behavior analyst can accompany the family on an upcoming family vacation.

d. All of the above

6. Self-reflection should include:

a. A review of your personal values, standards, and education, and how these might impact service delivery.

b. A review of your personal beliefs, misconceptions, and biases and how these might impact service delivery.

c. A review of your personal biases, standards, and misunderstandings and how these might impact service delivery.

d. A review of your personal values, beliefs, and biases and how these might impact service delivery.

7. How can you as a behavior analyst continue to address issues related to culturally sensitive service delivery?

a. Conduct research specific to the area of culturally sensitive service delivery.

b. Both A and C

c. Continue to conduct self-assessment activities to ensure you are implementing culturally sensitive behavioral services.

d. Neither A nor C

8. A culturally sensitive behavioral health practice should:

a. Mention culturally sensitive practice during orientation and no other time.

b. Create and implement general policies that address areas of culturally sensitive service delivery.

c. Provide ongoing education and training for behavior analysts regarding culturally sensitive service delivery and offer positive and corrective feedback.

d. Incorporating the words "culturally sensitive" into the mission and vision statement.

9. _____ best illustrates a multicultural guideline.

a. The behavior analyst will be aware of personal and professional biases.

b. Personal biases held by the behavior analyst cannot affect service delivery.

c. Behavior analysts will be aware of personal and professional biases in working with diverse populations.

d. Behavior analysts will be aware of personal and professional biases in working with diverse populations and will make referrals when appropriate.

10. A behavior analyst can incorporate culturally sensitive practices into their personal practice by:

   a. Self-evaluating their current level of culturally sensitive practices and seeking help in areas of deficit.

   b. Conducting communications across cultural groups to ensure cultural compliance and competency.

   c. Both A and B

   d. Neither A nor B

Chapter 3 Answer Key

1. A
2. C
3. D
4. C
5. B
6. D
7. A
8. C
9. D
10. C

Chapter 4 Exam Questions

1. An individual who engages in cultural practices that are unspoken and shared by the group is engaging in:

    a. Shared values.

    b. Group culture.

    c. Deep culture.

    d. Surface culture.

2. The Multidimensional Model of Racial Identity (MMRI) demonstrates all except:

    a. Racial regard.

    b. Racial identity.

    c. Racial centrality.

    d. Racial ideology.

3. When implementing behavioral interventions within the African American community, the behavior analyst should remain aware of:

    a. Historical biases against the African American community.

    b. Implicit biases.

    c. Personal biases.

    d. All of the above

4. The field of applied behavior analysis can:

    a. Provide education to African American communities specific to the diagnosis of autism and the benefits of ABA.

    b. Continue not to comment about the current needs of learners within the African American community.

    c. Generalize treatments derived from outside cultural groups without taking the cultural influences of those cultural groups into account.

    d. Do nothing. The field of ABA is doing a great job addressing the concerns of the African American community.

5. You have been asked to work with a 12-year old child within the African American community. Currently the child lives within the home with his biological mother, father, and sister. Within the same home resides his maternal grandmother and maternal aunt. Down the street resides his paternal aunt and uncle. Who would be considered the learner's community?

    a. All individuals living within a 20-mile radius of his home

    b. His mother, father, sister

c.   His mother, father, sister, grandmother, and maternal aunt

   d.   His mother, father, sister, grandmother, maternal aunt, paternal aunt, and paternal uncle

6. The cultural expression of African Americans:

   a.   Includes being a part of the African American racial group.

   b.   Includes being considered minorities in the United States.

   c.   Includes mainstream assimilation.

   d.   All examples are relevant to the cultural expression of African Americans.

7. A behavior analyst is currently working with an African American family and has been for several months. The behavior analyst is not religious; however, the parents have expressed the desire for the child to start attending church services. The behavior analyst is not fully comfortable attending church with the family. How should the behavior analyst proceed?

   a.   The behavior analyst should speak with the parents regarding the skills required during a church service.

   b.   The behavior analyst should speak with the family regarding the skills required during a church service and implement these interventions within the home. Once mastered, the behavior analyst should identify a staff member who has an established relationship with the family and is comfortable attending services.

   c.   The behavior analyst should speak with the parents about their objections related to interventions specific to church services.

   d.   The behavior analyst should conduct a self-assessment to identify what aspects of church they do not feel comfortable with.

8. A learner you have been providing services with for several weeks has communicated the desire to be identified as Afro-American. The behavior analyst should:

   a.   Comply with the learner's request.

   b.   Inform the learner you are unaware of the term and refuse to identify them as Afro-American.

   c.   Talk to your best friend about the day you have had.

   d.   Speak with your supervisor about the situation to identify any potential ethical violations.

9. How can a behavior analyst fully incorporate the Aversive Childhood Experiences (ACE) tool into service delivery specific to the African American culture?

   a.   Incorporate the assessment into the intake/assessment process.

   b.   Incorporate the assessment into the intake/assessment and identify effective behavioral programming, taking into consideration the results of the assessment.

c. Incorporate the assessment into the intake/assessment process but never utilize the information derived from the assessment.

d. Incorporate the assessment into the intake/assessment process and report the parents to the local authorities.

10. Specific to law enforcement perceptions, the BCBA should:

a. Incorporate aspects and concepts of law enforcement into behavioral programming.

b. Examine personal beliefs regarding law enforcement.

c. Evaluate African American concepts regarding law enforcement and evaluate the possible cultural implications of this understanding.

d. All of the above

Chapter 4 Answer Key

1. C
2. B
3. D
4. A
5. D
6. D
7. B
8. A
9. B
10. D

Chapter 5 Exam Questions

1. Specific to Latino communities, what factors can affect service delivery?
   a. Lack of access to health services
   b. Lack of access to behavioral services
   c. Lack of trained service providers
   d. All of the above

2. _____ is a professional group whose mission is to train, support and mentor the next generation of behavior analysts to serve underrepresented populations and to increase diversity in all facets of the field of behavior analysis.
   a. Association for Behavior Analysis International
   b. Latino Association for Behavior Analysis
   c. Multicultural Alliance of Behavior Analysts
   d. Association of Professional Behavior Analysts

3. Regarding communication barriers specific to the Latino community, behavior analysts should:
   a. Ensure adequate access to translators and/or written communications within the family's native language.
   b. Speak slowly and hope the parents can understand.
   c. Have a family member serve as a translator when needed.
   d. Gain a basic understanding of the family's native language.

4. Within the Latino community, barriers include:
   a. An increase in understanding regarding the special education or school system.
   b. The ability to locate a qualified professional to obtain a diagnosis.
   c. Both A and B
   d. Neither A nor B

5. A behavior analyst has completed an assessment for a young man within the Latino community. Both parents do not speak English; however, one of the younger children is fluent in both English and Spanish. The behavior analyst provides the family with an English language document and requests the younger sibling translate the document for the parents so approval can be obtained. This behavior analyst is in violation of which ethical code?
   a. Code 1.03
   b. Code 3.04
   c. Code 4.06
   d. Code 7.01

6. Within the assessment/recommendation process, what recommendations specific to the Latino community can a behavior analyst request to ensure appropriate and culturally sensitive service delivery?

a. Request a small amount of services to ensure the family is able to pay the copay.

b. Request a bilingual therapist to ensure appropriate and adequate communication.

c. Ensure programming materials only include icons and images directly related to Latino culture.

d. Request the same general services as done with a previous Latino learner.

7. When a behavior analyst provides substandard services, Latino community parents can:

a. Normalize their child's behavior.

b. Deny that a problem exists.

c. Mistrust the entire ABA/medical community.

d. All of the above

8. What should behavior analysts do when delivering services within the Latino community?

a. Slightly modify the same programs across all Latino learners to ensure programs are individualized.

b. Consider the cultural and environmental factors of the Latino community and how these factors can impact service delivery.

c. Consider how other ethnic groups implement behavioral services and apply those same principles into the Latino community.

d. Only accept individuals who speak English as a primary language.

9. A behavior analyst is asked to provide services to a Latino family. The behavior analyst has never worked with this community and has never received training regarding the specific cultural influences within this culture. The behavior analyst reaches out to an alternative colleague who has extensive experience within the Latino community. Which ethical standard is this behavior analyst in compliance with?

a. Ethical Code 1.02

b. Ethical Code 1.03

c. Ethical Code 3.03

d. Ethical Code 4.06

10. In accordance with Ethical Code 5.01, an individual seeking supervision experience hours should:

a. Identify a supervisor who is willing to provide supervision.

b. Identify a supervisor who is in close proximity to the learners' home.

c.   Identify a supervisor who has experience providing behavior analyst services within the Latino community.

    d.   Identify a supervisor who is willing to sign off on documentation.

Chapter 5 Answer Key

1. D
2. B
3. A
4. B
5. B
6. B
7. D
8. B
9. A
10. C

1. The School-Wide Positive Behavioral Support (SWPBS) system is:

    a. The implementation of a comprehensive behavioral approach utilized for one student throughout the school day.

    b. A behavioral intervention.

    c. A comprehensive behavioral approach that arranges contingencies to promote safer schools and reduce problem behavior to improve student behavior.

    d. A complex blend of technologies including precision teaching and talk-aloud problem-solving.

2. With respect to language within indigenous populations:

    a. It is recommended to use a tribe's original name.

    b. If unsure, it is OK to skip this and/or gloss over it.

    c. It is not important because indigenous populations typically speak English.

    d. None of the above

3. Which of the following events can contribute to Indigenous students having a lack of skills within the classroom?

    a. Missionary School Movement

    b. New Boarding School Movement

    c. Off-Reservation Boarding School Movement

    d. All of the above

4. You are a behavior analyst currently working with an Indigenous family. The family has requested you introduce the family's Native language into teaching targets for skill acquisition. You are unclear of the pronunciation of the requested targets. How should you proceed?

    a. Identify a YouTube video that provides you with generic native language examples.

    b. Speak with the parents to identify the Native language targets and if possible, include them into a parent implemented program.

    c. Inform the parents that these targets are not relevant to behavioral intervention.

    d. Inform the parents that you will implement these targets and never do so.

5. As a behavior analyst you have taken the first step by reading this chapter regarding Indigenous communities. Simply reading this chapter is not the end of your educational experience. What other actions can you take to increase your development of socially sensitive cultural skills?

    a. Attend conference presentations regarding socially sensitive cultural skills.

    b. Conduct self-assessment regarding your socially sensitive cultural skill delivery.

c.   Both A and B

d.   Neither A nor B

6. _____ means to honor the culture of Indigenous cultures by educating in the history and historical interacting within this group, while _____ refers to individuals utilizing the Indigenous culture for inappropriate purposes.

a.   Appreciation/Appropriation

b.   Understanding/Appropriation

c.   Appropriation/Appreciation

d.   Cultural Acceptance/Cultural Rejection

7. You are a behavior analyst providing services in a school-based setting with a small percentage of Indigenous students. Around November, you conduct an observation within a classroom during a lesson specific to the upcoming Thanksgiving holiday. During this lesson you observe the teacher portraying the Indigenous that represent the culture as savages with tomahawks and dressed in feathers. How can you address what you observed with the teacher following the conclusion of the school day?

a.   You are not a trained educator and it is outside of your scope of practice to address this concern.

b.   You go directly to the principal and demand the teacher be removed from the classroom.

c.   You refuse to interact with the teacher following the conclusion of the school day due to the observation.

d.   You ask to speak with the teacher and inform them of the inaccuracies within the observed lesson and offer culturally sensitive facts about Indigenous cultures.

8. Specific factors among Indigenous communities that lead to a lower life expectancy include:

a.   Higher rates of alcoholism.

b.   Higher rates of suicide among teens.

c.   Higher rates of tuberculosis.

d.   All of the above

9. The Morningside Model of Generative Instruction (MMGI):

a.   Includes direct instruction

b.   Includes precision teaching

c.   Both A and B

d.   Neither A nor B

10. A behavior analyst can establish a respectful rapport with an Indigenous family and community by:

    a. Providing services within the Indigenous community.

    b. Ensuring Indigenous families receive information regarding ABA.

    c. Appropriating the Indigenous culture.

    d. Fully integrating themselves into the community by attending social events and ensuring behavioral supports are generalized to the community.

Chapter 6 Answer Key

1. C
2. A
3. D
4. B
5. C
6. A
7. D
8. D
9. C
10. D

1. You are a BCBA working with an Asian American family. While working with the child you provide positive reinforcement in the form of a high five and verbal praise. The parents are upset with you for providing reinforcement to their child in this manner. What might be the cultural issue here that you would need to be aware of?

   A. In Asian American culture, parents often practice strict control and their parenting style provides low levels of affection.

   B. In Asian American culture, the BCBA should not be providing the therapy; only a relative or family member should.

   C. In this scenario you did nothing that was culturally insensitive.

   D. None of the above

2. Which of the following factors may impact an Asian American family's abilities to access ABA services?

   A. Asian American families may not be familiar with ABA therapy.

   B. Prejudicial and misguided beliefs of ABA may prevent Asian American families from wanting services.

   C. Barriers related to linguistic diversity may hinder an Asian American family's ability to participate in ABA services.

   D. All of the above may be factors.

3. In Asian American families, parents may not consent to using a traditional FA since problem behavior will be evoked; therefore, as a behavior analyst you should consider:

   A. Conducting the FA anyway.

   B. Conducting a precursor FA.

   C. Conducting an IISCA.

   D. Both B and C

4. When designing treatment plans and working with Asian American families, some families may view corporal punishment as an effective form of treatment. What should you do as a BCBA?

   A. Tell the family you are reporting them to child protective services and have them arrested.

   B. Discuss the legalities of corporal punishment and train other alternative ways for reducing problem behavior.

   C. Turn a blind eye and forget that corporal punishment is happening in the home.

   D. Both A and B

5. When providing parent/caregiver training to Asian American families, what must you consider?

    A. Language may be a barrier; therefore, having a bilingual behavior analyst will be useful for training.

    B. Plan for generalization in treatment with not only parents but also grandparents.

    C. Use behavioral skills training, in vivo training, performance feedback, and problem solving.

    D. All of the above.

6. Which of the following are not immigration-related stressors that Asian American families may face that behavior analysts should be aware of?

    A. Separation from family members

    B. Discrimination

    C. Higher socioeconomic status

    D. Cultural shock

7. How should behavior analysts cultivate cultural awareness?

    A. Identify a unit or individual that is responsible for ensuring cultural awareness.

    B. Incorporate cultural awareness into individual clinical supervision.

    C. Infuse cultural awareness into clinical training.

    D. All of the above are ways to cultivate cultural awareness.

8. Which of the following is not part of the guidelines for cultural adaptation for treatment?

    A. Identify a unit or individual that is responsible for ensuring cultural awareness.

    B. Use a conceptual adaptation framework to identify key elements in the adaptation.

    C. Carefully document all adaptations.

    D. Evaluate the integrity of the original treatment model vis-à-vis the adapted version.

9. What must a behavior analyst possess in order to initiate adaptations related to cultural values and traditions for Asian American culture?

    A. Know the native language and be able to translate treatment documents.

    B. Have cultural sensitivity and a comprehensive understanding of the client's culture.

    C. The behavior analyst's training is enough.

    D. None of the above

10. Which of the following is not a potential cultural mismatch of Western derived evidence-based interventions?

    A. Community consultation and readiness

    B. Language

C.   Years of experience

    D.   Country of origin

Chapter 7 Answer Key

1. A
2. D
3. D
4. B
5. D
6. C
7. D
8. A
9. B
10. C

Chapter 8 Exam Questions

1. You are working with an Arab family as a behavior analyst and you notice a pattern of behavior where the family is always 10–15 minutes late for meetings, parent training, and so forth. In this scenario, you should:

   A. Recognize in Arab culture that they are customarily not as time bound as Americans, who stick to a precise time schedule.

   B. Not tolerate this behavior and tell the family you will dismiss them from services if it continues.

   C. Come up with a corrective action plan for the family.

   D. None of the above

2. As a behavior analyst you are conducting a treatment planning meeting with an Arab family. During the meeting, the father answers a phone call from a relative in the middle of the meeting and does not step out of the meeting. In this scenario, you should:

   A. Shut down the meeting and reschedule when the family is able to be fully present for the meeting.

   B. Be patient and understand that family is important in Arab culture.

   C. Tell the parent that taking a call during a meeting is rude.

   D. All of the above

3. When working with an Arab-American family you are a male behavior analyst entering the home for the first time to meet the family. Which of the following should you not do?

   A. Shake the father's hand

   B. Work with a male learner

   C. Shake the mother's hand

   D. None of the above

4. What are some practice considerations and implications service delivery that behavior analysts should keep in mind when working with Arab populations?

   A. Develop awareness of Islamic language.

   B. Develop awareness of high context communication.

   C. Find a "cultural insider."

   D. All of the above

5. You are a behavior analyst working with an Arab family who has a child with autism. You are providing edible reinforcers (i.e., food and drinks) during your treatment session. When may you need to modify the use of these reinforcers?

   A. During Christmas

   B. During Ramadan

C. During Hanukkah

D. You don't have to modify giving these reinforcers.

6. When working with an Arab-Muslim population of clients, which of the following cultural norms must you be aware of for nonverbal communication?

A. Unrelated women and men often avoid eye contact.

B. Showing the sole of one's foot is considered highly offensive.

C. A man does not extend one's hand to shake that of a woman unless the woman extends her hand first.

D. All of the above are cultural norms to be aware of when working with Arab-Muslim populations.

7. As a behavior analyst you are aware that when working with Arab populations they are often considered to have high context communication. Therefore, what may be a common phrase you would hear a parent say about their child due to stigma in Middle Eastern regions?

A. The behavior occurred in the past but no longer occurs, even though it does.

B. The behavior happens all the time and needs to stop.

C. The behavior is driving me crazy.

D. The behavior happens sometimes.

8. Which of the following are formalities related to holding meetings that you should be aware of as a behavior analyst working with an Arab family?

A. The authority sits at the head of the table.

B. Men often do not sit next to women.

C. The speaker may orient toward a specific person even when speaking to the entire group.

D. All of the above are formalities to be aware of.

9. When using a cultural insider or interpreter, what should a behavior analyst be prepared to do?

A. Use technical language in applied behavior analysis.

B. Speak quickly to get the information across to the cultural insider or interpreter.

C. Use simple language and avoid behavior speak.

D. None of the above

10. Which particular ethical code may be difficult for a behavior analyst when working with an Arab family that may be disrespectful to their culture?

A. Not accepting food or gifts

B. Gaining consent for services

C.   Performing assessments

    D.   Designing interventions

Chapter 8 Answer Key

1. A
2. B
3. C
4. D
5. B
6. D
7. A
8. D
9. C
10. A

Chapter 9 Exam Questions

1. Gender is:
    A. Male or female.
    B. A person's expression of themselves as male, female, or something else entirely, such as a nonbinary or agender identity.
    C. Based on how other people see a person.
    D. Determined by someone's biological makeup alone.

2. Which of the following is NOT a sexuality?
    A. Gay
    B. Bisexual
    C. Transgender
    D. Lesbian

3. Which are components of someone's sex assigned at birth?
    A. The medical field designating someone male or female at birth.
    B. A binary gender system that works to keep sex as either male or female.
    C. A system that does not center gender-determination within the individual's own identity.
    D. A person's gender marker on their birth certificate.
    E. All of the above

4. In the original *Diagnostic and Statistical Manual of Mental Disorders*, which was NOT a sociopathic personality disturbance?
    A. Homosexuality
    B. Transvestism
    C. Pedophilia
    D. Depression

5. What is problematic about current structures of accessing gender-affirming surgery or hormone therapy?
    A. That LGBTQIA people can access it.
    B. That acquiring it necessitates obtaining a diagnosis of a pathologized identity and experience.
    C. That more and more insurance companies are covering it.
    D. That it can help affirm LGBTQIA identities.

6. (Select all that apply) Which principles of the BACB Code of Ethics does non-affirmative practice with LGBTQIA clients violate?

A. Discrimination

B. Engaging in behavior that is harassing or demeaning.

C. Seeking training when not competent to work with clients or referring them to practitioners who are competent.

D. Reliance on scientific knowledge

E. All of the above

7. How can a person's gender be ascertained?

A. Gender is determined by a medical professional at birth.

B. A person's gender is determined by their biological characteristics.

C. Only the person themselves can identify their gender and assign a label to it.

D. Gender can be ascertained by how well a person is seen by others in the world as a man or a woman.

8. (Select all that apply) Which of the following are means by which a behavior analyst can work to make their business an affirming space for LGBTQIA folks?

A. Ensure access to gender-neutral bathrooms.

B. Be clear and communicative on promotional and print materials about LGBTQIA-affirming hiring practices and protections in the workplace.

C. Work to consistently address implicit and explicit bias in themselves and in their employees, as well as the workplace culture.

D. Ensure intake documents and intake procedures reflect and make space for LGBTQIA identities and experiences.

E. Maintain a referral list of helping professionals and medical providers who are committed to best practice in their field and to LGBTQIA-affirming practice.

F. All of the above

9. What are ways that behavioral analysts can be allies to LGBTQIA folks when they are presented with homophobia or transphobia regarding affirming therapeutic practice in the workplace?

A. Provide information about the ineffectiveness of conversion therapy and the protective factors of affirming therapy.

B. Disregard it and work to provide affirming therapy to the client.

C. Ask the client to talk to the person who brought forth the concerns.

D. Ask an LGBTQIA staff member to handle the issue.

10. (Select all that apply) How can one can respect and make space for people's pronouns?

    A.   When you first meet people, ask them for their pronouns, regardless of whether you think they might be LGBTQIA.

    B.   Work to create a culture where pronouns are respected, and where professionals are willing to be corrected and to correct each other about their and other people's pronouns.

    C.   Create a culture where pronouns are considered a standard part of email signatures.

    D.   Ask someone if their pronoun reflects their sex assigned at birth.

Chapter 9 Answer Key

1. B
2. C
3. E
4. D
5. B
6. E
7. C
8. F
9. A
10. D

Chapter 10 Exam Questions

1. (Select all that apply) How can having shared components of identity enhance the therapeutic process?

    A. It can enhance a client's willingness to disclose.

    B. It lessens the time the client needs to explain their culture or values.

    C. It can make rapport-building a smoother process.

    D. It is impossible to connect with each other without some overlapping identity.

2. Currently, what is in place in the field of ABA to ensure multicultural competency is available?

    A. An abundance of trainings and workshops on multiculturalism.

    B. Diversity among ABA practitioners.

    C. An ethics code that asserts referral to a competent provider when a practitioner does not have competency.

    D. A large and robust movement to develop multicultural practices in the field.

3. Why does it matter that there is a lack of diversity in the ABA field, particularly when considering clients with autism spectrum disorder?

    A. It does not matter; identity and culture do not play a part in the work.

    B. There is both over- and under-diagnosis in minority groups of ASD, and it is important that these clients receive culturally competent services to ensure their impact.

    C. More diversity in ABA practitioners means ethics codes will change.

    D. Autism has been shown to be alleviated by exposure to new cultural experiences.

4. Culture includes all of the following but:

    A. Behaviors.

    B. Values.

    C. Ideas.

    D. All of the above

5. All of the following are ways to assess and develop cultural self-awareness except:

    A. Consultation with other professionals.

    B. Using assessments to ascertain cultural bias.

    C. Observing one's private events.

    D. Continuing to only take part in one's own culture and cultural practices and belief systems.

6. What is important to consider in terms of cultural awareness when working with a child diagnosed and in treatment for ASD?

   A. The meaning of an ASD diagnosis in the context of the client's culture

   B. The need for education about ASD

   C. The meaning expression of emotion has in a culture and how this might affect a child's diagnosis and treatment

   D. Culture has no impact on diagnosis or treatment of ASD.

7. Why is it important to not only have cultural competence when working with client but also to have cultural competence when working with their families?

   A. It promotes generalization of skills across other stimuli and environments.

   B. It only makes sense to pursue cultural competency if it is important to the client.

   C. There will be no roadblocks to treatment if the client is receptive to it.

   D. Families are rarely involved in client's treatment.

8. Which is not a self-assessment tool to develop cultural self-awareness?

   A. Beck Depression Inventory

   B. Diversity Self-Assessment

   C. Multicultural Sensitivity Scale

   D. How Do You Relate to Various Groups of People in Society Self-Test Questionnaire

9. Which is not a factor that might influence whether a family is participating in a treatment plan?

   A. Socioeconomic status

   B. Culture

   C. Lack of support

   D. All of the above

10. What is one way to become more aware of your private events?

    A. Practice mindfulness when working with clients.

    B. Process our private events with clients.

    C. Do not interact with people from other cultures.

    D. Do not notice difference or how you respond to it.

Chapter 10 Answer Key

1. A, B and C
2. C
3. B
4. D
5. D
6. D
7. A
8. A
9. D
10. A

Chapter 11 Exam Questions

1. To better serve consumers from various cultures, the ABA organization should be aware of cultural impact throughout the patient lifestyle. The patient lifestyle should include but is not limited to the following in a behavioral practice setting:

   A. Intake, treatment planning, caregiver training, all school services, fading, discharge

   B. Intake, billing, treatment planning, therapy delivery, caregiver training, fading, discharge

   C. Intake, billing, interfamily coordination, therapy delivery, caregiver training, fading

   D. Intake, all school services, interfamily coordination, therapy delivery, fading, discharge

2. In order for organizations to enhance their cultural competence, they should meet the following standards for cultural competence:

   A. Organizations should respond to current demographic changes in the United States, services should be expanded to provide therapy with a culturally competent approach, and an organization should meet the cultural and ethnic needs of the population they serve.

   B. Organizations should respond to current demographic changes in the United States, services should be expanded to provide therapy with a culturally competent approach if funds allow, and an organization should meet the cultural and ethnic standards of all populations in the United States.

   C. Organizations should respond to current and projected demographics, and an organization should meet the cultural and ethnic standards of all populations the company serves.

   D. Organizations should respond to current and project demographics, and an organization should meet the cultural and ethnic standards of all populations in the United States.

3. Regarding implementing assessments:

   A. The agency implementing the assessment should be able to asses in the home language or refer the individual to an organization who can provide multilingual services if English is a barrier.

   B. The agency implementing the assessment may assess the individual regardless of whether multilingual services are provided, but should refer the individual to an agency who provides multilingual staff for treatment planning.

   C. The agency implementing the assessment should be able to assess the individual in the home language, but during treatment it does not have to provide multilingual staff.

   D. The agency implementing the assessment may assess the individual regardless of whether multilingual services are available and should continue providing services during treatment regardless of whether multilingual services are available.

4. When providing parent training programs, the following cultural variables should be considered:

   A. Cultural gender roles, disciplinary practices according the family's culture, educational and literacy deficits

   B. Disciplinary practices according to the family's culture, educational and literacy deficits, both parents should be expected to complete all programs since the family is residing in the United States

   C. Cultural gender roles, educational and literacy deficits, and disciplinary practices according to the ABA

   D. Cultural gender roles, disciplinary practices according to the family's culture, educational and literacy deficits should not be taken into consideration

5. During the initial intake process it is important for the person conducting the intake to be aware of the following items:

   A. Initial phone calls should be in the home language, but after that all other services should be provided in English.

   B. All resources should be in English, but the ABA organization should provide the family with resources for free English classes.

   C. Racial and ethnic makeup of the community, all resources should be in English, ABA organization should provide free services for English classes

   D. Racial and ethnic makeup of the community, languages spoken, community resources for linguistically diverse populations

6. Ethical Standards are currently set through the following organizations:

   A. ABAI, BACB, APA

   B. ABAI, BCBA, APA

   C. ABAI, BACB, BHCOE

   D. ABAI, BCBA, BHCOE

7. When working with cultural competence within an ABA organization, it is important to ensure that the company:

   A. Only hires individuals who share a culture similar to that of the company and developing training related to the culture the company is representing.

   B. Should only serve one culture, but should become an expert in that culture through training, speaker series, and hiring practices.

   C. Should have a diverse hiring practice, checking for cultural competence throughout the interview process and creating sensitivity to language barriers.

   D. Should have a diverse hiring practice, checking for cultural competence through the interview process and only serving one type of culture.

8. The BHCOE provides the following standards for effective applied behavior analysis organizations:

   A. Collaborating among organizations, but not needed with parents; the participating organization provides training to ensure competency in clinical tasks; participating organizations obey all federal, state, and local laws related to health, safety, and employment

   B. Collaboration among participating organizations and parents; the participating organization provides training once a year (regardless of when new staff are hired) to ensure competency in clinical tasks; participating organizations obey all federal, state, and local laws related to health, safety, and employment

   C. Collaboration among participating organizations and parents; the participating organization provides training to ensure competency in clinical tasks, participating organizations obey all state and local laws

   D. Collaboration among participating organizations and parents; the participating organization provides training to ensure competency in clinical tasks; participating organizations obey all federal, state, and local laws related to health, safety, and employment

9. Regarding cultural competence according to the governing bodies of ABA agencies:

   A. Initial training in racial, ethnic, religious, and sexual identity in regards to the family(s) being represented is needed, but ongoing training is needed only one time a year.

   B. Initial training in racial, ethnic, religious, and sexual identity in regards to the family(s) being represented is needed, and continuous ongoing training is needed along with collaboration with families.

   C. Initial training in racial, ethnic, religious, and sexual identity in regards to the family(s) being represented is needed, continuous ongoing training is needed, and collaboration with families is needed only during the intake process.

   D. Initial training in racial, ethnic, religious, and sexual identity in regards to the ABA organization are needed, continuous ongoing training is needed, and collaboration with families is needed only during the intake process.

10. The BACB Professional and Ethical Compliance Code promotes cultural diversity through 1.02 and 1.05(c) by:

    A. Behavior analysts should only provide services only within the boundaries of their competence related to training, education, and experience or by seeking consultation with appropriate individuals who are competent in those areas.

    B. Behavior analysts should only provide services within the boundaries of their competence related to training, education, and experience.

    C. Behavior analysts should only provide services within the boundaries of their competence related to training and experience.

D. Behavior analysts should only provide services within the boundaries of their competence related to training and experience or by seeking consultation with appropriate individuals who are competent in those areas.

Chapter 11 Answer Key

1. B
2. C
3. A
4. A
5. D
6. C
7. C
8. D
9. B
10. A

Chapter 12 Exam Questions

1. The consumer is a part of various cultural groups in regard to the family and the contingencies that the child comes in contact with in the work and social environments; Caregiver training should reflect:

   A. The cultural values guiding the parent's values, guiding the family unit, and guiding the work and social environment.

   B. The cultural values guiding the parent's values and the family unit.

   C. The cultural values guiding the work and social environment and community.

   D. The cultural values guiding the work and ABA environment.

2. Accommodations in manualized therapies contain similar components in ABA to:

   A. Discrete trials.

   B. Behavior skills training.

   C. Response interruption and redirection.

   D. Classical conditioning.

3. The EVM model includes:

   A. Eight dimensions when creating a culturally sensitive treatment.

   B. Surface accommodations and deep accommodations.

   C. Three phases including setting the stage, initial adaptations, and adaptation iterations.

   D. None of the above

4. In regard to reviews of culturally accommodated caregiver training in psychotherapies:

   A. There have been no clinical findings in any studies to suggest the importance of manualized therapies.

   B. The studies did not find any significant gains in regards to culturally adapted caregiver training programs.

   C. The greatest effect was noted in deep-level accommodations and it accommodated for caregivers of many backgrounds.

   D. It was not found to be effective for caregivers of all backgrounds.

5. Although research and studies on effective assessments in regard to cultural competency in the ABA field are in the infancy stages, some initial findings include:

   A. There is no need for further studies; cultural competence is equal among all backgrounds.

   B. An interpreter can increase the effectiveness of parent training, and further studies are not needed.

C. Having an assessment that addresses what the caregiver finds most important does not have more social validity than an assessment that does not address the question.

D. An interpreter can increase the effectiveness of parent training but does not necessarily increase the overall gains by non-Caucasian groups in implementing the strategies.

6. Although currently there are no ethical codes that directly address the issues of cultural accommodations, there are features of cultures addressed in various sections including codes 1.02 and 1.05. Some ways that BCBAs can increase cultural competence include:

A. Knowing the federal, state, and local laws regarding language access for all written and oral services.

B. Being aware of individual biases.

C. A and B

D. Neither A nor B

7. Some ways to increase social validity for the ABA agencies by using cultural competence include:

A. Self-assessments, professional networks in which cultural and diversity issues can be discussed, and participating in cultural trainings.

B. Self-assessments and conducting English trainings for all new caregivers.

C. Gaining experience in working with other cultures only.

D. Studying other cultures only.

8. Providing language accommodations such as considering caregivers' literacy level, accommodations for the caregiver's dominant language, and including the use of bilingual staff is:

A. Best practice and often has legal protection.

B. Best practice but not legally needed.

C. Legally needed, but not necessarily best practice.

D. Not needed during all phases of ABA treatment but only during the intake process.

9. Although there is still much research to be done; the element found to have the most social validity in regards to caregivers was:

A. Sexual identity accommodations

B. Religious accommodations

C. Gender accommodations

D. Language accommodations

10. The major commonalties between psychotherapy manualized training and ABA practices include:

A. Language accommodations and collaboration.

B. Language accommodations and agency-centered ideas.

C. Language accommodations and caregiver-centered ideas.

   D. Providing services in English and caregiver-centered ideas.

11. The major difference found in current ABA practices when compared to similar fields is that

   A. There is no difference.

   B. ABA treatments should be individualized.

   C. ABA treatments should be more generic.

   D. No further research is needed.

Chapter 12 Answer Key

1. A
2. B
3. A
4. C
5. C
6. B
7. A
8. D
9. A
10. B

Chapter 13 Exam Questions

1. Parent engagement in implementing training depends greatly on the ABA company's:
    A. The ABA company's communication with the family regarding goals and desired outcomes.
    B. The ABA company's communication with the family daily or whenever the parent has a question.
    C. The education of the person implementing the treatment.
    D. Neither the communication nor the education is more important.

2. Children's reduction in maladaptive behaviors can be seen in regards to:
    A. The increase in effective parent training that leads to parents implementing procedures correctly.
    B. It is not tied to the increase in parents effectively implementing procedures.
    C. An increase in effective parent training with Caucasian families only.
    D. Effective therapy from the ABA company with no increases due to the parents.

3. Specifically in functional communication training studies in relation to parents implementing the strategies, the number one factor in parents implementing the strategies included:
    A. Meeting the goals set forward by the BCBA.
    B. Communicating daily with the parents.
    C. Individualizing the program to meet the daily routine.
    D. Meeting the goals set forward by parents.

4. Three factors that make it likely that all behavior analysts in the United States will serve individuals from other parts of the world include:
    A. An increase in the amount of BCBAs, the expected influx of immigrants, and the decreasing rates of autism spectrum disorders.
    B. A decrease in the amount of BCBAs, the expected influx of immigrants, and the decreasing rates of autism spectrum disorders.
    C. An increase in the amount of BCBAs, the expected decline of immigrants, and the decreasing rates of autism spectrum disorders.
    D. An increase in the amount of BCBAs, the expected influx of immigrants, and the increasing rates of autism spectrum disorders.

5. According to the studies in this chapter in regards to efficacy of parent training specifically in regard to Hispanic parents, the following were shown to increase effectiveness:
    A. Adaptation of parent training protocols and effective treatment of parents on the implementation of protocols regardless of language used.
    B. Adaptation of parent training protocols and implementing everything in Spanish.

C. Having an interpreter present for all phases of training.

D. Having multilingual staff present for all phases of training.

6. Another intervention shown to be effective for a group transition program for Hispanic families of youth with ASD included:

A. Identifying needs and interests of families, obtaining feedback from community partners, and not collecting any feedback.

B. Making changes based on feedback given, creating or translating and adapting the curriculum.

C. Both A and B

D. None of the above

7. In order to make sure BCBAs are following the BACB Ethical Codes, these specific adaptations based on the following should be included:

A. Family's culture

B. Family's beliefs

C. Family's values

D. All of the above

8. In order to make sure that BCBAs are implementing culturally competent manner based on the BACB Ethical Codes; BCBAs should:

A. Read about the culture that they will be working with.

B. Talk to community members only of the same culture they will be working with.

C. Involve the families and community members in the planning of the intervention.

D. Take ethical courses only.

9. In order for BCBAs to be more effective, they can engage in the following concepts to improve their best practice.

A. Acknowledge the importance of culture, develop cultural awareness of oneself, and develop cultural awareness of others.

B. Acknowledge the importance of culture and develop cultural awareness of others, but developing cultural awareness of oneself is not needed.

C. Acknowledge the importance of culture; developing cultural awareness of others is not needed, and developing cultural awareness of oneself is not needed.

D. Acknowledge the importance of culture; developing cultural awareness of others is not needed, but developing cultural awareness of oneself is needed.

10. Making a cultural judgment based on one's opinion:

A. Is not best practice but will not make a difference in the parent implementation of services.

B. Is best practice, yet could make a difference in parent implementation of services.

C. Is not best practice, and could make a difference in parent implementation of services.

D. Is best practice, but will not make a difference in the parent implementation of services.

Chapter 13 Answer Key

1. A
2. A
3. B
4. D
5. A
6. B
7. D
8. C
9. A
10. C

Chapter 14 Exam Questions

1. Currently in regard to race of the BCBA compared to that of the consumers (clients) according to a 2018 survey from Beaulieu and colleagues:

   A. The majority of BCBAs are white, and the majority of clients are white

   B. The majority of BCBAs are non-white, and the majority of clients are non-white

   C. The majority of BCBAs are White, and the majority of clients are non-white

   D. The majority of BCBAs are non-white, and the majority of clients are white.

2. According to two recent surveys from 2018 from Taylor and colleagues and Beaulieu and colleagues:

   A. The percentage of parents believing the BCBA demonstrated respect for their cultural values and beliefs was higher than BCBAs responding to the same question.

   B. The percentage of parents believing the BCBA demonstrated respect for their cultural values and beliefs was the same as BCBAs responding to the same question.

   C. The percentage of parents believing the BCBA demonstrated respect for their cultural values and beliefs was lower than BCBAs responding to the same question.

   D. The percentage of BCBA's believing they demonstrated respect for the cultural values of the clients they served was lower than the parents' responding to the same question.

3. According to code 1.05 of the BACB ethical code, when there are differences between the behavior analyst and client, then behavior analysts must:

   A. Obtain training, experience, consultation, and/or supervision necessary to ensure services or make appropriate referrals.

   B. Obtain training, experience, consultation, and/or supervision necessary to ensure services.

   C. Obtain training, consultation, and/or supervision necessary to ensure services or make appropriate referrals.

   D. Obtain training, experience, and/or supervision necessary to ensure services or make appropriate referrals.

4. Also according to code 1.05, behavior analysts must not discriminate against others or knowingly engage in behavior that is demeaning or harassing based on:

   A. Age, gender, race, culture, ethnicity, national origin, religion, sexual orientation, disability, language, or socioeconomic status.

   B. Age, gender, race, culture, ethnicity, national origin, religion, sexual orientation, disability, language, or socioeconomic status in accordance with law.

C. Age, gender, race, culture, ethnicity, national origin, religion (not protected if receiving state funds), sexual orientation, disability, language, or socioeconomic status.

D. Age, gender, race, culture, ethnicity, national origin, religion, sexual orientation, disability, language (not protected as long as someone in the family speaks English), or socioeconomic status.

5. Code 1.06d, which prohibits behavior analysts from accepting gifts from clients due to concerns regarding multiple relationships:

A. Is often cited by behavior analysts as being offensive culturally if they do not accept gifts

B. Is argued by some in the field as not offensive, since behavior analysts are not guests

C. Both A and B

D. Neither A nor B

6. Being mindful of the language used during treatment and assessment and following assessment making appropriate decisions is:

A. Protected ethically based on the BACB code.

B. Protected ethically based on the BACB code and best practice.

C. Not protected ethically and not a suggestion for implementing cultural competence.

D. Not protected ethically but is a suggestion for implementing cultural competence.

7. Currently in relation to cultural competence:

A. Discrimination is adequately defined, and what should be done to ensure the delivery of cultural competence is adequately defined.

B. Discrimination is adequately defined, and what should be done to ensure the delivery of cultural competence is not adequately defined.

C. Discrimination is not adequately defined, and what should be done to ensure the delivery of cultural competence is adequately defined.

D. Discrimination is not adequately defined, and what should be done to ensure the delivery of cultural competence is not adequately defined.

8. Currently according to BABC, APA, and ASHA standards:

A. Cultural competence is objectively defined in BACB, but not in APA and ASHA standards.

B. Cultural competence is objectively defined in ASHA, but not in APA and BACB standards.

C. Cultural competence is objectively defined in APA, but not in BACB and ASHA standards.

D. Cultural competence is objectively defined in none of the aforementioned standards.

9. Behavior analysts must consider the cultural differences between:

    A. Practitioner and client only, but not employees and employers

    B. Practitioner and client and employees and employers, but not professors and students

    C. All affected groups, including practitioner and client, employees and employers, students and professor, and supervisees and supervisors

    D. Supervisees and supervisors only.

10. Behavior analysts should take into consideration the cultural beliefs and norms in regards to daily living skills, feeding skills, toileting, self-care, and sleeping.

    A. The BCBA should implement programs based on all assessments without regard to the aforementioned skills.

    B. The BCBA should implement all programs except for toileting in regard to cultural consideration.

    C. The BCBA should implement all programs except for feeding skills in regard to cultural competence.

    D. All of the above

Chapter 14 Answer Key

1. C
2. C
3. A
4. B
5. C
6. D
7. B
8. D
9. C
10. D

1. Some issues that may result in regards to cross-cultural supervision between BCBAs and supervisees may include:

   A. There may be a different culture

   B. There may be a different geographic location

   C. Both A and B

   D. Neither A nor B

2. The BACB lays out specific topics, specifically in codes 5.01–5.07, which an ethical supervisor should follow and cover when supervising staff. Some of these include:

   A. The behavior analyst and/or supervisee could attend workshops or lectures.

   B. The behavior analyst and/or parents of the client could attend workshops or lectures.

   C. The behavior analyst and/or client could attend workshops or lectures.

   D. The supervisee and/or parents of the client could attend workshops or lectures.

3. Currently there is no specific requirement for culturally sensitivity training; best practice may include:

   A. Teaching the trainee under specific tasks but not requiring the trainee to practice what is learned.

   B. Not directly teaching or having the trainee practice best practices, instead asking them to read about the culture.

   C. Teaching the trainee under specific tasks such as the behavior-change procedures and having the trainee then model what they learn.

   D. Having the trainee work directly with the client without first receiving any training.

4. If a supervisee comes from a different culture of the BCBA, then ethically the BCBA should:

   A. Never take on this supervisee.

   B. Take on the supervisee and get any person available to interpret.

   C. Take on the supervisee but find a formal interpreter for all situations.

   D. Provide written and verbal feedback, and search for a formal interpreter if the person speaks a different language.

5. The supervisor can teach cultural competence through the BACB 5th edition Task List (2017). The supervisor can use the task list to teach various issues such as:

   A. Identifying what is appropriate with each culture in regards to reinforce selection specifically to the client.

   B. Recommending intervention goals based on the supervisee and supervisor culture.

C. Both A and B

D. Neither A nor B

6. According to the Assessment of Culturally Sensitive Practice in Behavior Analysis Algorithm, the supervisor should make sure the supervisee is providing culturally sensitive services. If the supervisee is not providing culturally sensitive services, then the supervisor should:

A. Remove the supervisee with the first offense.

B. Provide needed trainings, co-consult with the supervisee, and remove if ethical concerns arise.

C. Co-consult, but do not provide trainings, and then remove if ethical concerns arise.

D. Remove the supervisee and report to the BACB.

7. A good behavior analytic program should

A. Be individualized for each client.

B. Incorporate the individual's culture.

C. Be individualized for each client and incorporate the client's culture.

D. Be individualized for each client and incorporate the supervisee's culture.

8. The supervisor's acknowledgement of the existence of culture in the supervisory relationship, and active exploration of the impact of culture on the relationship, refers to:

A. Cultural sensitivity to the client.

B. Cultural sensitivity to the supervisee.

C. Cultural responsiveness in supervision.

D. Cultural secularism.

9. Although not behavior analytic, the seminal 1992 article outlines the following three multicultural competencies that a supervisor should address:

A. Self-awareness, skills, speaking a second language

B. Skills, speaking a second language, knowledge

C. Knowledge, skills, knowing about various religions

D. Self-awareness, knowledge, and skills

10. A specific challenge in providing cross-cultural supervision that is more difficult to overtly objectively see is:

A. The conscious or external component of culture.

B. The unconscious or internal component of culture.

C. Both A and B

D. Neither A nor B

1. B
2. A
3. C
4. D
5. A
6. B
7. C
8. C
9. D
10. B

Index

Note: Page numbers in *italics* indicate figures; page numbers in **bold** indicate tables.